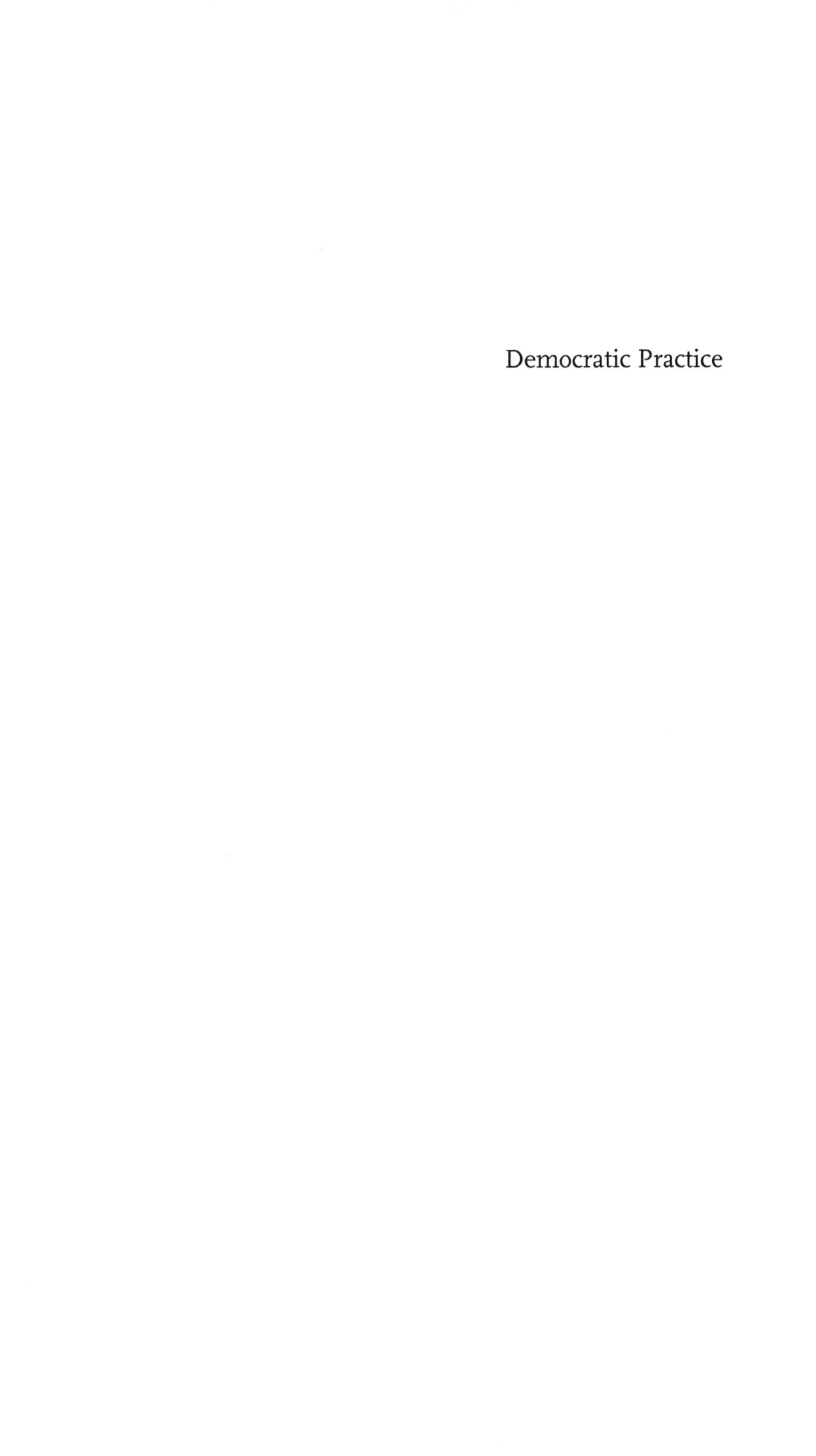

Democratic Practice

Recent Titles in
Oxford Studies in Culture and Politics
CLIFFORD BOB AND JAMES M. JASPER, GENERAL EDITORS

Contentious Rituals
Parading the Nation in Northern Ireland
JONATHAN S. BLAKE

Contradictions of Democracy
Vigilantism and Rights in Post-Apartheid South Africa
NICHOLAS RUSH SMITH

Plausible Legality
Legal Culture and Political Imperative in the Global War
on Terror
REBECCA SANDERS

Legacies and Memories in Movements
Justice and Democracy in Southern Europe
DONATELLA DELLA PORTA, MASSIMILIANO ANDRETTA,
TIAGO FERNANDES, EDUARDO ROMANOS, AND MARKOS
VOGIATZOGLOU

Curated Stories
The Uses and Misuses of Storytelling
SUJATHA FERNANDES

Taking Root
Human Rights and Public Opinion in the Global South
JAMES RON, SHANNON GOLDEN, DAVID CROW, AND
ARCHANA PANDYA

The Human Right to Dominate
NICOLA PERUGINI AND NEVE GORDON

Some Men
Feminist Allies and the Movement to End Violence
against Women
MICHAEL A. MESSNER, MAX A. GREENBERG, AND TAL PERETZ

Sex, Politics, and Putin
Political Legitimacy in Russia
VALERIE SPERLING

Democracy in the Making
How Activist Groups Form
KATHLEEN M. BLEE

Women in War
The Micro-Processes of Mobilization in El Salvador
JOCELYN VITERNA

Democratic Practice

Origins of the Iberian Divide in Political Inclusion

ROBERT M. FISHMAN

OXFORD
UNIVERSITY PRESS

Oxford University Press is a department of the University of Oxford. It furthers the University's objective of excellence in research, scholarship, and education by publishing worldwide. Oxford is a registered trade mark of Oxford University Press in the UK and certain other countries.

Published in the United States of America by Oxford University Press
198 Madison Avenue, New York, NY 10016, United States of America.

Library of Congress Cataloging-in-Publication Data
Names: Fishman, Robert M., 1955– author
Title: Democratic practice : origins of the Iberian divide in political inclusion / Robert M. Fishman.
Description: New York, NY, United States of America : Oxford University Press, 2019. | Includes bibliographical references and index.
Identifiers: LCCN 2018035434 | ISBN 9780190912871 (hc   ) |
ISBN 9780190912888 (pbk)
Subjects: LCSH: Democracy—Spain. | Democracy—Portugal. | Political culture—Spain. | Political culture—Portugal. | Spain—Politics and government—1975–1982. | Spain—Politics and government—1982– | Portugal—Politics and government—1974–
Classification: LCC JN8210 .F57 2019 | DDC 320.946—dc23
LC record available at https://lccn.loc.gov/2018035434

To Julia
And to the memory of Leo, Betty, and Ben.

CONTENTS

It is fitting that a book about the impact of history—and memories—on contemporary democratic practice should include some mention of its own history; in this case that history is a rather long one. It was more than fifteen years ago that I began a sustained effort to examine enduring legacies of the Iberian Peninsula's polar opposite pathways to democracy in the 1970s. In 2002, while I was completing a book on the quality of democracy in Spain and initiating more delimited studies on the cultural implications of Europe's common currency and on the impact of inequality on religious vocations, I agreed to write a conference paper analyzing the enduring consequences of the mid-1970s democratic transitions of Portugal and Spain. The American Political Science Association paper I gave in Boston in 2002, "Rethinking Iberian Democracy Twenty-Five Years after the Transitions," marked my first attempt to take up the themes ultimately developed in the work for this book. The initial research that I carried out while writing that paper had to compete with the demands of several other projects and with a moment when family matters also called strongly. Yet even so, the initial work I was able to do for that 2002 paper was sufficient to formulate the basic claim that Portugal should be understood as a post-revolutionary democracy and that, as a result, the smaller Iberian democracy was developing in certain ways that were fundamentally different from its larger neighbor Spain.

From the beginning I found the paired contrast between the two cases to be enormously interesting and enlightening. Indeed, I soon saw that the pairing of the two cases provided an analytical handle to systematically address many questions on which I had intuitions and tentative ideas about Spanish democracy, ideas that as of that point still lacked precision. I quickly decided that the matter merited book-length treatment, and my initial thought was that it would be a relatively quick book. That hunch was wrong—as the time elapsed in my research on this project clearly shows—but a number of hypotheses that I developed early in the research proved to be amply supported by a wealth of empirical evidence. For example, I suspected from my first work on the comparison that much light could be shed on the explanation for Spain's chronically high unemployment rate by examining contrasts with neighboring Portugal, which enjoyed a far more robust record of employment. However, I was not satisfied to make a few quick and telling comparisons. As a longtime student of Spanish politics and society I was determined to do all I could to get to know Portugal in real depth and as a theoretically minded social scientist I was committed to elaborating the conceptual and causal basis for the patterns of difference that I quickly identified. I had a great deal of work to do.

That work involved a highly eclectic multi-method approach to the collection and analysis of evidence. It also generated large intellectual and personal debts that I make some effort to delineate in this preface. But in a way, the project—just like all things—had in a sense begun even earlier than what would seem to be its "start date."

My effort to understand both Portugal and Spain by comparing the two cases to one another—and to advance our understanding of broadly theoretical questions through the insights provided by this unusually productive paired comparison—had begun earlier. Much of my work as a social scientist has focused on in-depth work on the Spanish case coupled with theoretical efforts to draw useful lessons from this case and its contrasts with others. Early in my career, while I was a junior faculty member at Harvard, I made use of the Iberian Peninsula paired comparison—and contrasts with the Greek case—to identify the crucial analytic importance of differentiating between state and regime in the context of broad-scale processes of political transformation. However, it was only when I began the work leading to this book that I took on the task of gaining an in-depth knowledge of the smaller Iberian Peninsula case.

I was fortunate to receive a great deal of help from Portuguese colleagues and friends in my turn toward sustained research on the Portuguese case. I cannot possibly thank here all of those who devoted time and effort to helping me in my work, but I do wish to mention a few of those who helped the most. At the Instituto de Ciencias Sociais of the University of Lisboa Manuel Villaverde Cabral was a constant source of advice and encouragement as were Pedro Lains, António Costa Pinto, Pedro Magalhaes, Marina Costa Lobo, and José Sobral. At the Universidade Nova de Lisboa and elsewhere Tiago Fernandes helped in countless ways and served as a conversational partner in innumerable discussions of areas of shared interest. Alan Stoleroff of ISCTE helped me get to know many crucial elements of Portugal's political realities and offered other types of friendly help. Boaventura de Sousa Santos and colleagues of his at the University of Coimbra also offered valuable suggestions and encouragement. Numerous Portuguese political actors, associational leaders, teachers, and journalists generously offered their time answering my interview questions patiently and in depth—as did their counterparts in Spain.

In Spain I also accrued numerous intellectual debts, many of them to old friends who offered renewed encouragement and help. Víctor Sampedro played an especially important role helping with interviews of teachers and others. At the Carlos III University in Madrid I am especially grateful to Ignacio Sánchez Cuenca for sustained in-depth commentaries and to many other colleagues in the Department of Social Sciences and the Carlos III/ Juan March Institute, including Lluís Orriols, Gema García Albacete, Juan Diez Medrano Pablo Simón, Juan Fernández, Damon Mayrl, Jonas Radl, Miguel Artola, Jordi Domenech, and Stefan Houpt, for highly useful feedback. Orriols offered especially in-depth commentaries on the chapter on the Catalan crisis. At the Universitat Pompeu Fabra in Barcelona first Rosa Virós and later Gosta Esping-Andersen, Stephen Jacobson, Luís Ortiz, Mariano Torcal, Ignacio Lago, Fernando Guirao, and Ferran Requejo offered valuable insights and feedback, as did Josep María Vallès of the Universitat Autónoma of Barcelona. Joan Font of the IESA in Córdoba and Xavier Coller of the Olavide University in Seville also offered generous insights and help. Many colleagues and friends at other universities in Spain, the United States, and elsewhere have joined in offering helpful feedback, especially Ken Roberts and Paloma Aguilar.

In the United States, friends and former colleagues at the Kellogg Institute and the Department of Sociology at the University of Notre Dame offered extraordinarily important advice and encouragement. At the University of Notre Dame I thank especially Omar Lizardo, now of UCLA, Samuel Valenzuela, Lyn Spillman, David Hachen, Scott Mainwaring, my late colleague Guillermo O'Donnell, Ann Miche, Michael Coppedge, and Andrew Gould. Also, colleagues at a Nanovic Institute faculty seminar on cultural change in modern Europe offered highly useful and insightful feedback. I thank in particular Julia Douthwaite, Thomas Kselman and Alex Martin.

With research support from the CONEX program at my new home institution, the Carlos III University of Madrid, I was fortunate to be able to organize a book workshop that offered in-depth commentaries on my first draft of the manuscript in June 2017. I am pleased to thank the funding sources for the CONEX program: the European Union's Seventh Framework Programme for research, technological development and demonstration under grant agreement n° 600371, Spain's Ministerio de Economía y competitividad (COFUND2013-40258), Spain's Ministerio de Educación, Cultura y Deporte (CEI-15-17), and the Banco Santander as well as the Carlos III University. The CONEX program has supported my research throughout my time at the Carlos III University.

At the book workshop, Igancio Sánchez-Cuenca, Mabel Berezin, Jeff Goodwin, Omar Lizardo, Tiago Fernandes, Laia Balcells, Eduardo Romanos, and Pedro Magalhaes offered extraordinarily helpful feedback on the manuscript as a whole. Several other Carlos III colleagues including Kostis Kornetis, Juan Diez Medrano, Javier Polavieja, Juan Fernández and Celia Valiente also offered generous feedback at the workshop.

Previously I had been fortunate to receive feedback on paper-length components of the work from scholarly colleagues at a number of universities and professional meetings. I especially wish to mention those who offered feedback in presentations at the Center for European Studies and the Ash Institute of Harvard University, the Kellogg Institute of the University of Notre Dame, the Watson Institute of Brown University, Columbia University, Cornell University, the University of Washington, Oxford University, the European University Institute, The Humboldt University (Berlin), the Universitat Pompeu Fabra of Barcelona, the Universidad Carlos III and the Universidad Autónoma of Madrid, the Pablo Olavide University of Seville, the Instituto de Ciencias Sociais and the Universidade Nova of Lisbon, the University of Coimbra, meetings of the American Political Science Association, the American Sociological Association, the Council for European Studies, the Society for Socio-Economics, and the International Sociological Association.

My work on this project has been long, and in this process I have incurred far more numerous intellectual debts than I can adequately mention in this context. Many other scholars, colleagues, and friends have offered highly valuable insights and help. I cannot possibly mention here all of those to whom I feel grateful, but I cannot fail to mention the greatest intellectual influence on my scholarship: I am particularly indebted to the in-depth intellectual feedback I received from Juan Linz on this project and all of my scholarly work prior to his death in 2013. Juan's insights, encouragement, and high standards have been a constant source of inspiration and guidance in my work.

I have also been fortunate to enjoy excellent research assistance from a number of scholars including Suzanne Coshow, David Everson, Timofii

Brik, Wilfried Kisling, and Nicholas Muench. Wilfried Kisling has generously and tirelessly helped bring the manuscript to final completion with numerous types of expert assistance. At Oxford University Press, Editor James Cook has been everything that an author can hope for: generous, rigorous, encouraging, and patient. The three anonymous readings provided by the review process at Oxford University Press were all helpful, strongly encouraging, and rigorous. I am also grateful to sociologist James Jasper, co-editor of the OUP Series in Culture and Politics for his enthusiasm about this book project and his helpful suggestions; to Assistant Editor Emily Mackenzie for her patient and skilled oversight of the post-approval publication process and her extraordinary commitment to getting everything right; and to Christina Nisha who has managed the production process with great generosity and skill as well as the willingness to allow corrections to be added up until the last possible moment.

The painting reproduced on the book's cover, *La Manifestación* by Antonio Berni, belongs to the MALBA Collection of the Museo de Arte Latinoamericano de Buenos Aires. I thank the Berni family owners of the rights to this work for granting permission for its use. This extraordinary painting portrays demonstrators in Argentina in the 1930s, a context that was in certain ways quite different from early twenty-first century Spain and Portugal, but in a deep sense the painting by Berni conveys the fundamental human significance of democratic inclusion, a central message of this book.

The most important support in my work on this project came from those closest to me. Julia Lopez has accompanied me with her insights, support, and encouragement in the exploration that led to this book and in the spaces that the book left for the rest of life as well. I dedicate the book to her and also to the memory of those who got me started in the approach to life that brought me to this project. My parents, Betty and Leo, promoted the curiosity and the ethical commitment to inclusion that motivated me to do this work. After they were both gone my step-father Ben did his best to keep that light alive—for Julia and me as well as for my sister Margaret and her family—until his final moments just as I was beginning work on this project. I dedicate this book on the importance of memories for confronting contemporary challenges to Julia and to the memory of Betty, Leo, and Ben.

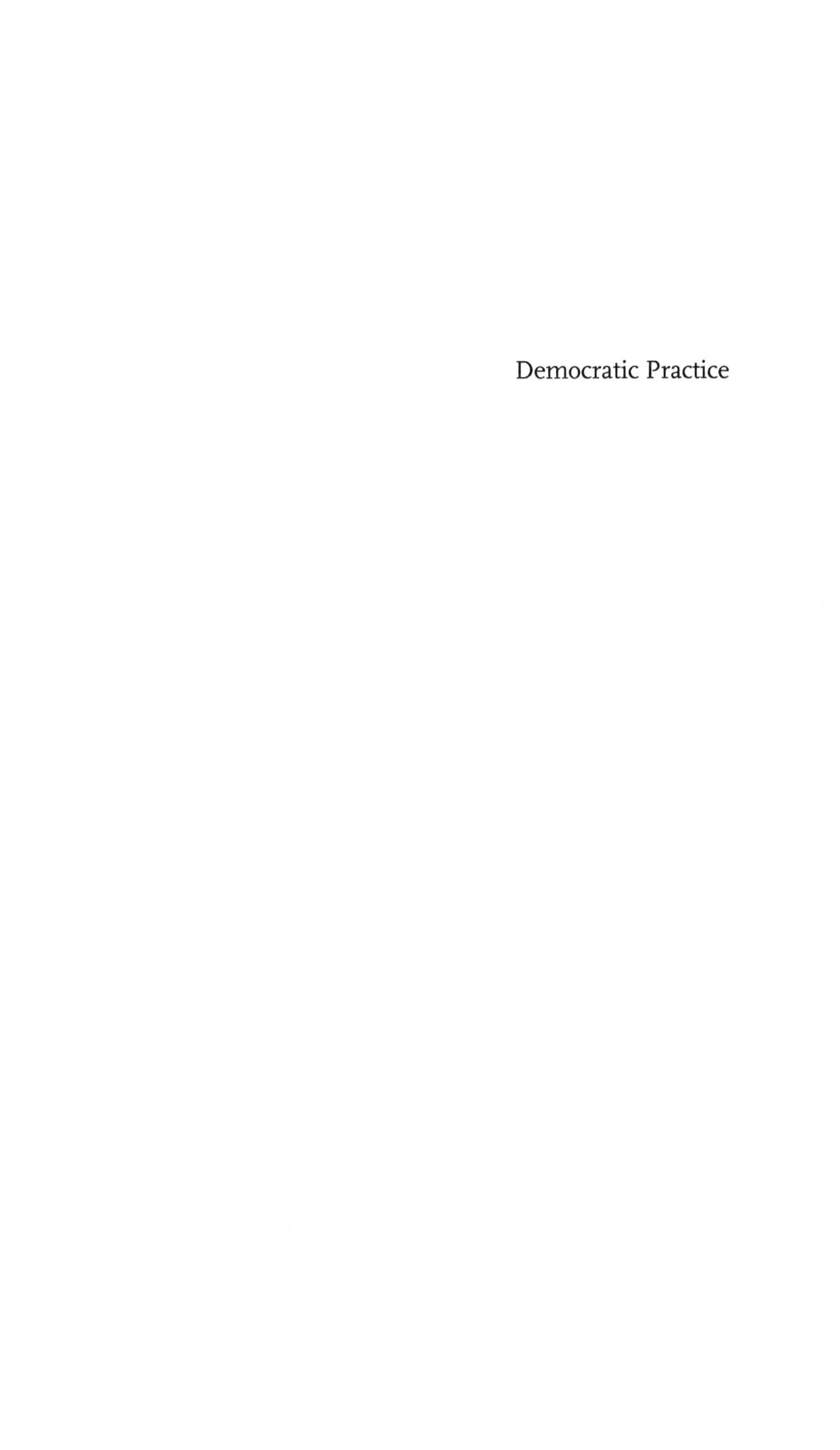

Democratic Practice

 How Democratic Practice Varies
by Country

Legacies of Historical Pathways to Democracy

I. Introduction

The global spread of democracy, after the initiation in 1974 of a historically extraordinary wave of regime change (Weyland, 2014; Huntington,
1991; Markoff, 1996; O'Donnell, Schmitter and Whitehead, 1986), fundamentally remade the political map of the world in ways that involved much
more than the straightforward increase in the number of democracies. The
worldwide process of change also put in place numerous new political and
social realities that ought to motivate scholars—and political actors—to understand democracy in new ways. With the large increase in the number
of democracies came growing evidence that such systems vary along several major dimensions of differentiation, thereby encouraging both scholars
and political actors themselves to search for ways to identify and understand
major elements of divergence among democracies. This book takes up this
challenge and shows how democratic practice itself—a term that I carefully
define in what follows—constitutes a major terrain of differentiation among
politically free representative systems. I draw attention to major elements
of difference among democracies in what actors actually do in pursuit of
their goals and interests—and in how they interact with other political forces
while pursuing their objectives. These differences in turn substantially determine whether democratic polities actually live up to central promises—
and hopes—of democracy's advocates. I argue that predominant forms of
democratic practice can be best understood as cultural legacies of large-scale
historical processes such as national pathways to democracy. It follows that

many fundamental determinants of how well democracies serve their citizens are rooted in the cross-case variation of national histories and in ongoing processes of cultural contention, the themes of this book.

I focus empirically on the veritable epicenter of the Third Wave's genesis—the Iberian Peninsula, located at the western end of continental Europe—in an effort to identify and analyze major cross-national differences in the mindset and recurrent forms of conduct of political actors in democracies. My objective is to account for the origins, substance, and consequences of such cross-national differences. Portugal and Spain—along with their southern European "cousin" Greece—initiated the democratizing quarter century that commenced in April 1974 but they did so in remarkably different ways and with starkly divergent results, many of which come into full view only when one makes use of the analytical prism developed by this book. Despite their long history of deep and pervasive similarity along many dimensions, contemporary Portugal and Spain have diverged substantially in their prevailing forms of democratic practice—thus leading to many other points of contrast. I refer to this fundamental difference between these neighboring countries as the "Iberian divide in political inclusion," placing its origins in the two countries' nearly polar opposite pathways to democracy in the 1970s.

For reasons that I outline in this introductory chapter, the paired comparison (Tarrow, 2010) of Portugal and Spain provides an especially useful empirical foundation for the broader comparative and theoretical effort to locate and make sense out of such cross-national differences. In a long-term project of research (discussed in the Preface), I have gathered multiple forms of evidence on the Portugal–Spain divergence in democratic practice and of its implications for these—and other—democracies' relative degree of success in approximating the central normative goal of full political equality among citizens. The dynamics analyzed in this study strike to the core of certain especially difficult challenges that democracies face in pursuing effective political equality. These challenges involve forms of political inclusion that cannot be easily attained simply by legislative rule-making. The elements of cross-case divergence that I emphasize in these pages stand in contrast to another quite important objective that democracies should, by definition, pursue, namely attempting to guarantee full equality for all citizens in their direct ability to shape election outcomes. The legal standards that underpin that guarantee are of undeniable importance; free, fair, and competitive elections for positions of political power constitute the institutional core of modern representative democracy.

However, the concerns of this book extend well beyond the voting booth and the institutional rules surrounding its role in representative political systems; in the pursuit of effective and full political equality among citizens the electoral arena is far from sufficient: Political equality limited to the casting and counting of ballots would be a rather shallow and inadequate marker of democracy. As the great democratic theorist Robert Dahl has persuasively argued (1998, 2006), the full attainment of genuine and robust political equality necessarily requires the primacy of that principle in the processes of agenda setting and policymaking as well as information acquisition. Indeed, it is in the interim between elections that the relative success of a polity in approximating political equality on these other terrains is determined. I argue that it is precisely on this point that nationally predominant forms of democratic practice prove to be determinant, thereby forging substantial cross-case variation in the breadth of political inclusion.

In what follows I aim to show both how and why democratic practice varies quite significantly between national cases. The book's intent is also to delineate the large implications of this phenomenon in the first instance for political inclusion and thus the relative approximation of formally free and representative systems to the normative goal of political equality. I seek to show that the disparity in effective political inclusion, in turn, leads to a wide range of differences in fundamental policy and societal outcomes—another theme of this book. I argue that historically rooted cultural understandings about the substance of democracy, and about the principles that should govern political interactions in such systems, carry enormous consequences for political inclusion and, as a result, the actual attainment of political equality. Thus, much of what follows is concerned with ways in which history leaves in its wake enduring legacies that shape collective life for many decades—if not far longer. Many of these legacies are cultural and it is on them that I primarily focus, but I also touch on other types of legacies of historical change—in formal institutional structures and economic arrangements. I turn to evidence from Portugal and Spain, two neighboring countries that are often assumed to be extraordinarily similar—but which nonetheless followed virtually polar opposite pathways to democracy in the 1970s.

The choice of Portugal and Spain as the empirical focus of this examination of the origins, substance, and consequences of national variation in democratic practice is intended to capture a wide range of differentiation in this object of study while controlling for numerous other elements of cross-national variation. These two early cases of Third Wave democratization present us with vast differences both in the historical processes that led them from dictatorship to democracy in the mid-1970s and in taken-for-granted assumptions about political inclusion or its absence, assumptions that were conditioned by those historical processes. I focus partly on the interactions between protesters and elected authorities, but the range of differentiation identified and examined here is far broader than that. The analysis that follows is concerned with many ways in which representative political systems either incorporate or effectively exclude hierarchical subordinates and other potentially marginal political actors. This book provides a challenge to existing approaches to the study of variation among democracies, arguing that certain historically grounded cultural phenomena are of vital importance in shaping quite important outcomes. Indeed, this book offers a forceful argument about how the historical origins of democratic systems, or equally weighty critical junctures, leave in place certain politically crucial tendencies that in turn powerfully condition the attainment of full political equality among citizens, a crucial normative goal in democratic theory, and a variety of other outcomes.

I treat democratic practice—the intellectual centerpiece of this book—as, in a sense, an intervening variable. Both its origins and its effects as manifested in various outcomes can be identified; they constitute much of the substance of what follows. But the linkage between those historical origins and their ultimate consequences in various socio-political outcomes cannot be adequately understood without specifying the more direct cultural product of national histories, namely democratic practice, and elaborating its intervening significance. All of this obviously needs to be placed in the much broader scholarly context of literatures on related themes. Although there is much in this book that is new—and that seeks to open fresh avenues of scholarly investigation, explanation and theory-testing—my analysis and arguments build in numerous ways on large bodies of excellent scholarly work that provide the essential foundation and intellectual context for this effort. Before we turn to a brief consideration of the scholarly approaches that serve as a foundation for this work, a few general words on this chapter and its role in the book are in order.

Although much of this chapter focuses on conceptual and theoretical matters of primary concern to social scientists working in this and related scholarly areas, most of the rest of the book examines the direct substance of political life—and of historical and cultural dynamics that shape its day-to-day dramas. The book's treatment of politics itself addresses both practical and ethical concerns meaningful to a wide segment of the citizenry, extending well beyond the professional scholarly world. The historical and contemporary cases taken up in the discussions found in the remaining chapters of the book provide the primary empirical substance for the book's rethinking of several interrelated theoretical debates. Thus the book is intended to speak to multiple overlapping readerships. The scholarly literatures on which this book builds are more or less equally divided between sociology and political science, but I draw also on works by historians, economists, and others. I rely especially heavily on sociologists in the conceptualization of culture and primarily on political scientists in the theorization of variation among democracies. In the remainder of this chapter I offer definitions of the book's central concepts and provide a roadmap to the remaining chapters. But first I examine foundations of the analysis in existing literatures. The book's theoretical and substantive innovations are developed in the following chapters.

Many scholars have developed arguments in which cultural phenomena serve as intervening variables that, in effect, mediate between causes located in historical process and consequences found in the contemporary world. A directly relevant recent example is the contribution of Juan Díez Medrano, *Framing Europe* (2003). With an empirical focus on three important member states of the European Union, Díez Medrano shows that cross-case variation in national histories generates cultural contrasts between the cases leading, in turn, to political differences in how matters related to the European Union are framed and understood. Other books, as well, show how historical and cultural variation across cases can provide scholars with compelling explanations of more proximate forms of cross-case divergence in political outcomes, but the use of history in social science explanations has been much more pervasive.

Growing numbers of social scientists have recently sought to identify multiple ways in which history matters for contemporary outcomes—such as democratization (Capoccia and Ziblatt, 2010; Pierson, 2004). A large literature shows how a variety of "critical junctures" in national-level historical development generate enduring differences between country cases that handle the challenges of the historical "critical juncture" in divergent ways (Collier and Collier, 1991; Collier and Munck, 2017). For the most part, the major works of scholarship in this important approach tend to emphasize formal institutional legacies that put in place political structures such as parties, unions, and carefully crafted public policies. I develop, instead, the significance of a major critical juncture—the mid-1970s pathways from dictatorship to democracy—for cultural legacies that condition numerous elements of political conduct. A crucial novelty of this book is to apply such an approach to the analysis of variation in forms of democracy—and above all in the breadth of political inclusion.

In a concrete sense, this book returns to a theme that attracted a good deal of debate in early research on the worldwide wave of democratization that began in 1974, namely whether different "modes of transition" generate distinctive consequences of an enduring nature (Stepan, 1986; Karl

1990; Hagopian, 1990; Karl and Schmitter, 1991; Valenzuela, 1991; Hunter, 1997). That debate did not generate scholarly consensus at the time, perhaps partly because it often focused on formal institutional dependent variables. Building on the insight that regime transitions can contribute to reshaping a variety of understandings and practices (Cook, Hardin, and Levy, 2005) the theory developed here specifies ways in which the legacies of transitions are broader and deeper than many analysts initially assumed, influencing ways in which new challenges and problems are confronted. I turn now to two important definitional matters.

II. Definitional Building Blocks of the Analysis

I define "democratic practice" as "the ways in which political actors— including ordinary citizens, groups that are organized or spontaneous, and institutional office holders—make use of the rights and possibilities for action provided by democracy and deal with others who are similarly engaged. The democratic practice of political actors encompasses their form of expression and interaction both within, and outside the bounds of, formal institutions" (Fishman, 2011a: 236). This concept is intended to focus our attention on a dimension of variation among democracies that is not fully captured by formal institutional rules or by what goes on exclusively within the boundaries of formal political institutions: "Although political life is powerfully shaped by institutional rules that specify—among other things—expected connections between power holders and other citizens, the actual practices constituting political life in a democracy can be more—or less—inclusive than formal institutional guidelines imply" (236). The study of democratic practice, understood in this sense, allows us to see and analyze ways in which democracies vary in their relative tendency to include low-income and socially or culturally marginal sectors in the substance of political life: Democratic countries differ from one another in the degree to which the most influential political forces welcome all actors to participate in democracy's recognized "conversation" or instead erect de facto barriers to the meaningful participation of political or social "outsiders" in political discussions and processes of import. Cross-case variation in the inclusionary practice of political elites is typically matched by the relative proclivity of social "outsiders" to pursue participation in institutional political life or alternatively to promote their objectives outside the bounds of the institutionally recognized arena. The type of democratic practice of a representative system is, in principle, reflected in the conduct of both elite and non-elite actors, given the relational character of political life that has been persuasively underscored by scholars of political "contention" (McAdam, Tarrow, and Tilly, 2001).

Of course, variation is to be found not only between but also to some extent within national cases. I understand democratic practice to be a culturally constituted phenomenon and as such, its substance tends to form a repertoire of possibilities rather than a narrow and homogeneous framework universally applied within national cases. Variation within countries is reflective of many types of differentiation: political contrasts between competing parties, cultural and historical differences between territorial units within a state, generational contrasts rooted in the distinctive historical experiences of individuals born and socialized in dissimilar times, and so forth. Nonetheless, I argue that democracies vary in their predominant form of democratic practice—in the center of gravity within their repertoire of practice—much as cultural sociologists tend to argue for other cultural objects of study (Swidler, 2001; Hall and Lamont, 2009, 2013). However, in some cases and at least for certain periods of time countries can be deeply divided by conflict over opposing conceptions of democratic practice. Such conflict may be confined to enduring tensions between segments of a polity that conduct themselves in quite different ways without really aspiring to change the unifying principles of the polity writ large. However, in other cases conflict may take the form of attempts to alter the shared conceptions and forms of conduct of the polity-wide set of actors. Cultural conflict can take multiple forms, a theme we will return to in chapter 7.

This book is about the central role that more or less enduring approaches to political conduct play in mediating between large-scale historical processes and outcomes such as the extent to which democracies approximate the normatively valued goal of full political equality among citizens. As noted previously, this centrally important outcome in turn carries with it numerous consequences reflected in a myriad of more specific societal and political outcomes. I conceive of "democratic practice," the book's centerpiece, as a cultural phenomenon. But what does it mean to say that? Without a clear definition of "culture" it is hard to know how to answer the question—so I offer here a short definition intended to work for this book's readers. My approach is heavily influenced by a great deal of scholarship in the field—especially the work of Omar Lizardo, (2004, 2017; Lizardo and Strand, 2010) Orlando Patterson, (2014) Ann Swidler, (1986, 2001) Michele Lamont, both in solo authored work (1992, 2002) and in an important collaboration with Peter Hall (Hall and Lamont, 2009, 2013), Pierre Bourdieu (1990), William Sewell (1996, 2005), Jeff Alexander (2006), Mabel Berezin

(1994, 1997, 2015), George Steinmetz (1999), Lynn Spillman (1997), Robert Wuthnow (Wuthnow and Witten, 1998), and others.

An earlier generation of scholars had tended to approach culture through an emphasis on values and perspectives manifested at the individual level and, as a result, subject to study through the valuable tool of survey analysis (Almond and Verba, 1963; McDonough, Barnes, and Lopez Pina, 1998). Although social scientists maintain an appropriate interest in operationalizing and measuring cultural phenomena (Polavieja, 2015), contemporary cultural sociologists have tended to move away from the earlier scholarly tendency to understand culture as above all a set of values orienting preferences and actions. Swidler's influential formulation sees cultures as repertoires that constitute "the set of symbolic vehicles through which such sharing and learning [about the meanings of the human world] take place" (Swidler, 2001: 12). She has also famously conceptualized culture as a set of constructs that offer persons tools they can appropriate or use for strategic ends (1986).

However, in their highly compelling studies of what cultural analysis can contribute to social science explanation, both Lizardo (2017) and Patterson (2014) conclude that predominant views in recent cultural theory, including those of followers of anthropologist Clifford Geertz's central focus on *meaning*, are somewhat too restrictive—failing to provide a conceptual home for many phenomena that ought to be seen as cultural. Patterson's (2014) review of the field and Lizardo's (2017) new analytical proposal both differentiate between what they conceptualize as a "non-declarative" type of culture that is learned through actual experience and a "declarative" form that is learned through words or other symbolic representations. I follow this approach, but doing so still leaves us with the need to formulate a simple working definition—as I attempt in what follows.

"Culture" may work better as an adjective—as in cultural phenomena—than as a noun, because so many kinds of "things" can be manifestations of culture: narrative and interpretive structures, cognitive frameworks, mindsets, practices, forms of expression, scripts and schemas, discourses, symbols—the list goes on and on. I suggest that we think of cultural phenomena quite simply as forms of human expression or practice that are learned and internalized, and their subsequent manifestations in human competences and in the orientation of practices, understandings, interpretations, and preferences.[1] Forms of human expression and practice become cultural once they are internalized or learned—whether by their initial creators or others. A spontaneous creative gesture or act is culturally irrelevant if it is never internalized or remembered by anyone. Cultural forms of expression are often verbal, but they may also be visual, musical, or representational in other ways. Whether in one sense or another, they can be understood as symbolic and in that sense as conveying—often constructing—meaning. However, culture involves much more than simply forms of expression: Forms of practice that are learned are inherently cultural, whereas those that are improvised or created more or less "ex novo" in response to new circumstances at a given time become cultural when they are learned and then used to orient practices or understandings at a subsequent (and potentially quite proximate) time. This conception of culture, following the work of Lizardo and Patterson, is broader than other current views (for example those that limit the concept to the important activity of meaning-making) and at the same time it offers clear analytical and explanatory advantages—especially for a study such as this one that seeks to understand the historical origins and enduring consequences of forms of political practice that vary by country.

Culture in this sense includes both implicit, taken for granted, assumptions or competences and explicit formulations of various sorts. The distinction of Patterson and Lizardo between declarative and non-declarative culture, analytically elaborated by Lizardo (2017) in his examination of differences in how these two forms of culture are internalized and then made use of, is of great usefulness for this book's analytic project. Indeed I see democratic practice as rooted in both types of culture—the internalization of lived experiences and the more formalized learning of the substance conveyed by expressive statements or representations about political life. This approach builds on Bourdieu's (1990) formulation of practice as resting on a "habitus" of internalized dispositions, and also on much subsequent theoretical work.

III. Studying Variation in Democracies: Concepts and Methodologies

The study of variation among democracies—conceived by one especially ambitious current project as the analysis of "varieties of democracy" (Coppedge et al., 2011)—is an area of growing interest among social scientists. That democracies can take quite different forms in their performance and handling of numerous questions is readily apparent to both scholars and other acute observers, prompting some to speak of the "global divergence of democracies" (Diamond and Plattner, 2001). But how should rigorous scholarly work conceptualize and study differences among democracies? Given that this book seeks to contribute one new way to do just that, it is important to place the effort in the context of other work concerned with the wider goal of understanding variation among democracies. One common approach is to group together under the generic heading of "the quality of democracy" a number of desirable and plausibly attainable features of such systems (Altman and Pérez-Liñán, 2002; O'Donnell et al., 2004; Diamond and Morlino, 2005). However, this approach, if not anchored in an analytically clear and conceptually well-developed framework clearly delimiting what features of democracies should be considered markers of their "quality"—and which features should be understood as markers of other dimensions of variation—is prone to producing what sociologist Ronald Burt (2005) referred to as a scholarly "Wild West" in his analysis of work on the concept of "social capital." If a widely used term is employed in quite varied and sometimes imprecise ways it is very difficult for the body of scholarship that uses the term to generate effective scientific accumulation. Scholarly works can easily end up "speaking past one another" despite the best intentions of their authors.

I have proposed a relatively compact framework of major dimensions of democratic variability (Fishman, 2016) intended to address the concerns of both normative and empirically oriented students of democracy, and in this book I make use of that framework. I differentiate between democratic quality, authenticity, depth, and consolidation. Whereas some students of democracy tend to assume that all good things go together—and on that basis search for determinants of favorable outcomes on all important dimensions of democracy—I conceptualize these objects of study as dimensions that may vary with independence from one another. I understand each of these four dimensions to constitute a cluster of attributes that is, in a sense, unified by the meaning that actors and/or scholars place on the attributes grouped together in such fashion. This approach to conceptualizing dimensions of variation in democracy is built on foundations elaborated in the work of social theorist Max Weber and democratic theorist Giovanni Sartori. Weber's methodology promotes the use of analytical distinctions that address questions that are *meaningful* from the standpoint of the values and normative concerns of actors (including social scientists themselves) while also facilitating objective empirical research (Fishman, 2007). Sartori's theorization of democracy emphasizes its inescapable connection to ideals that are typically imperfectly approximated in the humanly constructed institutional world (Sartori, 1987).

Those attributes that reflect the extent to which a system meets the minimum Schumpeterian criteria for membership in the genus of democracies—that is to say genuinely free and competitive elections for the highest executive and legislative offices in a polity—can be said to constitute "democratic authenticity." Shortfalls in "democratic authenticity" can be found in many systems that scholars universally place within the democratic genus. Absent this concept, limitations such as widespread electoral fraud or voter suppression, failures to guarantee the secrecy of the ballot, clearly political asymmetries in the reporting of the news, or in journalistic freedoms—and so on—may receive less attention than deserved. For reasons developed at length elsewhere (Fishman, 2016), I differentiate analytically between democratic quality and authenticity, reserving the concept of "quality" for normatively desired outcomes that *surpass* the minimum theoretically required for membership in the democratic genus, outcomes that can and should be pursued in cases that have at least some claim to "genus membership," even if shortfalls in democratic authenticity are present.

If democratic quality is, in this sense, understood to constitute the ability of discourse and debate in the public sphere to contribute to the full intellectual development of polity participants (Fishman, 2004)—an objective emphasized in normative and philosophic work on democracy since the classic formulations of Aristotle and Mill, more recently developed by Dahl (1998)—it becomes clear that democratic quality and authenticity can vary independently of one another. Social scientific analyses of what we can understand as the quality of public discourse and claims-making have established the systematic nature of the causal determinants underpinning this type of *quality* (Fishman, 2004; Ahlquist and Levi, 2013). Once we admit the existence of disparate logics underpinning democratic authenticity and quality, it becomes possible to understand how polities such as the antebellum United States could simultaneously experience severe shortfalls in democratic authenticity, reflected not only in limitations on voting rights but also far more flagrantly in the continued existence of slavery, alongside certain triumphs in democratic quality, perhaps best manifested by the historic Lincoln–Douglass debates of 1858 (Johannsen, 1965). The remaining two dimensions in this framework are democratic "depth" and "consolidation."

The terms "democratic depth" and the "deepening" of democracy have received a great deal of use in the literature on variation among democracies, but as with much else in this literature, that usage lacks a consensually shared understanding of what the term in question should be taken to mean; "depth" is widely used in two quite different ways and occasionally in others as well. In one common usage, democratic depth is understood to be roughly or fully equivalent to democratic quality and both terms are used for a large number of rather disparate attributes of political systems (Morlino, 2012; Diamond and Plattner, 2001). Despite the scholarly distinction of works that adopt this quite broad-ranging usage, I argue that the conflation of quality and depth unnecessarily impedes scientific accumulation. However, a second common conceptualization proves to be of great usefulness for this book's efforts and, I suggest, for much of the field of democracy studies. A large number of democracy scholars use the term "democratic depth" to mark the extent to which political systems provide opportunities for low-income or otherwise socially marginal sectors to gain effective influence over public policy formation and other political processes that take place outside the institutionalized arena of free and competitive elections to choose power-wielding representative of the *demos*. Whether this idea is formulated explicitly, or only implicitly suggested, the implication of important work by scholars such as Roberts (1998), Heller (2000), Fung and Wright (2003), Baiocchi (2005), Santos (2005), and others writing of *depth* in this sense is precisely this: that the exclusive reliance of political systems on the minimalist Schumpeterian formula of free and competitive elections for positions of political power yields a shallow form of democracy that fails to realize the underlying democratic ideal of government by the people, tending to exclude socially marginal sectors from equal influence over ultimate outcomes. Work of this nature on democratic depth may emphasize either the potentially important impact of social movements and popular protest on effective democracy or the hoped-for deepening effect of inclusionary institutions such as participatory budget-making. Both emphases—on the democratic contribution of social protest and the power-reallocating potential of participatory or deliberative institutions—reflect the view that capturing the will of the *demos* only at election time yields an inadequate approximation of certain fundamental democratic ideals.

There is a clear affinity between this conception of democratic depth and the insistence of democratic theorist Robert Dahl (1998, 2006), citizenship theorist Margaret Somers (2008), and others on vigorously pursuing effective political equality among citizens. Indeed, concerns over the attainment of effective political equality in contemporary democratic systems are quite broadly held among democracy scholars; this does not signify a lack of recognition for the fundamental importance of the Schumpeterian standard, which almost all students of democracy now accept as minimally valid. I take the concept of democratic depth as a highly useful way to strengthen the "state of democratic theory" (Shapiro, 2003) with a "Schumpeter-plus" sensibility that searches for avenues to pursue effective political equality not only in the electoral arena but also in the crucial periods of time between the institutionalized competition for votes, when fundamental processes such as agenda setting and public policymaking determine whether effective access to political power is highly skewed by economic position or relatively evenly distributed.

The central argument of this book suggests that cross-national variation in predominant forms of democratic practice exerts a strong impact on democracy's depth, shaping the bounds of political inclusion in ways that ultimately influence many other outcomes. The historical origins of this pattern of cross-national contrast, and the intervening significance of democratic practice, may to some degree also shape other outcomes primarily embedded in dimensions of democracy other than depth. For example, in the chapter on the Iberian divide in the politics of crisis, I argue that Portugal's post-revolutionary and inclusionary democratic practice has actually fortified the country's political institutions, allowing them to survive the new challenges of economic crisis more successfully than the equivalent institutions in those south European democracies lacking such an inclusionary form of democratic practice. Certain elements of inclusionary democratic practice may also lessen the danger of major shortfalls in democratic authenticity—for example through the robust autonomy of journalists and the communications media in cases such as Portugal.

The term "democratic consolidation" is widely used in democracy studies and has been understood in at least three different ways: Valenzuela (1990) emphasizes the importance of the elimination of "reserve domains" of non-democratic power in democratizing regimes, taking that indicator as a central measure of democracy's "consolidation." Schmitter (1995, 1999) and Morlino (1998) understand consolidation to refer partly to the stability of democracy's component institutions—such as party systems and so forth. Consolidation in this sense refers to the institutionalization and stability of existing forms of political representation and power in democratic settings. In this usage, democracy itself can remain in place even in the face of system "deconsolidation" as in the case of Italy, where democracy has survived over a quarter of a century after the implosion of that country's post–World War II party system in 1992–1994. However the predominant understanding of consolidation (Schedler, 2001; Fishman, 2016) is that of Linz and Stepan (1996), who use this term to identify the stability of democracy itself—that is, the likelihood that democracy will survive. A key component—perhaps even a guarantee—of democratic consolidation in this predominant sense is the presence of Dahl's "mutual tolerance" between governments and oppositions (Dahl, 1971). In extreme cases, democratic practice may actually influence democratic consolidation—especially in the third and most common sense of the term. Huntington's historically influential approach to conceptualizing political stability (Huntington, 1968; Crozier, Huntington, and Watanuki, 1975) would seem to predict that especially inclusionary democratic practice could undermine consolidation, but others would theorize precisely the reverse (Kadivar, 2018). I suggest that relatively exclusionary democratic practice may, in extreme cases, severely diminish democratic authenticity if some political adversaries of incumbent governments experience an outright denial of their capacity to effectively contest power in free elections. Moreover, the danger or perception of exclusionary tendencies of that magnitude can easily undermine mutual tolerance—and with it democratic consolidation. This possibility is not the main theme of this book, but I will return to it in the chapter on the Catalan crisis. However, that said, the central claim in what follows concerns the impact of nationally predominant forms of democratic practice on the attainment of *democratic depth*. I do not attempt to exhaustively develop the impact of this variable on other dimensions of democratic variability. There are, of course, other available frameworks for the study of variation among democracies. Among the most stimulating attempts to explain democratic variability is Robert Putnam's landmark book on regional variation in governmental effectiveness in Italy (Putnam, 1993). However, despite the great strengths of that study, in my view the reliance on the concept of social capital introduces unnecessary scholarly costs that ultimately render explanation more difficult than necessary (Fishman, 2004, 2009). Ian Shapiro's major recent synthesis of normative and empirical work—and his emphasis on political avenues to the reduction of domination (Shapiro, 2016)—constitutes another major perspective on ways to think about and study democratic variability. In my view, students of democracy would do well to draw eclectically on such approaches and on newer ones such the argument presented here.

IV. *Identifying the Determinants of Variation among Democracies*

Many conventional studies of variation among democracies tend to assume that the primary determinants of major differences among such systems lie in the formal makeup of their political institutions—such as constitutions, electoral systems, party systems, and the like. Such institutions are widely understood to establish the parameters determining whether free representative systems tend to empower or constrain majorities, whether they foster consensual or adversarial relations among contending political forces, and whether parties genuinely serve the public interest (Rosenbluth and Shapiro, 2018). In a fundamental sense, institutional rules and structures are assumed to put in place incentives that largely orient much of what goes on in political systems, for example in the fate of efforts to build and sustain coalitions in multi-party parliamentary systems (Mershon, 2002). This emphasis is to be found not only in scholarship by institutionalist theorists but also in major works by democracy theorists such as Dahl and Lijphart, who devote considerable attention to the institutional rules and procedures that provide greater power and leeway to electoral majorities in some cases than in others. This book's approach is not intended to question such arguments but rather as an important supplement to them.

Other schools of thought focus less on the design of constitutional and electoral institutions, or other factors put in place by legislative or judicial action, emphasizing instead variation in institutional determinants located in political or civil society. One important framework, that of "power resources" or "power constellation" theory (Korpi and Shalev, 1979; Stephens, 1979; Huber and Stephens, 2012) assumes that the organizational capacities and resource endowments of contending forces in society carry enormous consequences for distributional outcomes settled by democratic procedures. This approach yields readily operationalizable propositions, many of which have proven to be highly fruitful in explaining cross-national variation in major political and distributional outcomes. The power resources and power constellations approaches provide very useful ways to explain much variation in outcomes between democracies. Nonetheless, and despite its considerable usefulness, this approach has its weaknesses if employed as the sole instrument for explaining cross-national variation in distributional and other outcomes. The ability of social forces to engage in collective action and their capacity to shape public life or political outcomes is only imperfectly captured by their organizational strength and resources. In new democracies, and many long-established ones as well, the fit between, on the one hand, the organizational strength and resource endowments of contending forces and, on the other hand, their ability to condition public decision-making is quite inexact (Fishman, 2017). Both the ability of social forces to initiate collective action and their capacity to gain a hearing from others are conditioned also by cultural factors, which can generate outcomes that would not be anticipated on the basis of an exclusive focus on formal organizational strength or resources. Thus there is no escaping the importance of cultural factors—albeit in interaction with other determinants.

Indeed, a theoretically rich tradition of work has long emphasized the relevance of cultural factors for the study of politics in democracies. Tocqueville's classic studies of the contrasts between democratic dynamics in the United States and France incorporated the concept of mores into his overarching theory with its primary emphasis on the allegedly interrelated significance of voluntary associations and state decentralization. Much more recently, innovative studies of numerous other themes—such as the origins and nature of "apathy" (Eliasoph, 1998), the role of socially embedded imagination in citizen discourse (Perrin, 2006) and the construction of a post-communist public sphere in eastern Europe (Stamatov, 2000)—have strengthened the argument for studying politics from a perspective that draws cultural phenomena into the analysis. I apply this sensibility to the systematic study of variation among democracies, especially with regard to a crucial defining feature of representative systems: the breadth of inclusion that they afford to would-be participants in democratic life. The approach introduced in this book views the cultural sphere—and crucial historical developments that shape its emergence—as constitutive of fundamental parameters of democratic politics.

The approaches discussed thus far are, of course, not alone in the existing literature. Social scientists also focus on aggregate and distributionally oriented economic variables as well as the constellation of politically relevant ideologies and ideas—and other factors located in social or economic structure. Among these approaches are social network analysis, of special relevance when it is linked to the study of historical change (Bearman, 1993; Emirbayer and Goodwin, 1994; Ikegami, 2005; Mische, 2008). I take these analytic options —and others—to be quite valuable, but I focus on a different terrain of divergence, showing that it, too, has quite powerful consequences, especially for setting the bounds of political inclusion and, as a result, any given democracy's relative approximation to the goal of political equality. Thus this book offers a new way to think of and study the relative success of democratic systems in achieving the ideal of government by and for the people.

The ground that I emphasize is intended to be examined in combination, and often in interaction, with other determinants of political action, many of them well established by long traditions of scholarship such as those noted above. Yet I argue that a great deal of what matters—especially in shaping the bounds of political inclusion—is located outside those well-studied terrains. The new area of study that I advocate concerns assumptions that are often unwritten but which nonetheless shape individual and collective understandings of democracy and, as a result, the normal forms of activity in such systems. These understandings strongly condition how actors "do" democracy, how they make use of freedoms opened up by democratization, and interact with others so engaged. A great deal of my emphasis lies on the relationship between protesters and power holders—an area of much concern to social movement scholars (Markoff, 1996; Giugni, McAdam, and Tilly, 1998; Tilly, 1995, 2004, 2006; Tarrow, 2012; della Porta, 2013). Following the work of such scholars, I argue that the interaction between protesters and institutional office holders should also be of central concern to students of democracy. However, my emphasis here centers not on the contribution of protester contention to the emergence of democracy but instead on the linkage of this phenomenon to variation between democratic systems. My treatment of democratic practice also includes other dynamics, apart from social protest, that configure the overall propensity of representative systems to include socially marginal actors as full members of the institutionally recognized political community.

The claim that democratic life is to a significant degree shaped by what actors actually do and not only by the formal and written guidelines for political life is of course not a new one. Great theorists of modern democracy such as Robert Dahl, Arend Lijphart, and others have written of democratic practices, in the plural, as a significant element in the overall range of factors shaping the nature of democracies. Theorists of informal institutions such as Helmke and Levitsky (2006) have focused analytic attention on the substance of unwritten codes and rules that are intended to shape and constrain given outcomes. But the theory proposed here is quite different from earlier discussions of democratic practices in the plural or of informal institutions. Unlike observations of the political relevance of democratic practices in the plural, the approach introduced here attempts to delineate an overarching logic and general theoretical significance of democratic practice in the singular. This is not to say that I conceptualize national patterns of democratic practice as being thoroughly homogeneous or univocal. Far from it. But even if we conceptualize cultural phenomena as typically constituting repertoires replete with internal contradictions and complexities, the view that central tendencies and nationally predominant forms of practice can be specified clearly sets this approach apart from those that simply note particular practices in the plural. This book's undertaking is also quite different from the very useful project of theorists of informal institutions. Whereas the subject matter of Helmke and Levisky as well as their collaborators focused on informal yet enforceable rules, the argument proposed here emphasizes instead cultural understandings, frameworks, and practices that condition or orient numerous elements of democratic life without regulating and constraining those elements as tightly as enforceable rules aspire to do. The scope of impact of culturally rooted forms of democratic practice is broader, but the regulation of conduct is weaker than in the case of informal institutions.

It is useful to mention here one crucial point: Whereas some analysts have focused on interactions between protesters—or other civil society actors—and political power holders, others have instead prioritized interactions among political actors located within recognized political institutions. This book's concept of democratic practice does both things. These two terrains of analysis are linked by the way in which conceptions of democracy shape what goes on within them. In linking these two terrains, this book offers a new way of understanding cultural determinants of democratic inclusion.

V. The Logic Underpinning the Comparison of Portugal and Spain

I examine the substance, origins, and consequences of nationally distinctive forms of democratic practice through a focused comparison of two neighboring cases—Portugal and Spain. This paired comparison has proved highly useful because the two countries were remarkably similar in numerous ways before they diverged in the 1970s in the context of their remarkably different pathways from dictatorship to democracy. For centuries Portugal and Spain were marked by structural similarities in society and the economy, a series of notable historical parallels in their political development and multiple instances of cross-border diffusion in which the countries influenced one another. Their historical turn toward liberalism, most significantly in the nineteenth century, was in both cases later and more limited than in many successful societies of northern Europe. And in both country cases the early twentieth-century experience with democracy collapsed in the face of severe polarization, the decline of mutual tolerance between political adversaries, and the rise of anti-democratic forces during the interwar years (Linz, 1978). The breakdown of democracy in 1926 in Portugal and 1936–1939 in Spain led to many decades of harshly repressive authoritarian rule in both countries.

This pattern of persistent similarity and historical parallelism was fundamentally broken in the 1970s—a shift that presents social scientists with a historically rare opportunity to study and assess the consequences of such a large-scale macro-historical shift. The Iberian Peninsula neighbors' remarkably dissimilar pathways from dictatorship to democracy constitute a "critical juncture" or historical "turning point" of just the sort that comparative historical social scientists (Collier and Collier, 1991; Abbott, 2001; Mahoney and Rueschemeyer, 2003; Pierson, 2004; Collier and Munck, 2017) find especially useful as an analytic tool facilitating the effort to isolate the historical causes of meaningful outcomes. Portugal moved from dictatorship to democracy through a social revolution that upended hierarchies and remade cultural structures, repertoires, and frameworks, while also thoroughly transforming the political system. The Portuguese experience, in what was arguably the most radical transition process of the Third Wave, linked social revolution to the construction of new democratic institutions. The Spanish transition was, in contrast, one of the least radical democratic transitions during the wave of worldwide change. In the Spanish case the partially consensual and reform-oriented transformation of the authoritarian regime into a democracy allowed for certain elements of symbolic and legal continuity even in the midst of thorough-going regime change. The two transitions were fundamentally different—making this pairing of countries an especially useful empirical basis for research on the enduring legacies of divergent pathways to democracy (Stepan, 1986).

Thus the rationale in favor of systematically comparing democracy in Portugal and Spain is quite a powerful one. Numerous works by social scientists have taken up this paired comparison, investigating contrasts or similarities between the neighboring countries on a wide range of matters (Bermeo, 1987; Blanchard and Jimeno, 1995; Bover, García Perrea, and Portugal, 2000; Durán Muñoz, 2000; Esping-Andersen, 1994; Fernandes, 2015; Fishman, 1990a, 2005, 2010, 2013, 2017; Fishman and Lizardo, 2013; Glatzer, 2000; Gómez-Fortes, 2009; Gould, 2009; Jordana, 2002; Linz, 1977; Magalhaes, 2003; Magone, 2001; Montero, Calvo, and Martínez, 2008; Radcliff, 2017; Royo, 2002; Royo and Manuel, 2003; Rowe, Lago, and Lago, 2014; Stoleroff, 2013; Torcal, 2014; Watson, 2015; Wiarda, 1989). Some of those comparisons have taken the intrinsic interest of the pairing to be obvious and have simply concentrated on empirical findings, whereas other studies have elaborated a theoretical and/or methodological rationale for the pairing. Works by economists, sociologists, and political scientists have presented the comparison of the Iberian Peninsula neighbors as an especially useful way to pose and answer a number of important questions—including the causes of persistently high unemployment, and a number of social or political matters potentially shaped by pathways to democracy. The most far-reaching claims have presented this two-way pairing as a natural experiment allowing social scientists to isolate the effect of one or another point of recent variation between the two cases. That understanding is an attractive one—especially for the challenge taken up by this book—but the view that this pairing can be taken as a fully valid natural experiment is probably somewhat overstated.

Despite the numerous structural similarities between Spain and Portugal and the myriad elements of historical parallelism prior to the 1970s, the two cases were not fully identical even before the 1970s. One can identify several points of causally relevant contrast between the neighboring countries prior to the beginning of the democratizing wave in revolution on April 25, 1974. These points, to which I turn below, can be conceived of as what Slater and Simmons call "critical antecedents" (Slater and Simmons, 2010). That is to say that these elements of differentiation were in place prior to the critical juncture of divergent pathways to democracy in the 1970s and we should expect them to causally interact with the fundamental divergence that fully crystallized at the time of the 1970s transitions. These antecedent differences include several rather obvious points: the greater size of Spain and its internal linguistic and national diversity (Diez Medrano, 1995; Linz, 1973); the somewhat lesser economic development of Portugal and crucially the historically late introduction of universal access to education in the 1950s in Portugal (Candeias et al., 2007); the differing timing of decolonization in the two cases;[2] and the far greater magnitude and destructiveness of the Spanish civil war of the 1930s (Jackson, 1965; Casanova, 2010, 2013), when it is compared to the mini–civil wars experienced by Portugal during its early twentieth century First Republic (Wheeler, 1999). All of these differences are potentially of causal relevance, and I take them up in appropriate places, asking whether the existence of such points of added contrast contributes to the outcomes analyzed here—thereby detracting from the force of the book's central argument.

Crucially, when this issue is addressed, none of these "confounding factors" of national difference between the cases seems to play a crucial causal role in the dynamics emphasized here. The contemporary differences that I establish in democratic practice cannot be detected earlier in the history of the two countries—even during the twentieth-century interwar period. As recently as the beginning of the democratic transition period in the 1970s, the initial demands of protesting workers in the two societies were remarkably similar, as the major research study of Durán Muñoz (2000) has persuasively shown. Hence it seems reasonable to conclude that the pairing of the two cases is an exceptionally useful strategic comparison that provides us with an unusually strong basis to pose and answer certain questions of theoretical relevance. Nonetheless, the two-way comparison fails to fully meet the extremely demanding test of constituting a completely valid natural experiment. Our two-way comparison is promising, but it will be important to pause from time to time to ask whether factors other than the contrast in national pathways to democracy may contribute significantly to currently observable differences between the countries.

The Iberian contrast also offers one rather more specific type of theoretical promise. The Portuguese case stands as a historically exceptional exemplar of a fully democratic social revolution—one that partially inverted hierarchies of many sorts and rearranged culture phenomena while also putting in place the basis for constructing new and fully free democratic institutions. The scholarly analysis of causes and features of large-scale revolutions (Goodwin, 2001; Skocpol, 1979) is of crucial relevance for understanding the Portuguese case and its contrasts with Spain. However, as research by these and other scholars has shown, social revolutions have often led to anti-democratic regimes of one type or another or, at best, to periods of ambiguity characterized by instability and at least temporarily "hybrid" outcomes, as, is reflected in scholarly debates over how to characterize the post-revolutionary Nicaraguan regime prior to 2007 (Mainwaring and Pérez-Liñán, 2005; Anderson and Dodd, 2009; Levitsky and Way, 2010). That country's unmistakable turn away from democratic authenticity after Daniel Ortega's return to the presidency in 2007 altered the empirical basis for that debate. In contrast, the El Salvadoran insurgency (Viterna, 2013) and its connection to the democratization of what had been an exclusionary and violent regime (Wood, 2000; 2003) may be construed as an instance of social revolutionary democratization. The classic French case offers an obvious example of social revolutionary origins of a major democratic tradition, but the linkage of the French Revolution to consolidated democratic rule was highly historically discontinuous and involved anti-democratic interludes.

Fully democratic revolutions (Thompson, 2003), including those recently studied by della Porta (2016) have tended to be exemplars of strictly political transformation. Portugal's Carnation Revolution is, thus, a historically unusual case of a genuinely social revolution that led quickly to uninterrupted democratic rule—making it possible to use the analysis of this case to ask how social revolutionary beginnings can shape democracy. The Iberian Peninsula comparison allows us to focus on specifically post-revolutionary elements of contemporary collective life in Portugal as a way of addressing enduring consequences of revolution. This question obviously holds an important place among the broader issues posed by the book; but given the particular significance of the search for enduring consequences of revolution, especially in democracies (della Porta, 2016), it seems useful to bring this query into clear view. The discussion in what follows addresses both general issues on the cultural and political legacies of national pathways to democracy and specific questions on the enduring impact of revolutions, especially social ones.

VI. *The Approach Adopted by This Study*

The analysis presented in this book takes up a wide range of social, cultural, economic, and political dimensions of national life in Spain and Portugal— drawing out the comparative implications for democratic inclusion elsewhere. The focus is quite macroscopic, and the methodologies employed are eclectic. I have sought to investigate and theorize the interconnections between elements of collective experience that are often not seen as causally interrelated. In that way the book is much influenced by the broad effort of Hall and Lamont (2009, 2013) to draw out the usefulness of interrelating cultural, social, and political causality in the shaping of large-scale societal outcomes. The book's aspirations are in large measure theoretical ones, hoping to elaborate a basis for tracing out and making sense of causal patterns and contrasts of potentially great significance for the attainment of normatively valued goals in democracy. During the development of the book's arguments I have been concerned to search for evidence of all sorts as the basis for rejecting, reaffirming, or amending my earliest formulations of the argument. I have relied on a wide range of scholarly tools in the research including the secondary analysis of survey data and other quantitative indicators of relevance, in-depth qualitative interviewing, ethnographic observation, and a thorough reading of the available literature.

The central argument of the book is in effect a theory—one based on a great deal of historical, observational, and qualitative evidence as well as conceptual work linking such evidence to theoretical and empirical literatures in political science and sociology. However in certain respects the argument pushes theoretically beyond what the available evidence can fully prove. Without this added theoretical effort, the implications of the argument would be constrained unnecessarily—diminishing the significance of the study. Theoretical endeavors of this nature obviously play a crucial role in social science, but their ultimate utility rests on the use that can be made of them and, quite obviously, the tests to which they are subject. Given this emphasis on broadly theoretical aspirations and the considerable breadth of the claims advanced in the book, I have attempted several partial tests of the usefulness of the book's theoretical argument. These tests are by necessity somewhat selective and partial. After all, theories cannot be definitively proved to be correct. They can only be definitively disproved, but when theories pass various tests, even partial ones, that contributes to their plausibility. The evidence offered in the book is intended to strongly contribute to that objective. These partial tests include some centered on evidence afforded by macro-level historical experience and aggregate indicators as well as others that rely on the data provided by survey analysis. Together, they add plausibility to the argument, but the full range of usefulness of the theory can only be adequately established through future tests of various sorts. The impact of the argument on ongoing work by social scientists has already been significant; the findings of such work and of future studies by others will contribute greatly to assessing the pathway of explanation that this book aspires to set out.

Thus the earliest published versions of the book's core arguments (Fishman, 2005, 2010, 2011a, 2012a) have already helped to shape the research agenda of other social scientists who found in those arguments ideas or hypotheses worth pursuing. For example, a team of scholars led by Donatella della Porta, building on their major contributions to the field of social movement studies, has published two valuable works that provide important independent confirmation of the enduring impact of transition scenarios on social protest dynamics and related phenomena (della Porta, Massimiliano et al., 2017; della Porta et al., 2018). Those works are discussed in chapters 5 and 7. Other significant scholarly works on social protest have provided additional independent confirmation of the usefulness of arguments emphasized here (Accornero and Ramos Pinto, 2015; Baumgarten, 2017). Ongoing work by Tiago Carvalho on protest events is already underway[3] and surely more will follow. I conceive of all social science as an invitation to efforts at testing or even replication by others, and that is much the case here.

VII. The Organization of the Book

The book consists of eight chapters as well as a preface. Following the introduction presented in this chapter, chapter 2 examines the substance of the two Iberian Peninsula countries' transitions to democracy in the 1970s. A great deal has been written on both transitions—including studies by country specialists and works by comparativists. I draw extensively on the available literature on both the Portuguese and Spanish pathways from dictatorship to democracy, but in certain respects I seek to move beyond existing claims, drawing out the significance of under-emphasized elements of the two cases for the outcomes under investigation here. The chapter's central objective is to identify the components of the two countries' democratization pathways that hold causal relevance for the legacies highlighted in the rest of the book.

Chapter 3 is, in a sense, the book's centerpiece. It presents the essence of my claims on democratic practice in Portugal and Spain, showing how different the predominant pattern is in the two cases. Much of the discussion focuses on the nexus between social protest and institutional power holders, but in parallel fashion it also takes up the treatment that low-income and socially marginal actors receive from office holders in the two countries. The chapter is concerned with political actors "across the board," so to speak, including ordinary citizens, organized groups, and professional politicians. The chapter also takes up the significance of action and understandings inside two institutions that hold special importance for democracy's substance and future—the communications media and the educational system. The chapter argues that underlying understandings and ubiquitous forms of practice inside these two institutions and in the political system writ large are actually more inclusionary than required by formal institutional rules in Portugal and frequently less than implied by formal institutional rules in Spain. In essence the chapter argues that historical legacies dating from the 1970s have culturally conditioned the practice of democracy in both countries, generating substantially more inclusionary and anti-hierarchical outcomes in Portugal.

Chapter 4 turns to evidence on effects of this pattern of cross-national variation in democratic practice. This effort can be seen as a partial test, or a series of partial tests, of the theory's usefulness. I argue for the relevance of democratic practice for a range of socio-economic outcomes in the two cases, emphasizing the so-called Iberian employment paradox, which has long interested economists, political scientists, and sociologists. I suggest that Portugal's consistently superior performance in providing employment to those seeking jobs is in large measure an indirect effect of the national contrast in democratic practice. I examine also a variety of other outcome variables related to the welfare state and public policies. Additionally, I provide evidence drawn from two collaborative efforts that made use of survey data. I joined forces with experts in cultural sociology and the study of citizenship—jointly investigating contrasts between the two countries in one study on cultural tastes and another on forms of citizenship practice. Those collaborative efforts, both of which led to co-authored journal articles, provide us with findings of real importance for this book's exploration, findings that can be seen to represent two additional partial tests of the approach. Both of these additional partial tests draw on survey evidence, and find that the age cohort born, educated, and socialized under democracy—after the two transition pathways had put in place cultural understandings and practices conditioning the educational systems—shows effects strongly congruent with the book's central argument. Particularly significant is the demonstrable success of Portugal's post-revolutionary educational system in generating enhanced cultural capacities and forms of civic practice among those with at least a secondary education. In analyzing differences between the two cases in several outcome variables I stress the explanatory significance of democratic practice as an intervening variable, but I also identify and briefly discuss the significance of economic and formal institutional legacies of the two countries' pathways to democracy. The book's analysis of enduring legacies emphasizes cultural ones but is not limited to them. The material and the outcomes discussed in that chapter are drawn entirely from socio-political realities already in place—and on which data was available— when I formulated the initial versions of the argument that ultimately led to this book. From the standpoint of a truly rigorous conception of theory testing these partial tests could be seen as faulty or inadequate since the data that is presented in these "tests" was available when I initially formulated the argument on democratic practice. For that reason I treat these partial tests as less robustly satisfactory from the standpoint of theory testing than the subject matter of chapters 5, concerning the effects of democratic practice on the politics of crisis after 2010, and 6, on political conflict in Spain over the status of Catalonia.

Thus I treat separately these two recent test cases. The economic crisis— and especially the difficult turn that it took in southern Europe beginning in 2010—presented social scientists and actors with multiple new challenges. The magnitude of those challenges for citizens and residents of the southern European cases was of truly historic proportions, far greater than the impact of the great recession in the United States, Germany, and many other countries that proved more fortunate than Portugal, Spain, Greece, and others in the most affected area of Europe. Although not in any sense comparable, the new challenge faced by social scientists was also quite real. In my case, having already elaborated a comprehensive theory of historically rooted political differences between Portuguese and Spanish democracy, the new crisis posed the question of whether this large shock would erode—or reaffirm— the contrasts I had identified and written on in the period leading up to the new scenario. In a sense the crisis stood as a large scale "test" of the theory. I examine evidence on this test case in chapter 5.

Chapter 6 offers a different sort of partial test of the theory, examining the implications of the Catalan independence movement, and conflict over its objectives, for the book's arguments about Spain. Unlike the other substantive chapters, the analysis of the Catalan case essentially leaves out Portugal, for rather obvious reasons. In the Portuguese case there is no real equivalent of the bitter conflict over Catalonia's status within—or outside—Spain. The matters taken up in this chapter involve developments and conduct that are still quite recent as this book goes to press. For that reason, the chapter's empirical treatment of the Catalan case is, out of necessity, more exploratory or provisional than in the empirical analysis found in other substantive chapters. Nonetheless the significance of the Catalan conflict for the state of democracy in Spain and for assessing this book's argument seems inescapable. Moreover, taking up the Catalan case allows us to address—and weigh the importance of—a clear asymmetry between the Portuguese and Spanish cases: Whereas Portuguese politics are marked by the country's unitary and largely unquestioned national identity, Spanish politics are strongly conditioned by conflict over national identity and the existence of multiple national sentiments within the country's borders. The chapter provides strong evidence for its central claim that Spanish democratic practice contributed significantly to the gravity of the crisis, shaping the conduct of multiple actors on opposite sides of the conflict.

Chapter 7 addresses the large question of how cultures change—or reproduce themselves. Drawing on material from the comparison of Portugal and Spain and on relevant literature, the discussion examines the role of collective memory, of grievances both old and new, of exogenous shocks and endogenously generated sentiments, and of the "reselection" of relevant actors such as political parties capable of seriously contesting national elections. The chapter makes extensive use of fieldwork on commemorations, protest, and institutional political life in both Iberian cases, seeking to draw out lessons of usefulness for this book and the broader literature. This discussion also takes up the way in which democratic practice is culturally constituted and the mechanisms that contribute to its reproduction or transformation.

Chapter 8 aspires to identify the broader theoretical significance of the book's arguments for several areas of study and thought. The chapter also seeks to specify the comparative reach of the argument, which is to say its applicability or relevance for cases that lack the specific histories of the two Iberian Peninsula countries. A number of cases in Europe and the Americas are brought into the discussion, making the argument that significant elements of the constellation of causal factors found in one—or the other—of the two cases studied here can also be found in countries lacking the precise historical trajectories of Portugal and Spain. I link this effort to extend the argument's reach beyond the Iberian Peninsula to methodological claims found in the work of Max Weber and more recently Charles Ragin (1987, 2008). I also return to the central claims about Portugal and

Spain, addressing alternative possible treatments of the differences between them and assessing the implications of the analysis for our understanding of the two pathways to democracy. An examination of the argument's significance for theoretical understandings of democracy and for methodological claims in favor of the historical approach to social science close out the scholarly analysis prior to final thoughts on implications for contemporary democratic actors.

 | Messages of Transition
Fundamental Contrasts between Portugal and Spain

I. Introduction

The Third Wave got under way in the mid-1970s with two national experiences of self-transformation that sent extraordinarily different messages about democratization—and democracy itself. In assessing the import of the Portuguese and Spanish transitions for an overarching understanding of contemporary democracy, most scholars have focused on the message sent to actors in other countries. The external "messages" transmitted by these two cases seemed, at a minimum,[1] to offer suggestions about how actors could transform an anti-democratic regime into a democratic one. First, in the impact of Portugal's wave-initiating Carnation Revolution on the unraveling of late authoritarian rule in neighboring Spain (Sánchez Cervelló, 1993), and then in the "demonstration effect" of both transitions on political actors in countries governed by autocrats, the two cases contributed to democracy's spread worldwide (Weyland, 2014). In a sense Portugal could be seen to offer anti-democratic rulers evidence of the risks posed by not reforming their own house through a regime-initiated process of democratization, whereas Spain provided incumbent anti-democratic rulers with hope that they could avoid retribution for repressive conduct if only they participated in making democratic reform happen.

Without questioning the global importance of the Iberian Peninsula's external message to political forces in countries potentially "available" for democratization attempts, I instead emphasize the internal message of the two transitions to actors within each country itself. The images of change generated by these two processes of political transformation and the conceptions of democratic politics they encouraged were different enough to make the internal impact of the transition pathways at least as analytically important as the external influence—both at the time and afterward. In this chapter I seek to identify the major features of the two cases that exerted lasting effects on what followed internally within the two new democracies— Portugal and Spain. My emphasis lies on elements of transition that hold implications for cultural understandings of politics and, relatedly, for enduring forms of practice historically rooted in the two transitions, broadly construed.

Of course, there was a third regime transition in southern Europe during the mid-1970s, the collapse of military rule and the return to representative government in Greece in 1974. The Greek transition was in a sense intermediate between the other two both in historical time and in certain aspects of the mode of transformation. I take up the Greek case in this book's conclusion, hoping to specify analytical differences between that instance of democratization and the transitions in Portugal and Spain as part of a broader effort to elaborate comparative and theoretical implications of the Iberian Peninsula cases. I also offer there a limited conceptualization of elements of democratic practice in Greece after the demise of the colonels' military junta in 1974. The emphasis of this chapter lies on an analysis of the enormously different twin processes of democratic change in the Iberian Peninsula cases, highlighting ways in which that initial contrast between Portugal and Spain set the stage for the rather recalcitrant Iberian divide in political inclusion.

From their inception the Spanish and Portuguese transitions were fundamentally dissimilar in numerous respects. In certain ways—to be taken up later in this chapter—those differences continued to grow in magnitude during the unfolding of the two pathways to change as well as the crucial early years of democracy in which the two national party systems took shape. The most succinct possible rendition of the cross-case contrast is rather obvious: the long-lived Portuguese dictatorship was overthrown in late April 1974, whereas the Spanish regime reformed itself (under pressure from the opposition) after the death of longtime dictator Francisco Franco in November 1975. However that simple formulation would miss much of significance for understanding the enduring legacies of these two paths to democracy. The two cases are extraordinarily different in numerous respects: the identity of the central actors and their forms of interaction with one another, the breadth and depth of transformation, the venues within which the crucial processes took place, the types of demands that came to the fore during the transitions, the effects generated in society and the economy, the character and durability of the cultural dimensions of change, and—in a point of central importance—the role of the state apparatus in the pathway of change, to name but some of the many points of contrast.

There were nonetheless at least two elements of similarity in the pathways of change experienced by the neighboring countries in the 1970s. First and foremost, both transitions necessarily and centrally involved the calling of free and fair elections first for the bodies charged with writing new constitutions and then for the selection of office holders to govern under those new constitutions. This point of similarity made both countries into democracies; indeed all transitions to democracy share in that point of similarity. The elements of difference made them into different kinds of democracies. But one other element of similarity merits mention here for it underscores the theoretical usefulness of this paired comparison. In his important comparative study of worker mobilizations in the two democratization scenarios, Rafael Durán Muñoz (2000) finds that the initial content of demands formulated by labor in the context of transition was virtually identical in the two cases, even though those early demands ultimately led to highly dissimilar forms of collective worker action. The mobilization of social discontent became "transgressive" in Portugal—challenging existing ownership structures and forms of control—but was systematically blocked from following that route in Spain despite the shared nature of initial demands. This straightforward evidence of underlying similarities between the two societies at the time of democratization serves to confirm the usefulness of comparing cases that diverged strongly from one another in their mode of transition despite the prior existence of many strong parallels between the two societies. The juxtaposition between numerous underlying similarities and the radical divergence between the cases in the road taken to democracy is what makes this pairing so interesting—especially for the purpose of theory development.

II. Antecedents to Transition

Before we turn to an examination of the two transitions as such, it is important to first identify and take note of certain important antecedents to democratization in both cases. Neither instance of regime change can be fully understood without taking into account crucial elements of prior history that reflect some types of cross-national contrast even before the critical juncture of transition itself. One might think that any analytical nod to cross-case variation in crucial factors that were contextually in place prior to the Iberian neighbors' polar opposite pathways to democracy in a sense undercuts the claim that the trajectories of democratization constituted a historical turning point or critical juncture, placing the cases firmly on new path-differentiated avenues of development. However, important methodological work on the comparative historical approach argues strongly for incorporating "critical antecedents" into analyses of path dependency (Slater and Simmons, 2010). Slater and Simmons show how the causal dynamics at work during critical junctures operate in the way they do partly because of their interaction with certain antecedent variables. In their formulation, critical antecedents put in place conditions or processes that allow a large new historical bifurcation to generate fundamentally diverging pathways. To put the matter slightly differently, without their causal interaction with historically prior conditions or processes, the large-scale historical phenomena that we think of as critical junctures would not be able to produce their powerful effects. The comparison of the two Iberian Peninsula transitions to democracy confirms the usefulness of this approach. We cannot fully understand the cross-case contrast without incorporating into our analysis the significance of certain antecedents.

In both Portugal and Spain the regimes that ruled through authoritarian repression until the mid-1970s had been in power for decades. Portugal's right-wing authoritarian system, ultimately formalized as the Estado Novo, initially came to power in 1926, replacing the country's First Republic, which had been subject to polarization, severe government instability, and civil conflict that twice reached the status of brief mini–civil wars (Wheeler, 1978; Schwartzman, 1989). Spain's Franco dictatorship began with the attempt to overthrow the larger Iberian country's socially progressive but polarized Second Republic in July 1936, initiating a long and brutal civil war between supporters of the Republic and proponents of Franco's nationalist and anti-democratic military uprising. In the course of the war, areas of the loyalist Republican zone experienced social revolution or—in some contexts—a deepening of regional nationalist self-government (Casanova, 2010; Jackson, 1965). The political forces that mobilized in support of Franco's military uprising extended from Spain's domestic fascist party, the Falange (Payne, 1961), to ultra-monarchists in the Carlist movement, anti-democratic corporatists, and other extremely conservative sectors whose antagonism to the Republic's progressive agenda led them to support its violent overthrow. On the Republican side, Socialists, Republicans, progressive Catholics, Communists, regional nationalists, anarchists, Trotskyists, and others fought alongside loyal elements of the military and foreign volunteers. The Spanish civil war served as a battleground between virtually all of the major ideological tendencies to be found in interwar Europe. The victory of Franco's forces, aided by the military intervention of Germany's Nazi regime and Italy's fascist government gave way to decades of right-wing repression. Once the war ended, at least 50,000 people were executed and many thousands more imprisoned (Casanova and Gil Andres, 2014), an episode of repression so severe that historian Paul Preston has conceptualized the early years of Franco's rule as "the Spanish Holocaust" (Preston, 2012).

The two countries' systems of anti-democratic rule were similar in certain respects. Both of them drew support and political inspiration from a range of anti-democratic sources including among others anti-liberal strands of corporatism, ultra-conservative tendencies within Catholic thought, and classical fascism itself (Linz, 1964; Schmitter, 1979; De Lucena, 1979; Makler, 1979). Neither regime formally entered World War II, but Franco formed a "Blue Division" of regime-supporting volunteers who fought with the Axis Powers alongside the Nazis on the Russian Front. The Spanish dictatorship provided the empirical basis for Juan Linz's pioneering conceptualization of such systems as "authoritarian regimes" characterized by limited internal pluralism among regime loyalists despite their repressive character and lack of electoral accountability (1975). Linz differentiated authoritarian from totalitarian regimes not on the basis of their degree of repression—in fact he argued that some authoritarian systems were more harshly repressive than the least repressive totalitarian systems—or the spaces made available for participation but instead in other ways. Linz theorized totalitarian regimes to be committed to preventing dissent within their monistic center of power while aspiring to mobilize the broader society in pursuit of large ideologically defined ends. In contrast, Linz's authoritarian regimes permitted some forms of disagreement and limited political diversity within the center of power itself, among those historically supportive of the regime, and also allowed some freedoms for non-political or apolitical types of associations. The aspirations of authoritarian regimes were more limited than those of totalitarian ones (despite the presence of totalitarian tendencies within some authoritarian regimes in their early years), but faced with anti-regime opposition or sentiments, authoritarian regimes could prove at least as repressive as totalitarian systems if not, in some instances, more so (1975). Despite the monumental misreading of his work by those who mistakenly see in it a justification of authoritarian systems, Linz's Weberian ideal-typical (Fishman, 2007) typology has proved crucial to scholars' (and political actors') analytical ability to understand the capacity of some authoritarian regimes—but not others—to transform themselves.

The two Iberian Peninsula authoritarian systems did prove dissimilar in their capacity to transform themselves, but in both instances dictatorial rule was brought to an end in the transitions of the mid-1970s; whereas the Portuguese regime suffered a crisis of failure in 1974, the Spanish regime was ultimately subject to a different type of crisis, one of "obsolescence" (Fishman, 1990a). Both societies experienced rapid economic growth in the 1960s and early 1970s, bringing the two countries to a level of development at which democracy is the norm[2] (Boix and Stokes, 2003; Przeworski et al., 2000), but at the dawn of the 1970s it seemed far from evident that the two long-lived regimes could be transformed into democracies. Moreover, the Portuguese system was thoroughly committed to maintaining its colonial presence in several large African territories and smaller outposts elsewhere. Long after the events of the 1970s, the broadly global transformations of the Third Wave in the decades that followed its Portuguese beginnings made the turn to democracy in these initial cases seem somehow inevitable, but in fact both of the Iberian Peninsula pathways of change were fraught with difficult challenges, moments of deep uncertainty, and significant types of opposition to the path ultimately followed.

The Portuguese authoritarian dictatorship[3] persisted for six years after Marcelo Caetano replaced longtime ruler António Salazar, who was medically incapacitated in 1968. Caetano initially introduced limited liberalizing reforms, but whether due to pressure from right-wing stalwarts inside the Estado Novo, his own instincts, or the logic imposed by the regime's commitment to maintaining colonial rule in Africa, that opening ended unsuccessfully. The demise of reform efforts led to a renewed hardening of repression. Thus the regime proved incapable of reforming itself despite the presence of limited forms of controlled electoral competition and the existence of an internal liberal wing that had aspired to greater change (Fernandes, 2006). However, the regime's commitment to sustaining the country's colonial presence in several African territories and smaller outposts elsewhere would soon lead to a massive crisis of failure that severely undermined state capacities during the revolutionary period. In precisely the way formulated by Skocpol's paradigmatic theory of social revolution (1979), the Portuguese effort to occupy what proved to be an unsustainable position in the world system—as the last significant European colonial power—ultimately generated the tendencies within the state apparatus that led to the April 1974 revolution. The country's colonial overreach may seem especially puzzling given Portugal's economic backwardness and relative poverty in the twentieth century, but the historic Portuguese role in worldwide exploration and imperialism helps to explain this paradox. Without the difficult colonial wars that the country faced in Africa, the Portuguese route to democracy cannot be understood.

Tendencies internal to Portuguese society also played a role in the unfolding of revolution once the captains' movement had turned the precondition of the colonial war into an acute state crisis following the coup of April 1974. These tendencies included the growth of progressive Vatican II Catholicism, the development of forms of class solidarity and political opposition to dictatorship, and the diffusion of radical ideologies within crucial strata such as the middle ranks of the military. Nonetheless, none of these internal antecedents would have generated the effects that ultimately prevailed were it not for the state crisis induced by the colonial wars in Africa and the captains' coup on April 25.

Spain's Franco regime was also quite unable to reform itself into democracy prior to the death of the longtime dictator in November 1975; a change of such a fundamental nature was never remotely plausible during Franco's long rule as "Caudillo." Although the death of Franco seemed to open new possibilities, the challenge faced by pro-democratic forces in 1975 was a considerable one. There was no obvious crisis of failure—equivalent to Portugal's colonial wars in Africa or the humiliation of the Greek colonels in their military confrontation with Turkey over Cyprus—to which the opposition could appeal in an effort to delegitimize the regime. Instead, the regime was in effect rendered "obsolete" (Fishman, 1990a), even for many of its one-time supporters, as a function of several processes of change at work in Spanish society under authoritarian rule. The Franco regime had sought to legitimize itself by presenting its repressive authoritarian formula as the only way to "save the country" from conflict and disorder. Obviously, the regime was intrinsically illegitimate for all steadfast supporters of democratic principles and for the defenders of progressive social priorities but a democratizing appeal directed exclusively to those long active in opposition to the regime was not sufficient to bring authoritarian rule to an end. In the Spanish context, absent an endogenously produced collapse of the existing system, and given that the opposition's strength was insufficient to directly dislodge the regime, the hope for democratic transition rested in part on gaining support for democratization from sectors that had supported Francoism. There was no plausible path to democracy without gaining the support of at least some one-time supporters of the Franco regime. Undermining the regime's legitimacy formula by asserting its historical obsolescence was one avenue toward that objective.

At least three large processes of change at work in Spanish society contributed toward this end during the 1960s and early 1970s. One underlying

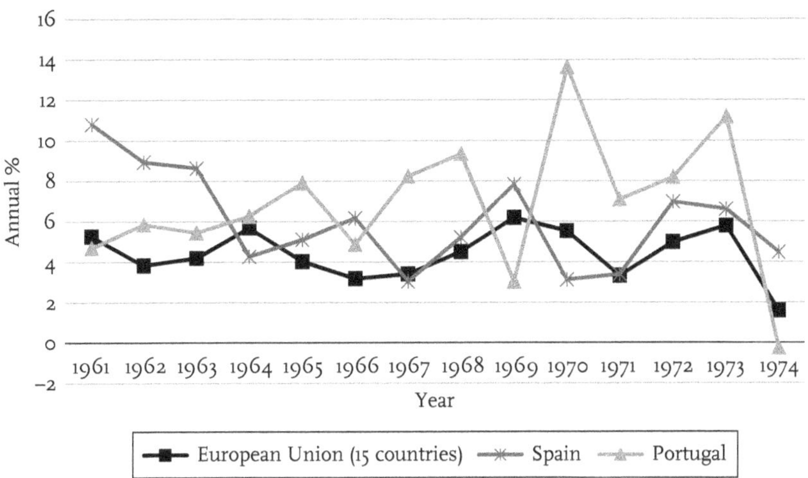

FIGURE 2.1 GDP per capita growth—EU15, Spain, Portugal—1961–1974 (annual %)
SOURCE: World Bank—World Development Indicators—Date extracted: 05.05.2018: http://data-bank.worldbank.org/data/reports.aspx?source=world-development-indicators. Note: The information on the EU15 is not indicated separately in the statistics. The calculated average of the fifteen member states is used and until 1971 does not include data for Germany and Ireland.

process was primarily economic. As the data presented in Figure 2.1 show, Spain's economy grew rapidly, as did Portugal's, during most of the 1960s and early 1970s. As a result, both Iberian Peninsula countries experienced a large decline in the rural and agricultural population, a transformative increase in per capita income, massive urbanization, and growth in the middle class. From the standpoint of theories that view economic development as highly beneficial to democracy's prospects (Przeworski et al., 2000; Boix and Stokes, 2003), these elements of change seemed quite beneficial. Other changes that took on fundamental importance as antecedents to the transition were socio-political and cultural (Pérez-Díaz, 1993; Maravall, 1978; Linz and Stepan, 1996). The two elements of transformation that I emphasize are first the growth of a remarkably effective labor movement in opposition to the regime and second the cultural rethinking of Spain's conflictual history.

During the 1960s a powerful labor opposition formed despite the repression to which it was subject (Maravall, 1978; Fishman, 1990b). From the 1950s onward, political opponents of the regime on the left had made the strategic decision to turn away from the post–civil war use of armed struggle by maquis in isolated mountain areas. Instead, they decided to employ all institutional spaces available in the authoritarian context in the hope of using them to mobilize mass civil resistance. This contributed to the growth of various types of civil resistance including neighborhood movements (Castells,

1983) and above all an increasingly effective labor movement. Opposition labor activists in Comisiones Obreras (Sartorius, 1977) and other union movements led major strike waves and also frequently won election to representative positions within the official regime "vertical union," which had been intended as an institutional vehicle of the Franco system to displace class and industrial conflict. The Franco regime's response to the growth of massive labor opposition was deeply contradictory: in some moments and contexts, officials of the regime attempted to incorporate worker activists within the authoritarian system by providing them certain limited institutional instruments for the pursuit of worker interests within the official regime union. Yet at the same time, the regime carried out major campaigns of repression, jailing some of the very same labor activists, often repressing strikes with coercive violence, and blocking many aspirations of worker representatives located inside the official vertical union that incorporated both employers and employees in the same obligatory structure.

In general terms, these contradictions promoted two rather different consequences, both of which proved favorable for the success of the democratic transition of the 1970s. The inherently contradictory nature of the regime's labor policy strengthened the opposition worker movement and fortified its political opposition to the Franco system (Fishman, 1990b:117–120). At the same time the (inconsistent) efforts of the regime to find institutional avenues to incorporate the genuine social reality of the labor relations field within official structures promoted a way of thinking within certain sectors of the Franco system that emphasized the virtue of adjusting legal forms to fit actual reality (Fishman, 1990b). The growth of a strong labor opposition provided the regime with pressure to change, constructed an ever wider social base for opposition activism and served as the motivation for an important cognitive development: the search by some elements of the regime for ways to bring legal formulae into congruence with social practice. All of this entailed a large human cost for those involved; a very high proportion of the activists in the opposition labor movement suffered arrest, spent time in jail, and experienced other types of repression.

A large and quite complex antecedent to the Spanish transition was primarily cultural in nature, although political analyses and calculations played a role in its genesis and evolution. Predominant interpretations of the country's past, and above all, ways of thinking about the civil war of 1936–1939, changed significantly during the long years of authoritarian dictatorship and especially during the last decade and a half of Franco's rule. The emergent re-interpretation was in a sense thoroughly anti-Manichean and for the most part sought to overcome the divisions of the past. As the important scholarship of Paloma Aguilar (2002; Aguilar Fernández and Payne, 2018)—author of the most extensive investigation into this theme—has shown, the increasingly predominant understanding of the war came to see it as a collective disaster in which both the blame for what happened and the costs paid for the descent into armed conflict were broadly shared. This way of viewing the past was not inconsistent with seeing the Second Republic as both morally and politically superior to the Franco dictatorship, but it implied that Spaniards should seek to move beyond the war's extreme polarization—searching for new avenues of reconciliation. Variations on the overall trend in re-interpretation could and did develop; this tendency was an internally varied one—just as Ann Swidler's conceptualization of culture (1986, 2001) as a repertoire of constructions and narratives would lead one to expect. The repertoire changed due to cultural work that served as a crucial antecedent to transition, but the uses made of that repertoire during the transition were a matter of politics.

Many eminent analysts see the cultural energy spent on re-interpreting the past as a vital component of the dynamics leading to democratic transition. For the sociological theorist Víctor Pérez Díaz, the rethinking of past divisions and of the civil war itself was one component of broader transformations in civil society that prepared Spain for the transition and for political coexistence between left, right, and center in democracy (Perez-Diaz, 1993). Theorists Juan Linz and Alfred Stepan, in a major work that emphasizes the strictly political dimensions of democratic transitions, argue that "through the 'cultural work' of civil society before the transition and the cultural work of civil society and almost all elements of political society during the transition, Spain had transformed the lessons of the civil war into a positive factor that aided the transition" (1996: 88). The game theoretical analyst Colomer (1995) suggests that the fear of civil war played a role in many transition-era decisions. Indeed, the growing emphasis on reconciliation—and in a related vein, on the search for consensus—emerged as a major theme in public discussions and in the contemporary press coverage during important phases of Spain's pathway to democracy (Edles, 1998; Sánchez-Cuenca, 2014a). However, just as Swidler's (2001) framework on cultural repertoires theorizes, in this case political actors made use of those elements of the new constructions of the past that served their strategies. The repertoire was selectively employed. Moreover, the interpretation of the past continued to evolve. We return to this theme in this chapter's concluding section, examining scholarly debate on legacies of the two transitions, but first we turn to the substance of the two Iberian roads to democracy.

III. *Democratization through Social Revolution in Portugal*

In analyzing the two processes of change, I begin with the Portuguese case—if only because it was chronologically first. The Carnation Revolution of April 25, 1974, was in its inception a military operation led by veterans of the country's increasingly unsuccessful colonial wars in Africa.[4] Crucially, it was captains rather than generals or colonels who led the rebellion. The fact that the coup was led by hierarchical subordinates or, to be more exact, hierarchical intermediaries, was to hold enormous consequences for what followed and for the cultural construction of its meaning. The challenge to hierarchies—initiated when captains overrode the chain of command and took charge of soldiers in several barracks, leading columns of tanks to march on Lisbon—began to spread while the coup was underway and continued doing so for much time afterward. Shortly after the forces led by the rebellious captains reached Lisbon on April 25, a brigadier general loyal to the Estado Novo unsuccessfully ordered a tank crew and other soldiers under his command to fire on the insurgents; these soldiers disobeyed the general's order, deepening the erosion of military hierarchy.

Crowds of ordinary citizens spilled into the streets, joining the tanks and soldiers in rebellion, well before they had secured the surrender of Dictator Marcelo Caetano in the military barracks where he sought refuge on the Largo do Carmo, a small square in old Lisbon. The columns of tanks that the "captains of April" brought into the streets of Lisbon overthrew not only the right-wing dictatorship that had ruled the country for nearly fifty years but also the institutional hierarchy and discipline of the Armed Forces. From the beginning of the Portuguese revolution, the captains were joined by others in challenging existing hierarchies, in many instances directly disobeying those above them in the institutional line of command. In this and other ways, the actors engaged in the uprising—including the civilians who entered the streets in support of the captains and in celebration—placed in question conventionally restrictive conceptions of the nature of politics and institutions. By the end of the day on April 25, the authoritarian Estado Novo had been defeated; in the process of rapidly achieving that goal, the captains and their allies had initiated a broad process of transformation that would remake central features of culture, society, and the economy—along with the political system.

The swift and successful overthrow of authoritarian rule by the Armed Forces Movement (MFA) and its allies, including the civilians who poured into the streets in support of the rebellion, soon undermined the ability of both the military and the police to employ state repression to contain social mobilization within existing legal boundaries. The Portuguese pathway to democracy was decisively marked by the location of the initially central actors inside the state apparatus as such, rather than within the political organs of the incumbent regime (Fishman, 1990a), a crucial difference with Spain. Analytically, it is useful to distinguish in this fashion between states and regimes even though they may be very tightly intertwined in some cases. A regime can be understood as the "formal and informal organization of the center of political power and of its relations with the broader society" (428); the distinction between democratic and anti-democratic political systems concerns regime type. The state can be understood as "a (normally) more permanent structure of domination and coordination including a coercive apparatus and the means to administer a society and extract resources from it" (428).

This distinction has proved highly useful to many students of systemic political change. In contexts of macro-political transformation state structures may be left largely intact when a regime is fundamentally altered or they, too, may be subject to basic reformulation, or in unusual circumstances outright collapse. The location of crucial actors involved in processes of macro-political change may also vary across cases; in some instances such as Spain significant political leaders of the authoritarian regime itself played a crucial initiating role in the transition. In contrast, in the Portuguese case it was state actors who had held essentially apolitical positions of only intermediate importance—namely, captains in the army—who played the most important initiating role in the demise of authoritarianism. The Portuguese location of the initiators of the transition inside the state gained deep significance above all because of the coup's rejection of existing institutional lines of command. The challenge to hierarchy and, related to that, the growing political divisions within the Armed Forces, decisively eroded the discipline and institutional capacity of the military and police after April 25. In this respect, the Portuguese road to democracy was thoroughly unlike that of Greece, several months later in 1974. In Greece the institutional leadership of the Armed Forces reasserted hierarchical lines of command, ousting the junta that had ruled the country since 1967, and returned that country to democratic rule.

Portugal's Carnation Revolution, and its crucial antecedents in the country's difficult colonial war in Africa (Bermeo, 2007), had generated a classic "state crisis"—the central precondition for a successful social revolution in Theda Skocpol's highly influential formulation (Skocpol, 1979). A great deal of excellent scholarly work on the Portuguese revolution clearly establishes the causal significance of this precondition for the turn to social revolution (Bermeo, 1986; Hammond, 1988; Durán Muñoz, 2000; Palacios Cerezales, 2003; Ramos Pinto, 2013). In this new and radically changed context a large number of subordinate social groups pushed their demands—and their projects of transformation—considerably further than would have been possible under normal circumstances. In the process they changed Portuguese society and themselves. With the severe erosion of the coercive capacity and will of the police and Armed Forces, both old and new movements could transform social circumstances in many fundamental ways. Workers occupied factories and other economic enterprises, in many cases leading to their nationalization. Agricultural laborers occupied large farms and there, as well, overturned their ownership status. Urban residents mobilized to change their lived environment and in many instances occupied vacant dwellings or constructed new ones on land owned by others (Hammond, 1988; Ramos Pinto, 2013). Those involved altered not only their social environment but also their self-conception and in some cases their collective identity. Their sense of efficacy and political relevance increased along with their success (Bermeo, 1986; Hammond, 1988; Ramos Pinto, 2013).

This new context encouraged subordinate or disadvantaged social groups— and those who sought their support—to see democracy as an instrument allowing all sectors of society, including the poor, to pursue solutions to their concerns and grievances. Urban residents of low-income neighborhoods were among the newly emergent actors who shaped the political direction of the country in the period that followed (Ramos Pinto, 2013). In this setting even parties on the right developed a social sensibility. The most right-wing party of electoral significance, the Partido do Centro Democrático Social (CDS), articulated its appeal to voters in the first elections, held on April 25, 1975, around the slogan "Queremos Responder"—"We Want to Respond." The party's election posters featured representations of poor Portuguese citizens—people of very limited economic means—alongside this slogan.[5] The social mobilization made possible by revolution conditioned political appeals across the ideological spectrum. The largest party to the right of the Portuguese center, initially called the Partido Popular Democrático (PPD) before changing its name to Partido Social Democrata (PSD), defined itself as social democratic and unsuccessfully sought admission to the Socialist International. The political impact of the revolution's social turn was quite broad. Decades later, survey data on the very widespread commitment of the Portuguese public to redistributive economic policies point to the congruence of contemporary reality with those democratic beginnings (Villaverde Cabral, Vala, and Freire, 2003).

Much of what went on during the revolution took the form of a partial inversion of hierarchies. This process generated widespread bottom-up, and generally alegal, purges (Costa Pinto, 2001, 2006). As anthropologist José Sobral put the matter, "It was the whole world turned upside down."[6] Supporters and alleged supporters of the now-defeated Estado Novo were ousted from positions of authority in government ministries, private enterprises, the news media, and educational establishments. In secondary schools and universities students and left-wing teachers met in assemblies and ousted those held to be linked to the old authoritarian order. The challenge to existing hierarchies also reshaped gender relations. The revolution quickly incorporated women's issues into its agenda for change (Ferreira, 1998), implementing new guarantees for women workers, thereby facilitating the work/family life balance. Participation by women in the labor force rose quickly, making Portugal the only southern European country in which at that time the presence of women in the work force surpassed the average level for the European Union (Fishman, 2010).

The social revolution quickly restructured the economy and a large range of cultural phenomena. The revolution came to articulate socialism as its economic goal, but its social character was both prior to and broader than that systemic economic objective. The widespread nationalizations of the period encompassed the country's entire financial system along with much else. Through the ownership of many enterprises by Portuguese banks and savings institutions, the overall scope of nationalization was actually broader than indicated by a simple accounting of enterprises directly nationalized by the state. Although much of the economy remained in private hands, the rapid expansion of the state-owned sector, and the ideological commitment to socialism of a sort by parties and political forces enjoying majority support (Jalali, 2007; Lisi, 2015), placed Portugal in the position of attempting to simultaneously construct a more or less conventional representative democracy and a socialist economy (leaving plenty of room for the private sector). One crucial enterprise, the country's largest bank, the Caixa Geral de Depositos, was already publicly owned, making its nationalization unnecessary in the new context.

The Portuguese revolution wove together various forms of transformation—social, political, economic, and cultural (Fishman, 2018a). The fundamental unity of the process as a historical phenomenon should not be lost from view. After all, each form of transformation conditioned— and in turn was conditioned by—the others.[7] The revolution's process of cultural renewal was deeply affected by the fact that it took place alongside the partial inversion of social hierarchies and the expansion of the terrain for political action well beyond the boundaries of official institutions. The political dimension of change was, in turn, conditioned by the social, economic, and cultural processes at work. But the political component of the overall set of transformations, with its defining essence in state crisis, clearly conditioned all else, making possible the overturning of hierarchies, widespread nationalizations, and fundamental cultural change as well. Yet even though these dimensions or arenas of change were tightly interconnected in the mindset and the actions of many actors at the time, it is both useful and reasonable to analytically disentangle them from one another. Doing so seems reasonable partly because the actors of the period disagreed among themselves in the relative priority they placed on each of these dimensions of transformation. Additionally, the drawing of analytical distinctions—for example between the political and cultural components of the Portuguese process of change—is necessary in order to examine and understand similarities and differences between this case and other national instances of democratization that lacked such robust processes of social and cultural transformation. We turn now to a consideration first of political dimensions of change and then of cultural ones.

IV. The Politics of April—and Its Aftermath

The captains who launched Portugal's extraordinary road to democracy were veterans of the increasingly unsuccessful colonial war in Africa who sought to bring to an end not only that war but also the authoritarian Estado Novo, which remained committed to preserving colonial rule. Just after midnight on April 25, 1974, the uprising began when members of the MFA played "Grandola," the now-famous folk song of José Afonso, over Radio Renasença, sending a signal to those involved in planning for the coup attempt that operations were underway. Captains and others involved in the movement assembled support in the barracks at Santarém and other points outside Lisbon, organizing columns of tanks and soldiers to march on the nearby capital city. When the forces led by captains of the MFA reached Lisbon they met only scattered resistance. The refusal of some rank-and-file soldiers to follow the orders of commanders loyal to the regime and the massive support of civilians who spilled into the streets in support of the rebellion soon established the dominance of the captains' movement. The incumbent authoritarian ruler, Marcelo Caetano, fled to the military barracks located at the edge of the Largo do Carmo, a square in old Lisbon, but by the end of the day he had surrendered and the institutions of the old regime were left in a state of collapse.

What followed was a politically complex process that involved new forms of mobilization and participation alongside the construction of new institutions—first within the Armed Forces themselves and then in the emergent political system. The military authorities who replaced the repressive structures of the Estado Novo quickly committed themselves to a program of democratization through elections, decolonization, and development. However, their institutional definition as the new center of political power was less than fully clear, as was the political balance of power within the military, leading to both conflict and uncertainty within the Armed Forces during the ongoing revolutionary period. The MFA's role in the trajectory of change was accompanied throughout the larger process by politically charged popular mobilizations both in the streets and within numerous institutional venues. The crucial actors in the new context included military officers of various positions in the hierarchy of the Armed Forces, as well as civilians who mobilized either spontaneously or in actions led by political parties and associations. This varied set of actors gave rise to a great proliferation of new demands and forms of practice while also building new structures and approaches for resolving political matters. With the collapse of the old order, and absent clear rules or even an unambiguous line of command for acting within the emergent revolutionary order, virtually everything political was subject to discussion and the potential for redefinition. Political conflicts over the direction of change, the speed of transformation, and the scope of the larger process soon engulfed the MFA and in a broader sense the military at large as well as politicized sectors of the citizenry who were increasingly involved in the process. Political conflicts also took place in schools and universities, newspaper offices and radio stations, neighborhoods and economic enterprises.

The Portuguese revolution clearly involved both bottom-up and top-down dynamics of change, rooted in the spontaneous or weakly organized projects of ordinary citizens and the plans formulated by the new revolutionary authorities as well as organized political parties with their own internal hierarchies. Yet, one central point cannot be ignored: The institutions and power holders of the old authoritarian order were essentially totally absent from the process of change. The location of key events, decision-making, and demand making was in military barracks, in assembly halls, in the streets, inside party headquarters, and within secondary institutions—such as the news media and schools—which had been thoroughly external to political power in the old order. Political action unfolded in new venues and took on new forms. Once a new Assembly of the Republic had been chosen by voters, demonstrators began to take their causes to the steps of that representative body—thus anticipating a central feature of Portugal's post-revolutionary democratic practice. At one point in the fall of 1975 workers who were on strike actually besieged the parliament, but instead of provoking a state of crisis or the use of official coercion, this incident instead led to negotiation and settlement (Maxwell, 1995: 156). From the revolution onward, Portuguese protesters often achieved their ends through conversation with institutional power holders (Fishman and Everson, 2016). Pictures from the period convey perhaps more effectively than words the thorough interweaving of civilian and military mobilization in the toppling of the old order and in the process that followed. All of this is thoroughly unlike what was to happen in Spain following the death of Francisco Franco a year and a half after Portugal's "liberation by golpe" (Schmitter, 1975).

The political process that led from the April 25, 1974, coup to Portugal's full democratization was quite complex and frequently subject to redirection—in one fashion or another—as a result of political or military actions by elements of the Armed Forces. New coup attempts, mobilization in the streets, and struggles for control within new revolutionary institutions pushed the process of change steadily to the left—and then back toward the center, particularly after the outcome of the April 1975 elections and the brief military confrontation between radicals and moderates in November 1975. The political divisions within the Armed Forces extended from militant ultra-Marxists well to the left of the Communist Party to orthodox Communists, Socialists, social democrats, and conservatives. The ultimate direction of change, which in the end fused the ongoing social revolution with the construction of relatively conventional representative institutions chosen through free democratic elections, seemed unclear at several points along the way (Maxwell, 1995; Manuel, 1995; Linz and Stepan, 1996). Some students of the period emphasize the risk that the process could have ended in a new dictatorship of one form or another— given the ideological preferences of some key participants. It is unquestionably true that some sectors active in the revolution stood opposed to the standard liberal guarantees and freedoms needed for democratic life to function. They viewed liberal representative democracy as intrinsically antagonistic to the revolution's social agenda—adopting the perspective of those social revolutions that have ended in non-democratic forms of rule. However, those who pursued such ends were in the minority; they lost out to advocates of both social revolution and democracy. The key struggles during the Portuguese revolution included conflict in many institutional venues—including the news media, educational establishments, and other contexts.

Ultimately, the outcome of ongoing conflict within the Armed Forces, in competing demonstrations in the streets, at the ballot box, and inside institutions such as the news media gave clear predominance to forces that favored the fusion of social objectives of the revolution with the political commitment to build a representative democracy anchored in the guarantee of conventional liberal freedoms. As Mário Soares put the matter, emphasizing the complementarity of demonstrations and the ballot box "everything was discussed in the streets. We demonstrated in the streets. We won in the streets, not only in elections."[8] The Constitutional Assembly elected on April 25, 1975—precisely one year after the initiation of the Carnation Revolution—wrote a guiding document for the new political system that was situated well to the left of other Western constitutions but that at the same time guaranteed all of the crucial political and civil liberties of liberal democracies. The new Constitution included robust social guarantees of many sorts, an institutional determinant of much that followed, and in its initial version prior to subsequent amendments, committed the country to the construction of a socialist economy (Magalhaes, 2013; Brito and Carreira Silva, 2010). Indeed social theorist Boaventura da Sousa Santos has argued that the new political formation, unlike other Western democracies, should not be conceptualized as a capitalist state until the Constitutional Reform of 1989, which permitted the reprivatization of firms nationalized during the revolution (de Sousa Santos, 1990).

The central components of political development during the revolution included some rather conventional ones—such as the development of a new party system (Jalali, 2007; Lisi, 2015)—and other quite unconventional ones such as the major presence of demonstrations and popular pressure in the streets as a predominant influence on the direction of change. The initial electoral dominance of the Socialist Party (PS) led by Mário Soares, and the role played by parties to its right and left, clearly helped to establish the balance of power reflected in the writing of the Constitution and later in governing the country. But what went on in the streets and inside typically secondary institutions such as the news media and the educational system also played a crucial role in shaping the direction of change and the character of the new order. In a highly telling observation, Mário Murteira, an economist who served as a Minister in several governments during the revolutionary period, remarked to an interviewer, "Several times when I was engaged in important conversations with [Prime Minister] Vasco Gonçalves, in his office, we would go to the window to see those who were passing by in demonstrations. In the end and to a great extent we were more spectators in a grand popular movement than actors" (Silva et al., 2007). The April revolution and its aftermath put in place not only new institutional arrangements but also new ways of doing politics and thinking about politics—as the words of Murteira clearly underscore.

V. *The Cultural Impact of April—and Its Aftermath*

From the beginning, Portugal's Carnation Revolution was as much an episode of fundamental cultural transformation as of rapid political and economic change. The crowds of civilians and columns of troops that filled streets and squares in Lisbon on April 25, 1974, did as much to reshape cultural as political life, as a prelude to their meta-political forging of wide new spaces for "doing politics" in the months that followed. From its first moments, the revolution created new symbols, forms of discourse, understandings, meanings, and practices. The initiation of the revolutionary coup with the playing over the radio of a banned protest-folk song that eloquently conveyed the egalitarian and republican essence of democracy was more than a mere operational device; it also transmitted the meaning of what was beginning. The popular embrace of red carnations—on the revolution's first day—as a form of celebration and as a symbol to be placed in the barrels of guns and tank cannons initiated a period of widespread creativity of a certain sort. The revolution was a time of cultural effervescence through both bottom-up and top-down dynamics that generated new ways of understanding Portuguese identity and the essence of politics. The process of cultural awakening quickly produced numerous forms of expression to represent and convey such conceptions. Poetry and song, posters and graffiti, innovative discourses and changed forms of practice all carried the message that the time had arrived to think and act in big new ways.

Political posters were among the favored media for expressing prevailing hopes for remaking the country. Lisbon's *Diário de Notícias*, one of the country's oldest newspapers, published a commemorative volume celebrating those posters some thirty years after the events of 1974. As that volume related the matter, "With people ceasing to fear who was listening to them, the most varied forms of art arrived in the cities, towns and countryside of Portugal, in many cases spontaneously, trying to express a new way to live. [This was] The way it was imagined that through the success of the Armed Forces Movement the future could be constructed" (Diário de Notícias, 2004: 6). Produced by Sérgio Guimaraes, one of the most widely remembered posters from 1974 simply showed a young girl placing a red carnation in the barrel of a machine gun held by soldiers. A poster produced in June of that year by the Democratic Movement of Plastic Artists made the connection between culture and politics quite explicit. Its message read "Flower, Freedom, Fire, Imagination, Strength, Unity, Art, Revolution" (Diário de Notícias, 2004: 26, 20). The artist Maria Helena Vieira da Silva produced several versions of what became the most emblematic poster of the revolution. It depicted people demonstrating in Lisbon alongside the message "The Poetry is in the Streets" (Diário de Notícias: 11, 110). The discursive and representational linkage of revolution to both poetry and public demonstrations has lived on in numerous ways in Portugal's post-revolutionary democracy. Of course, posters and poetry were not the only forms of cultural expression. The *Diario de Notícias* volume also took note of one of many revolutionary songs: " 'Song is a weapon' assured the lyrics of a musical piece of the period" (6).

The cultural innovations of artists and song writers as well as political activists who forged new ways to think about, do, and speak of civic action did not stand alone. The new revolutionary authorities and political party leaders also undertook efforts to activate new cultural capacities—typically linking cultural change to the goal of civic activation. A major component of this more-or-less "top-down" effort of the revolution's leadership was the "cultural dynamization campaign" that commenced in the fall of 1974. Elements of the military, accompanied by civilian artists, musicians, or activists traveled to rural areas of the country, attempting to bring cultural change, new capacities, and political perspectives to relatively traditional communities (Vespeira de Almeida, 2007; Bermeo, 1986: 39). The effort was quite controversial. Many Portuguese saw the campaign as an attempt by revolutionary sectors within the military to push the country to the left of where its own instincts led it. The campaign was also viewed by its critics as intended to erode religiosity and other traditional commitments or perspectives. Given the continuing existence at that time of low levels of educational attainment, and in many cases outright illiteracy, in rural areas, the effort to promote cultural dynamization and change also had its strong supporters, but it was eventually abandoned. The simple claim of the campaign that "culture is the freedom of the people"—the words conveyed by one of its posters (Diário de Notícias, 2004: 16)—serves to underscore the importance of cultural innovation and initiatives for the revolution, even though this top-down effort at activation was relatively short-lived. In contrast, much of what the revolution did in the cultural sphere was the result more of bottom-up than top-down initiatives.

Both the educational system and the news media attracted the attention— and interest—of activists and revolutionary leaders committed to the goal of cultural change. The concerns and impact of the revolution touched numerous venues and forms of cultural life. The revolution brought about efforts to create new cultural artifacts and forms of expression, but it also reshaped taken-for-granted assumptions and forms of practice underpinning political life. The cultural implications of revolution were multiple in number. Revolutions typically devote great attention to education, often promoting innovative or transformational pedagogies (Ewing, 2005), and Portugal was no exception to this general rule. The revolution's perspective on education resonated with the objectives of the cultural dynamization campaign and also promoted flexible and inclusionary organizational forms for the school system, empowering both students and teachers (Stoer, 1982, 1983, 1986). A bulletin that the MFA published in the fall of 1974 conveyed this perspective on education quite clearly: "We have to win the cultural battle, which is not only what the books teach. The schools must go out to the streets and the streets must go into the schools, through musical bands, folklore, orchestras, songs, dances, poetry, theater, the circus, the cinema, artisanry, and the plastic arts" (cited in Stoer 1986: 155). As this document clearly suggests, the new cultural energy generated by the Carnation Revolution included changed ways of seeing and making use of cultural production, and induced inclusionary understandings of the boundaries between formal institutions—such as schools—and the world external to them. This shift in the understanding of the boundaries between formal institutions and the world outside them was among the most important effects of social revolution. The cultural renewal made possible by Portugal's revolutionary transition involved not only discourses, symbols, and cultural products but also forms of practice and the underlying understandings linked to them.

The new understandings and forms of practice tied to efforts at cultural activation in the school system and in rural areas of the country were primarily linked to political mobilizations situated in one way or another on the left side of the political spectrum. The political battles of the revolutionary period were in this sense difficult to disentangle from cultural contention of various sorts. The educational system was not the only institutional terrain in which this mix of political and cultural contention emerged. In the communications media as well, battles over control of the news content and the editorial slant of newspapers, radio stations, and other media outlets took on great significance during the revolutionary period. The argument that not only journalists but also printers and other members of the technical staff of media outlets should play a role in deciding the editorial and news content of radio stations or newspapers was employed to strengthen the hand of organizations well to the left of the Socialists within the journalistic field. Their "workerist" view, widely criticized at the time as a de facto form of news censorship, was defeated, but the more moderately left-wing view that journalists should share in the setting of editorial policy and news content fared far better. This view guaranteed a plurality of perspectives in the news media and protected professional journalists from the political manipulation of their work by the owners of media outlets. In the news media as well as in the educational system the revolutionary period left in place a set of assumptions and forms of practice that rejected traditional and hierarchical conceptions of how such institutions should function. Relatively anti-hierarchical conceptions that affirmed the autonomy of teachers and journalists and that valued both political and cultural pluralism came to predominate during the revolution. The cultural assumptions shaping practice not only in the political system writ large but also in crucial institutions such as the news media and schools showed the marks of Portugal's synthesis of the social commitments of revolution with the democratic and liberal guarantees of pluralistic and representative democracy.

VI. *Transition through Regime-Guided Reform in Spain*

Although the Spanish pathway to democracy was powerfully conditioned by antecedent processes of change or resistance rooted in civil society, and by ongoing pressure from the political opposition, most crucial decisions shaping the transition and the new democracy were taken inside official institutions. The institutions left in place by the Franco regime when the longtime dictator died in November 1975 made the crucial decision one year later to approve Adolfo Suárez's plan for genuinely competitive elections for a parliament charged with writing a new democratic constitution. And the elected parliament chosen by voters on June 15, 1977, made the remaining major decisions—often following top-level meetings between political leaders of opposing parties and in a process that ultimately led to a popular referendum on the new constitution in December 1978. The role of the Spanish public at voting booths in June 1977 and December 1978 was crucial, but the epicenter of the process of change was located firmly within official institutions that maintained their own formal legality and continuity throughout the transition. In the newly elected parliament chosen in June 1977, parties led by political veterans of the Franco regime—the Unión del Centro Democrático (UCD), the reform-oriented party of Prime Minister Adolfo Suárez, and Alianza Popular (AP) the more conservative party led by Manuel Fraga Iribarne—held a majority of the 350 seats. Both Suárez and

Fraga had held high-level positions inside the Franco system, as had many other important members of UCD and AP; not only Francoist institutions but also political leaders of the old regime played a central role in the system's transformation into a democracy.

The pivotal role of institutions and leaders linked to the Francoist past is not fully captured by simply identifying those who made crucial decisions on the road to democracy. Of course, the process of democratization involved much more than the actions and decisions of those individuals and institutions. Opposition parties, social movements, civil society actors, and ordinary voters all engaged in decisively important activities during the transition years—shaping outcomes in numerous ways (Radcliff, 2011). But in the overall architecture of the process of change, power holders within official institutions such as the parliament, municipal governments, and so forth sought to establish clear and impervious barriers between the internal workings of those institutions and the dynamics of change afoot in the larger society. Moreover, through both top-down and bottom-up processes to be delineated later, the impact of social pressures from below on the evolution of the system was significantly contained. Spanish politicians used considerable skill and—in some moments—genuine courage in dismantling a repressive dictatorship and replacing it with a democracy. But the process of change was one that left in place a set of asymmetries that lived on in cultural legacies of the transition, thereby limiting greatly the space for de facto inclusion in the informal side of policy making and agenda setting in the new democracy.

I argue that the general characteristics of Spain's regime-guided transition and the impact of civil society pressures on that process of change were mutually constitutive; they co-evolved during the pathway to democracy, as actors both inside and outside official institutions such as the country's legislative chamber adapted to one another's strategies and forms of power (Fishman, 2017). In that sense, even though the elite-led interpretation of the transition captures some important features of this case, that conceptualization, most famously identified with political scientist Richard Gunther (1992), misses much of significance. Although democratization in principle leads to the growing salience of citizen preferences in politics, and for that reason the imposition of the central principle of political equality among those citizens, for all of its successes in dismantling a long-lived authoritarian regime, the Spanish transition also generated increasingly asymmetric cultural assumptions about democratic politics that curtailed the realization of political equality to something rather close to the minimum required for representative democracy. Under the new system, these cultural assumptions have tended to insulate political office holders from pressures from below, thereby limiting the boundaries of effective political inclusion more sharply than required—or beneficial—for the survival of representative institutions. The most complex and expansive conceptualization of the Spanish transition—the landmark analysis of Linz and Stepan in their important volume on democratic transition and consolidation—captures many of the most important challenges and contours of Spain's process of change, and new works of major scholarly significance continue to appear (Sánchez-Cuenca, 2014a), contributing to what we know as social scientists. However, I suggest that the full implications of the Spanish transition for the boundaries of political inclusion in the new democracy can only be adequately understood by incorporating cultural dynamics within our analysis of the transition itself and its legacies.

I argue that in the Spanish case a growing predominance of asymmetric cultural assumptions about democracy and normal political life have their origins in the transition itself; the polar opposite Spanish and Portuguese transitions were remarkably dissimilar not only in the identity of the principal actors but also in culturally emergent assumptions about normal political life that were put in place by the two roads to democracy. The cultural emphasis in Spain on historical reconciliation had served as a crucial antecedent to transition and was given added weight during the transition itself (Edles, 1998), facilitating needed negotiations over the new constitution, but in the end—and in practice—the predominant understanding of this and related objectives ended up generating asymmetric results, insulating institutional representatives from dissatisfied citizens who felt excluded from power, and establishing remarkably different principles for the treatment of the memories of the two sides in the country's civil war of 1936–1939. These asymmetries did not recede during the transition as one might have expected, but instead grew in magnitude, contributing to a predominant form of democratic practice that has set significant limits on political inclusion—with numerous unfortunate consequences manifested in ultimate social outcomes.

VII. The Politics of Spain's Regime-Guided Transition

The political challenges faced by those leading Spain's regime-guided transition were quite large ones and could not have been overcome without significant political skill and—when necessary—true courage on the part of many of the principal actors. On the basis of a rigorous program of research, political scientist Ignacio Sánchez-Cuenca has persuasively argued that the

Spanish transition should be seen above all as an instance of institutional suicide by the system that Franco left in place (2014a). Sánchez-Cuenca shows that consensus emerged as a main theme only in a second phase of the transition, once the Francoist legislature had voted in favor of Prime Minister Adolfo Suarez's proposed Law for Political Reform with its promise of calling free and competitive elections for a new assembly with constituent powers. The history of this pathway to change has its puzzles, carefully analyzed by Sánchez-Cuenca: Following the plan of the late dictator himself, the first institutional steps of change after Franco's death in November 1975 led to the return of the monarchy—with Juan Carlos I succeeding Franco as head of state—and to the continuity of the conservative Carlos Arias Navarro as head of government. With Franco removed from the power equation, those in power began work on altering the system. Paradoxically, Arias Navarro's cautious and inadequate proposal for a highly limited political reform failed to receive majority approval in the Francoist legislature, but the much more ambitious and fully democratizing plan of his successor—Adolfo Suárez—was able to win the needed approval from the Francoist legislature, which voted in November 1976 to end its undemocratic powers and call free elections for a new representative body. How and why this happened—the theme of important recent research by Sánchez-Cuenca—is an important component of the transition story, but the political pathway of change also required action by others—outside the authoritarian center of power of the regime put in place by Franco.

The conceptualization of the Spanish transition by Linz and Stepan as a *reforma pactada/ruptura pactada* captures two additional elements of importance in the overall multi-year transition scenario, extending beyond the crucial first phase theorized by Sánchez-Cuenca. The Linzian emphasis on the *ruptura pactada* component of the Spanish model captures at least two important facts about this national case: not only that the commitment to new fully competitive elections stood as a clear break with the past but also that regime reformers had a need for legitimation that could only emanate from their democratizing acts and from the willingness of the opposition to both accept the new framework and agree to participate. The opposition had hoped for a genuine clear break with the past—a *ruptura*—in the identity of the governmental body exercising control over the calling of competitive elections for the constituent process of the new democratic regime. The assumption of longtime opponents of authoritarian rule was that a clear break in the identity of the authorities overseeing the process would shift the nature of democratization. Important research on precisely that question by Braulio Gómez Fortes (2009) has confirmed the wisdom of that intuition.

However, the general strike called by the opposition in November 1976, hoping to push the government to accept such a course of action, failed to generate the breadth of support needed to dislodge the regime-led reformist approach and replace it with the *ruptura* framework. The inability of the opposition to displace the existing reformist government, and the knowledge that many actors within the remnants of the Franco regime sought to prevent any genuine democratization, ultimately led the mainstream opposition to agree to participate in the reform process initiated and guided by the Suárez government. This lent the reform an air of legitimacy and a certain claim to offering a clear break with the past in the shift to elections as the allocator of positions of institutional power (albeit in keeping with rules established by the incumbent government).

One key action of the Suárez government did more than any other to establish a clear symbolic and practical line of demarcation with the Francoist past. In April 1977 Suárez legalized the long banned Communist Party (PCE), the best-organized party in the democratic opposition and the focus of much of the Franco regime's propaganda. Even though the PCE was above all a source of moderation within the Republican zone during the long civil war of the 1930s, favoring a broad socio-political alliance incorporating as many sectors as possible within the Republican coalition, and opposing the anti-capitalist social revolution that took place in much of the loyalist zone during the war, the Franco regime had concentrated much of its political communication on the effort to demonize the Communists. The April 1977 decision of Suárez to legalize the PCE ran counter to assurances he had offered to some of the regime actors whose support he had needed to press the reform forward inside Francoist institutions in 1976. In reaching this crucial decision, a major concern of Suárez and his circle of advisers involved the likely reaction of the Spanish Armed Forces—the institutional inheritors of the victorious Franco forces during the civil war. Once he had legalized the PCE, that concern proved to be well taken; the response of military leaders was sharply critical (Molinero and Ysás, 2017: 196–208; Gómez Rosas, 2007: 130–135). The closest approximation to a symbolic break with the past in the pathway from Franco's succession in November 1975 to free elections in June 1977 was a moment in which the source of pressure most feared by regime reformers was the coup potential of hardline elements in the military rather than the socially progressive potential of crowds in the streets.

A key determinant of the direction taken by the Spanish transition—one that is strongly reflected in the story of the legalization of the PCE—was the continuity in both the capacities and the institutional identity of the state apparatus during the entire process of regime change (Fishman, 1990a). State institutions linked to the Franco regime remained firmly in place, with their legality, internal hierarchies, and mentalities essentially unaltered during the regime transition. Without the analytic distinction between state and regime,[9] this fundamental feature of the Spanish transition and of its strong contrasts with Portugal would be very difficult to grasp. Throughout the Spanish transition, government officials such as the Minister of the Interior under Adolfo Suárez, Rodolfo Martín Villa, and his predecessor under Arias Navarro, Manuel Fraga, made effective use of the police to prevent opposition demonstrations and strikes from exceeding legally established limits. As Martín Villa relates the matter, during his tenure as Interior Minister under Adolfo Suárez, "Every day first thing in the morning I met with aides to see what demonstrations were to take place throughout Spain."[10] This allowed him to prepare police units to prevent demonstrations from pushing the process of change beyond the institutional channels designed by regime reformers.

Whereas in Portugal crowds in the streets helped move that country's process of change in directions that reflected social concerns and pressures expressed "from below," in Spain such pressures were strictly controlled and at best kept within legal bounds by the government and the police. At times, keeping demonstrations under control proved to be a somewhat violent matter. Indeed, as the data collected by political scientist Ignacio Sánchez-Cuenca show, there were annually at least twenty mortal victims of the state's use of coercive force in every year of the Spanish transition, some of them in the context of demonstrations, others at police checkpoints or under other circumstances. During the crucial period of time between the death of Franco and the first democratic election in June 1977, 71.1% of those victims were ordinary citizens and not members of terrorist organizations or criminals (Sánchez-Cuenca, 2014a: 86–87). The most serious incident occurred in Vitoria, in Spain's Basque Country, in March 1976, during Manuel Fraga's time as Minister of the Interior. Armed police attempting to dislodge striking workers from a church where they were holding an assembly killed five of the participants and wounded many others.

The impact of the continuity and repressive capacity of Spain's state apparatus on the transition was not limited to the use of the armed police by reformist governments. Fears among pro-democratic actors about potentially democracy-impeding actions by hardline factions in the still unreconstructed military—that is to say those sectors of the military opposed to the democratizing reform—tended to push activists toward moderation and self-limitations in the making of demands. Such fears were present to one degree or another throughout the transition, but they became especially acute after the early decisive years of the process. The very serious coup attempt of February 23, 1981, more than two years after a new democratic Constitution had been approved in referendum, obviously accentuated such concerns but did not give birth to them. The pre-coup atmosphere in which open enemies of democratization searched for ways to roll back the political reform, mobilizing support for their views in newspapers such as *El Alcázar*, had put in place a basis for such concerns far earlier than February 1981. Many political actors harbored a fear of hardline anti-democratic sectors, tending to contribute at least to some degree to self-limitations in the making of demands by the left and its social base (Fishman, 1990b); this dynamic was one of the elements of Spain's transition scenario that contributed to its considerable asymmetries. The impact of such fears was disproportionately felt on the left.

A common interpretation of Spain's pathway to democracy stresses heavily the search for consensus. One variant of this approach—the argument that the essence of the Spanish model of democratization lay in agreements or "settlements" among political elites, which is to say in a top-down process of consensus-seeking pacts—is most clearly and succinctly formulated in influential work by political scientist Ricard Gunther (1992). Despite the fact that this perspective captures important and very real elements of the Spanish transition, a great deal of scholarly work has shown it to be insufficient as an overall theorization of what happened. Much research has shown how pressures from below contributed significantly to both the initiation and the advance of the transition process toward democracy (Maravall, 1982; Foweraker, 1989; Fishman, 1990b; Threlfall, 2008; González Martín and Martín García, 2009; Herrera and Markoff, 2011; Radcliff, 2011). Even in the forging of moderation itself, bottom-up processes with their roots in social realities located far from nationwide elites and centers of power played a significant role. Such bottom-up dynamics included the reluctance of many workers to support strikes once economic conditions deteriorated (Fishman, 1990b). But perhaps most importantly, the most definitive research on this theme shows clearly that the search for consensus was a guidepost of the second phase of transition, after the holding of national elections in 1977, and not of the initial phase when the Francoist Cortes was persuaded to essentially vote itself out of existence (Sánchez-Cuenca, 2014a). The path-establishing early steps of the Spanish transition were conditioned by both regime reformists and the democratic opposition, but these forces did not act consensually in much of that first period of regime transformation, despite occasional meetings scheduled to generate the minimum area of agreement needed for elections to be held.

The turn toward consensus after the elections of 1977 led to a number of agreements reached by the national leadership of most major political parties; in some instances they were joined by civil society organizations such as unions and/or employer associations. The period of time characterized by the politics of consensus generated the first outlines of the country's new party-system and the drawing up of the new Constitution (Gunther et al., 1986; Linz and Stepan, 1996). The politics of this period of time facilitated difficult-to-reach agreements on many points, including the provision of special autonomy frameworks for the country's nationally distinctive periphery in the Basque Country, Catalonia, and Galicia; a variety of religious and educational matters; economic agreements; and accords on basic institutional rules of the game. A broad amnesty for political acts committed in the past was one of these matters of broad agreement, a question that most of the political elite—and many rank-and-file activists in the democratic opposition—felt had to be dealt with in order to reduce the danger of hardline efforts to restore authoritarian rule. The broadly consensual decision to grant amnesty for deeds committed in the past—including both infractions of legality by the opposition to Francoism and the regime's numerous acts of repression—could be seen as a major achievement for pro-democratic forces (Aguilar, 1997), but it also provided those involved in suppressing the opposition during the long years of dictatorship with the guarantee of never paying a price in the future for that conduct. As should be obvious, many of those protected by this guarantee retained positions of power and importance. Many other matters were also resolved through broadly consensual agreements between socialists, communists, regional nationalists, reformist veterans of the Franco regime, and others.

Some points in the scholarly interpretation of the period in which consensus predominated—at a minimum from June 1977 through the approval of a new Constitution in December 1978—remain open to debate. Whether the tendency to seek consensus reflected a broadly shared cultural preference for agreement as a way to avoid a renewed descent into destructive polarization reminiscent of the country's conflictual past (Edles, 1998), or more simply a pragmatic need to reach agreements in the context of a split balance of power produced by the first elections (Sánchez-Cuenca, 2014a), the practical effects at least in the short run were essentially the same. Political leaders in Madrid reached a large number of broad agreements that allowed the country to successfully install a new democracy, but they did so in a way that had at least two large costs: First, the accords generated, at a minimum, a good deal of skepticism or loss of enthusiasm among those who had wanted their political representatives to pursue a stronger version of the objectives favored by the electorates that voted for them—whether on the left, the right, or the center, and second, within the universe of democratic political forces, the substance of consensus implied especially large renunciations by those located to the left of the political center. The politics of consensus generated internal divisions and discontent within political parties and their electorates, thereby contributing to a profound remaking of the party system in 1982.

Thus the political contours of the Spanish transition established strong points of contrast with Portugal well before the first free elections of the new era were held in June 1977. From the perspective of an ahistorical conceptualization of democracy, one might expect such differences to fade in intensity once citizens were given the right to freely choose their representatives in free and competitive elections. I argue, however, that the important points of contrast actually grew in magnitude in certain respects after the holding of free elections when newly chosen political representatives got to work. Some points of contrast in the drafting of the new constitutions by those elected representatives can be seen to constitute a direct result of rules put in place by what Gómez Fortes has aptly called the "convoking powers," namely the rebellious military in Portugal and the regime reformists in Spain (Gómez Fortes, 2009). However, I argue that much of the dynamic at work and many of the strong legacies of this period that have shaped ongoing political life in the two cases are located outside the institutionally defined terrain of conventional politics. It was in the cultural work and implications of the two transitions that the full magnitude of the Iberian divide in political inclusion came to life and was sustained. For this reason, our understanding of the transitions needs to incorporate the cultural dimension—the theme to which we now turn.

VIII. *The Cultural Dimensions of Spain's Regime-Guided Transition*

The Spanish transition lacked Portugal's massive outpouring of cultural innovation with its crafting of new symbols and types of expression as well as the rethinking of forms of practice on multiple fronts—beginning in April 1974. The larger Iberian Peninsula case had no Sewellian great event (Sewell, 1996) leading to the rapid reconfiguration of cultural expression and practice as well as underlying assumptions—as happened in Portugal in the context of revolution. Sewell's theoretical masterpiece on how the fall of the Bastille in France rapidly generated a revolutionary recasting of cultural structures—and as a result, political realities—in that country in 1789 (Sewell, 1996) proves extraordinarily suggestive for understanding the Portuguese case. Nonetheless, the Spanish transition, as well, was both conditioned by and later generative of multiple cultural phenomena. These phenomena included the evolution of underlying assumptions and preconditions, shifting ways of representing and discussing the nation's past and its ongoing political life, the construction of new assumptions and arguments about what normal democratic life should look like, and the forging of practices that established clear boundaries between institutional centers of power and expressions of political sentiment outside such institutions. Both in the substance of what went on during transition and in the consequences generated, Spain's path to democratization had its cultural dimensions. In her major study of the cultural symbols, discourse, and rituals of the transition, cultural sociologist Laura Desfor Edles argues that the pursuit of reconciliation was treated as culturally "sacred" during the crucial period of the politics of consensus, encouraging political leaders to seek agreements with one another. Yet she argues that after the Constitution was approved in December 1978 in the maximum expression of broad consensus "the effervescence of the core symbols receded" and they came to be "taken for granted" (Edles, 1998: 147). To this claim on the eclipse of the "core symbols" of consensus and reconciliation, we should add the evidence of Sánchez-Cuenca that consensus only came to predominate after the democratic elections of June 1977 took place. Whether we focus primarily on political arrangements, cultural messages, or the interconnections between the two, it is clear that the theme of reconciliation and consensus predominated during one crucial period of the Spanish transition but was not a "constant."

This raises the question of whether there was any cultural "constant" among politically dominant sectors during the Spanish transition. I argue that a crucial development concerned the construction of a sense of politics that differentiated sharply between social pressure in the streets and the decision-making of official institutions, conceptualizing demonstrations as potentially destabilizing and dangerous. In a speech justifying his legalization of the PCE in April 1977, Suárez reasoned "Sincerely, is it not preferable to count in the ballot boxes what otherwise we would have to measure on the poor basis of unrest in the streets?" (Linz and Stepan, 1996: 97). Suárez's decision to legalize the PCE was a crucial move providing much needed full democratic authenticity (Fishman, 2016) to a reform process led and guided by veterans of the Franco regime, but in doing so he articulated an unnecessarily dichotomous opposition between the institutionalized expression of voter preferences at the ballot box and the mobilization of citizens in the streets. The framing of mobilization in the streets as "unrest" opposed to the logic of electoral democracy conceptualized politics in the streets as antagonistic to the essence of representative democracy—instead of as its complement.

This was not an isolated formulation or framing. Article 77 of the Spanish Constitution explicitly prohibits Spanish citizens from presenting their country's legislative chambers with petitions through demonstrations. Petitioning is of course permitted in writing, but the Constitutional text, approved in the maximum expression of broad ideological consensus, ex- plicitly rules out the presentation of petitions by demonstrations. The assumptions about politics that predominated during the brief politics of consensus period included the erection of a very strict boundary between the realm of official institutions and the sphere of public mobilization in the streets. Thus the Spanish transition encouraged the development of a view of political processes that set down strong lines of demarcation, in- deed separation, between official institutions and their environment while implicitly reaffirming established hierarchies related to such demarcations. Much earlier in the transition, the actions and words of Manuel Fraga—the Minister of the Interior of Arias Navarro and founder of AP—regarding the Vitoria killings in March 1976 sent an even stronger message questioning the political legitimacy of protest in the streets. In a press conference held after the police action that killed five workers, Fraga remarked, "El que no haya aprendido la lección de Vitoria, él verá lo que hace" (Sánchez-Cuenca, 2014a: 91). These words can be roughly translated as "Those who fail to learn the lesson of Vitoria may find out where that leads them." The threat was implicit but unmistakable. During his time as Minister of the Interior, Fraga was also famously reported to have warned, "The streets are mine!" but there is lingering debate over whether he actually made that second remark.[11] In any case, all of this was a far cry from the Portuguese transition's claims and assumptions about the role of protest demonstrations in politics.

Key actors in the Spanish transition generally avoided top-down efforts to comprehensively transform the country's culture in a fashion designed to promote both civic involvement and individual self-realization among citi- zens. Those objectives, historically linked to some republican conceptions of democracy, were embodied in educational efforts of Spain's Second Republic in the 1930s and in the Portuguese revolution's campaign of cultural dynamization beginning in the fall of 1974. However, both of those attempts at cultural activation led to conflict with conservative sectors of the Catholic Church—exactly the sort of outcome that leading forces in the Spanish tran- sition sought to avoid. During Spain's period of consensual decision-making, when the new Constitution was being drafted, political forces on the left and right reached agreement on an "educational pact" (Maravall, 1995; Fernández Mellizo-Soto, 2001), that preserved significant space for traditional forms of Catholic education, limiting any possibility for a culturally transformative recasting of the public education system. In this environment, the Socialist Party (PSOE) came to see educational policy primarily as a vehicle to promote new economic opportunities for workers and lower income sectors (Fernández Mellizo-Soto). The classically republican goal of seeking cultural transformation and growth through the educational system was essentially abandoned as politically dangerous and potentially polarizing.

Whether bottom-up processes of cultural transformation were at work during the consensus-oriented period of the Spanish transition, after the first elections in June 1977, is a point on which some debate is possible. There is ample evidence that the predominant turn toward moderation by activists on the left was not simply a top-down imposition driven by elite-level agreements but also was generated by processes rooted in the lived experience of rank-and-file Spaniards during the transition years (Fishman, 1990b). On a variety of matters dealing with economic and political goals, cultural representations of the country and its history, and ways of "doing politics," many on the left who had been active in opposition to the Franco regime shifted their views and practice, adopting positions closer to the center of the political spectrum in the new political universe brought into being by democratization. The case for restraint was internalized by many rank-and-file activists. At the same time, many longtime supporters of the Franco regime came to accept the political rights of the opposition and of ordinary citizens. Public opinion research covering the entire transition period shows much evidence of an evolution in public attitudes, with a decline of both anti-democratic right-wing views and left-wing perspectives radically opposed to the existing status quo (Linz et al., 1981). Pérez-Díaz (1993) has conceptualized this process as one rooted in the transformation and reinforcement of Spain's civil society.

The shift in perspectives on the left included the increasing tendency to abandon symbols and aspirations linked to the dream of restoring the defeated Second Republic. The monarchy and its flag came to be accepted by large majorities of the public despite an initial reluctance on the part of many socialists and others on the left for whom the flag of the Republic was still of symbolic power in the first stages of the transition. In this sense, the shift in attitudes that took place during the transition served as a crucial precondition for the consolidation of what many have called the "Pact of Forgetting" (Encarnación, 2014; but see in contrast Juliá, 2003), which is to say the tacit decision to avoid politically reopening the civil war's outcome. That tacit pact was widely seen as precluding a cultural policy of rehabilitating Republican symbols or heroes and of devaluing Francoist ones. The obvious question posed by this outcome is whether it simply served to consolidate democracy in a country with a conflictual past or, instead, put in place fundamentally asymmetric understandings (Aguilar and Payne, 2018) with consequences for the limits of political life that set Spain apart from at least some other democracies. In a very real sense, the most important question about the implicit Pacto del Olvido—and the cultural processes to which it was linked— concerns the effect of this understanding and the broader cultural tendencies in which it was embedded on predominant forms of democratic practice and political inclusion. This very complex question helps to motivate this book, but before we turn to an examination of contemporary democratic practice and its consequences in the Iberian Peninsula cases, it is important to complete this examination of the transition by examining its tail end or "coda" in each case. Indeed, I argue that in both Iberian Peninsula cases, political developments that were quite directly conditioned by the transitions but that took place after democracy was clearly already in place served to accentuate or partially reorient certain legacies of the transitions.

IX. The Transitions' Codas and Their Effects on What Followed

I argue that before the stage was fully set for the form of democratic politics that currently prevails in Portugal and Spain both transitions produced a "coda" which finally closed processes that had begun in the context of democratization. Some conceptualizations of democratic "consolidation" (Schmitter, 1995, 1999; Morlino, 1998) include such matters in their understanding of the solidification of democratic rule, but following the most general usage (Linz and Stepan, 1996; Schedler, 2001), I understand democratic consolidation to refer simply to the process that more or less assures the survival of democracy itself by weakening opponents and strengthening supporters of free and representative government, leaving the process that I discuss here beyond the limits of consolidation as such. I find it useful to think of a transition's tail end as its "coda" and I turn now to that theme. I understand the Spanish transition's coda to consist of the rapid and deep transformation of the new democratic party system in the elections of 1982—the third national vote on the composition of the country's legislative chambers and government after the death of Franco. In contrast I view the reprivatization in 1989–1990 of firms nationalized during the Portuguese revolution (Asensio Menchero, 2001; Freire de Souza and Cruz, 1995) as the coda of that transition. In both cases these processes were strongly shaped by the initial outcome put in place by the transition yet at the same time the codas changed important transition-era outcomes in ways that have conditioned the nature of contemporary politics. Democratic politics in twenty-first century Spain and Portugal would not be what it is without these two readjustments of the transitions' initial "settlements."

In the Spanish case, the parliamentary elections of 1982 decimated the governing UCD (Hopkin, 1999)—the party forged by reformist Prime Minister Adolfo Suárez—which won first place in the elections of 1977 and 1979, and greatly weakened the third-place Communists of the PCE, who lost more than half of their electoral support (Gunther et al., 1986). As many analysts of the transition have noted, the parties most closely and indelibly identified with the politics of consensus were the victims of the rapid and deep recasting of the country's party system. Severe internal divisions within both the UCD and the PCE proved decisive in generating this large electoral shift. However, what is not commonly noted is how this profound shift in the party system changed the basic political and cultural foundations for the country's new democratic life. The PSOE grew dramatically in support, drawing some voters and a few party leaders from the virtually destroyed former party of government, the center-right UCD. The Socialists won a strong absolute majority of seats in the Congreso de los Diputados, to be precise 202 out of a total of 350 deputies, and became de facto the country's natural party of government for well over ten years. The deeply divided UCD was overtaken by its right-wing rival, the AP, as the main alternative to the Socialists and the primary party to their right. A new party founded by Suárez, the CDS, attempted to occupy political space between the AP and the Socialists and proved somewhat more durable than the decimated remains of the UCD. The Communists lost more than half of their electorate and were left with only four deputies, a loss of nineteen seats. Ultimately the AP renamed itself the Partido Popular (PP) and attracted many former members of the UCD, allowing it to compete effectively with the Socialists especially after winning power in March 1996. The new party system continued to permit alternation in power, but in certain key respects it was fundamentally different from the first post-Franco party system, and I argue that the shift held significance for the legacies of the transition that lived on after 1982.

The most important change in the underpinnings of politics generated by the new party system was the shift in the identity and the nature of the primary party located to the right of the political center. Both the UCD and

AP—later the PP—had their origins in sectors of the Franco regime that participated in the design of the new democratic system; they both qualify as what Loxton and Mainwaring (2018) call "successor parties." However the two parties had rather different perspectives on a variety of matters involving the essence of democratic politics. Whereas the UCD under Adolfo Suárez was a steadfast defender of compromise, showing a repeated willingness to cede ground on both symbolic and material matters, the AP was a defender of authority and order, and of a rather traditional understanding of the national "essence," taking those principles to be important elements of durable political systems. The differences between the two parties came to the surface many times during the transition, sometimes on matters involving the culture of politics. The AP resisted important elements of the consensual agreements of the transition period, although its top-level leadership did ultimately support approval of the new Constitution (with some internal party dissension). On the crucial matter of peripheral nationalism—especially in the Basque Country and Catalonia—whereas Suárez and the UCD showed a willingness to cede important symbolic ground in order to achieve workable compromises, AP was reluctant to do so. Manuel Fraga, the founder and leader of AP, opposed the use of the term "historic nationalities" in the Constitution's treatment of Spain's multinational periphery, arguing, "the concept of 'nationalities' is, without a doubt, a time bomb for the national unity and strength of the State" (in Edles, 1998: 120). On another occasion during the Constitution-drafting process, Fraga had asserted, "in the midst of easy consensuses AP has the difficult role of acting as the conscience of Spain" (112).

The principal right-of-center space in the party system was no longer occupied by a party that defended the virtues of compromise with former adversaries but instead by a party that feared such compromises as a potential avenue to the violation of a traditional sense of the Spanish "essence." Transition-era Spain had erected strong barriers between official institutions and their external socio-political environment, but for several years it also promoted the inclusion of a wide range of parties within the sphere of conversation and compromise inside the elite world composed of participants in representative institutions. The transition's coda reinforced an older way of thinking and talking about politics which valued a variety of conservative positions, above all the presumed virtue of adamancy in the defense of a unitary sense of national identity—rejecting the conception that many Basques and Catalans held of Spain as a plurinational state. The predominant understanding of democratic politics during the transition proper differentiated sharply between representative institutions and the expression of citizen perspectives outside their walls, but at the same time, prior to the 1982 transformation of the party system, that dominant view also valued the willingness to reach compromises, to cede ground, and to welcome longtime adversaries into official institutions.

With the "reselection" of principal organized actors in the transition's coda, the impervious boundary between representative institutions and the external political world took on more asymmetric properties than in the earlier days of the transition, essentially excluding future compromises of the magnitude of those achieved during the transition, thereby tending to fix in place the symbolic imbalance in the treatment of the two sides during the civil war. This shift also generated effects on the left side of the political spectrum—as developed below—thus yielding a form of political practice that was significantly less inclusionary than appeared likely during the transition. The transition plus the closely associated 1982 redefinition of the party system which I refer to as the transition's coda had this combined effect. In what remains of this chapter I also address the effects of this "coda" on the Socialists and on an approach to democracy shared by the two main parties. Finally I turn to a brief consideration of how the coda of Portugal's transition—the change of the Constitution in 1989 intended to provide for the reprivatization of the Revolution's nationalizations—ended up changing the character of that transition's legacy in a way that preserved its social character while essentially ending, or at a minimum vastly reducing, its socialist nature.

For the Spanish Socialists the remaking of the party system in 1982 had at least three effects: First it changed the structure of electoral competition that the party faced—weakening its main competitors on the left and on its immediate right. This would force the Socialists to look well to their right for allies, or at least for cooperation, on any matter that institutionally required a strong super-majority of votes in the parliament. At the same time it freed the party from the need to compete energetically for support in the center and center-left of the ideological spectrum. Secondly, the new party system changed the internal balance of power within the PSOE, adding both members and some leaders who had previously been active in UCD, thereby strengthening the party's most moderate sector. Third and finally, the electoral shift rapidly made the PSOE into a natural party of government despite its relatively low membership (Morlino, 1998). Given the large number of offices won by the Socialists in the new electoral climate, this last consideration strengthened the hand of office holders in internal party matters and weakened the influence of more or less ideologically motivated party militants. These three points tended to move the PSOE at least somewhat toward the right. In the new environment there would be little pressure inside decision-making institutions to take up and rethink matters that were shut out of the transition's agenda in the interest of promoting reconciliation and consensus. The transition's coda increased the odds that the enduring legacies of the transition manifested in democratic practice would be relatively exclusionary ones—shutting certain dissatisfied sectors out of the polity's central "conversation" and processes.

The "coda" of the Portuguese transition as I conceptualize it was thoroughly different in nature, but in certain crucial ways it, too, represented a readjustment of the transition's initial settlement. An important initial feature of the system put in place by Portugal's Carnation Revolution was its quite explicit commitment to socialism—along with democracy. Much of the economy was nationalized, and the Constitution explicitly prohibited the reprivatization of nationalized firms. As a result, much of the social content of the revolution was initially anchored in the constitutional commitment to public ownership and in the political management of the state sector of the economy. The consequences of this model will be taken up in chapter 4, but for now suffice it to say that this major legacy of the revolution decreased the pressure on policy makers to develop the country's welfare state. However, in 1989 the two largest parties—the then governing PSD on the center-right and the Socialists of the PS on the center-left—joined together to amend the Constitution, changing it to permit reprivatization of the post–April 25 nationalizations (Asensio Menchero, 2001; Freire de Souza and Cruz, 1995). This shift could be seen as a turn to the right and from one perspective it was, yet it inaugurated a period of relatively rapid growth in the social expenditures lying at the heart of the country's welfare state. In a real sense, in the transition's coda the social legacies and commitments of the revolution were transposed from the sphere of enterprise ownership to the terrain of the welfare state (Fishman, 2010).

The reprivatization process begun in 1989 moved ahead quickly, returning the massive revolutionary-era nationalizations to private hands in a move that among other things added significant funds to the public treasury (Freire de Souza and Cruz, 1995). The growth of the welfare state during the 1990s took place under governments of both the center-left and the center-right—enjoying widespread multi-party support. Further growth of anti-poverty and redistributive measures continued after the turn of the century. When I asked Mário Soares in the first of two interviews with him whether these two developments could be seen as a sort of de facto political exchange between the country's two principal parties, he replied that the complex area of agreement was "tacit but not explicit."[12] Leaders of the PSD have never shared that assessment, but the substance of their actions is congruent with the claim that the social commitments of the revolution were transposed from enterprise ownership to the field of welfare state development. This point is of crucial significance for understanding policymaking in post-revolutionary Portugal, because it helps to explain why the robust phase of welfare state development began only in the 1990s. Granted, the revolution itself did immediately produce an increase in social expenditures by the Portuguese state (Esping-Andersen, 1994), but a sustained program of welfare state development awaited the re-focusing of the revolution's social character in 1989–1990.

It follows that for many purposes comparisons of public policy outcomes in the two Iberian cases make most sense if they focus on the post-1990 period—once both of the transitions' codas were in place. This is not to argue against comparisons that include the period from 1975 to 1990. Clearly that decade and a half holds much substantive and theoretical relevance. But until both codas were in place in 1990, there was no reason to expect "outcome variables" in the two countries to take on a stable and sustainable form. The full and surprisingly sustainable legacies of the polar opposite Iberian pathways to democracy came into full view in the 1990s, once actors in both countries had had an opportunity to readjust certain aspects of the transitions' initial settlements. Before we examine the substance of those legacies, focusing first on the cross-national contrast in democratic practice and then on its consequences in a variety of ultimate outcomes, we turn to a brief consideration of debates in the scholarly assessments of the two transitions and their legacies.

X. Scholarly Debate over the Transitions' Legacies

This book's analysis of cultural legacies of the Iberian Peninsula democratic transitions builds on some existing tendencies or intuitions in earlier work, but also moves well beyond the prior literature in various ways. It was the decision to focus on a sustained contrast between the two Iberian Peninsula stories that made it possible to identify and draw into clear view aspects of the enduring legacies that had not been specified in earlier work. Whereas many Spaniards have developed a rather general sense that some of their country's democratic travails may be somehow linked to the post-Franco transition, the effort to tie current dynamics of Portugal's democratic politics to the system's revolutionary origins has, until recently, been much less common.

The intuition that Spain's often celebrated democratic transition left in its wake legacies that have proven unfortunate has been articulated even by some analysts who hold a generally quite positive view of the country's pathway to democracy. Thus, in his first game theoretic analysis of the Spanish transition, Josep Maria Colomer suggested that after the transition was successfully completed, some of its major tendencies produced "stagnation, exclusions, the falsification of political wills and disinterest. The virtues of transition have turned into vices of democracy" (Colomer, 1990: 306). Unlike Colomer, critics of the transition have seen vices rather than virtue in the democratization process itself. A prominent voice of that strong critique is the public health and policy analyst Vicenç Navarro. Navarro has suggested that shortfalls in the transition process are in some sense connected to weaknesses in the country's social welfare policies, but in doing so has not specified the mechanisms involved (Navarro, 2006). Other writers have focused on the very significant terrain of cultural legacies. For example, the astute journalist Guillem Martínez recently assembled a group of writers to explore the "culture of the transition," producing a highly critical volume of essays that addresses a wide array of themes in the country's collective life. The focus of the essays extends well beyond the political sphere, including discussions of music, literary criticism, and film (Acevedo et al., 2012). Despite the value of such insights, general critiques and intuitions are insufficient. As I seek to show here and in earlier analyses (Fishman, 2005, 2010, 2017), the systematic comparison of Portugal and Spain greatly facilitates the scholarly task of specifying mechanisms that can account for outcomes reflected in the concerns of many writers.

In contrast, in Portugal until quite recently the linkage between the country's revolutionary route to political freedom and the current dynamics of its democracy has been under-appreciated. Large literatures focus on the country's revolution and on its contemporary democracy, but the linkage between the two has elicited much less scholarly attention. Some enthusiasts of the revolution have tended to see institutional democratic life as leading to a betrayal and reversal of revolutionary conquests. In this vein, the Nobel laureate José Saramago has lamented, "when I say that nothing is left [of the revolution] it is that not even the spirit of the revolution remains."[13] At the same time, many scholarly analysts of the country's democratic politics have been eager to establish fruitful comparisons with other democratic polities without treating the revolutionary origins of the political system as a variable requiring sustained theoretical and empirical treatment. This book seeks to show not only how the political life of both countries can be understood through a prism emphasizing legacies of the road taken to democracy but also how each country's experiences can be best understood by placing them comparatively alongside the experiences of the other Iberian Peninsula case. This paired comparison is of great usefulness for theory development, just as Tarrow (2010) has argued is often the case with carefully chosen two-way pairings.

There is, however, one theme on which a large scholarly literature on legacies of democratization has developed, namely that of historical memory, transitional justice—and forgetting. Some analysts of Spain's transition, and of the historical antecedents to it, in effect treat the predominant conception of the civil war almost entirely as a cultural "prior," put in place before the transition and—for some analysts—a necessary precondition for successful democratization. Defenders of the Pacto del Olvido—which is to say the tacit decision to eschew efforts to assign blame for the long decades of repression and to avoid reopening the divisions of the civil war—have portrayed this shared understanding of many actors as a crucial contributing component of the country's pathway from dictatorship to democracy. The relative reticence of Spanish institutions to pursue transitional justice or even a truth commission charged with bringing to light violations of human rights by the dictatorship is, from this point of view, seen as a necessary element of a larger constellation of factors constitutive of the country's road to democracy. However, this view has been subject to increasing criticism. As analysts of this question have noted, the tendency to avoid assigning blame for the ethical transgressions of the Franco regime and the forces that brought it to power during the civil war solidified significant asymmetries in the handling of the past (Golob, 2008; Druliolle, 2015; Escudero Alday, 2016; Aguilar Fernández and Payne, 2018). In effect these asymmetries established cultural preconditions for life under democracy that were different from those found in most democracies (Acevedo et al., 2012), due to the tacit exclusion of certain types of judicial and political initiatives—including most of those that fit under the broad heading of "transitional justice." Symbolic reminders of the Francoist past such as the Valle de los Caídos in the mountains north of Madrid and numerous street names in Madrid and other large cities were kept in place, but veterans of the Republic's fight for survival—and victims of Francoist repression—lacked equivalent forms of recognition, except in certain highly localized settings.

This pattern of relatively enduring asymmetry raises at least two important questions: First, was the perspective on the past that produced the Pacto del Olvido put entirely in place prior to the transition as a result of the society's efforts to grapple culturally with the memories and consequences of the civil war, or was it at least partially constructed during the transition as a cultural byproduct of political strategies—and of the balance of power among adversaries—during that period? Second, was this approach to the past really required for democracy to be successful in Spain? Although neither of these questions can be taken up at great length here, they both deserve brief treatment.

The first of these questions raises a rather complex matter. It is clear that some of the cultural work rethinking the civil war in a way that promoted reconciliation had taken place prior to the beginnings of the transition; this is a clear conclusion of the most important work on this theme, that of Paloma Aguilar (2002). Nonetheless, even in the relatively early work on this question there is a strong evidence—for example in the scholarship of Aguilar— that actors made strategic use of civil war memories and, as a function of the ongoing nature of the transition's trajectory, at times shifted their positions on handling the past. This point is even clearer in the important new work of Aguilar and Payne (2018), which documents the shift in the handling of the past by key actors during the transition and in the early years of the new democracy. Thus, for example, after the first democratic elections in June 1977, the PSOE abandoned its earlier perspective on dealing with the past and essentially renounced its longtime commitment to symbols and memories of the Second Republic. The transition substantially remade crucial actors' perspectives on the past and on how to deal with it. It is hard to avoid the conclusion that the shift in viewpoints on the past would have taken another direction had political conditions and constraints followed a fundamentally different path during the transition. Thus even though some elements of the country's collective memory of the past can be seen as a cultural "prior," in place before the transition began, the fully developed and sharply asymmetric handling of the past that had become dominant by the time the Socialists won power in the elections of 1982 was at least in part a result of the Spanish pathway to democracy. Moreover, a prominent analyst of the Pacto del Olvido has emphasized that the tendency of the PSOE to, in effect, forget the past grew in magnitude after the party won power in 1982 (Encarnación, 2014).

The second question is somewhat easier to answer. As has already been suggested above, many of the practices and assumptions that oriented Spain's treatment of the past came into full view after the new democracy had gained consolidation during the first term of the Socialist government of Felipe González, elected in 1982. In that sense, the decision of some on the left to leave in place numerous symbols of the Franco period may be more a feature of an already consolidated democracy than a bitter pill needed to produce that result. From a comparative perspective, a useful point of reference is the Chilean transition to democracy. That transition, after the defeat of the Pinochet regime in a 1988 plebiscite, was carried out under circumstances as least as challenging as Spain's post-Franco transition. After all, Pinochet remained a player to be contended with and he retained certain institutional resources (Valenzuela, 1990). Nonetheless, Chilean defenders of democracy were able to take steps to address the human rights violations of the Pinochet regime even before the dictator was subject to arrest in London ten years after ceding power (Valenzuela, 2006). Chile did much more than Spain to pursue transitional justice (Aguilar, 2013) and its transition was not any less successful as a result of that point of contrast (Aguilar and Payne, 2018).

Thus, I argue that the cultural perspective on the past that tended to produce sharp asymmetries should not be seen as a fixed and unchangeable condition of Spanish society prior to the return to democracy in 1977. The trajectory of transition analyzed in this chapter influenced the ongoing reinterpretation and use of the past. If political conditions had, instead, opened the way to a very dissimilar democratization scenario, the likelihood of a very different form of cultural work of a rapid sort during the transition would have been very great, as the extraordinary example of Portugal clearly suggests. In studying the two Iberian transitions, the comparison between the two provides numerous insights into what happened in each case. Moreover, in the Spanish case, the transition's "coda" in 1982 seems to have contributed to the dynamics that produced deep asymmetries in the treatment of the past. In this sense, historically contingent features of Spain's pathway to democracy rather than systematic requirements of democratization led to the most exclusionary side of this chapter's story. Growing numbers of Spanish analysts have come to recognize the existence of cultural asymmetries in the country's treatment of its past. This book draws into clear view factors that produced both that outcome and a series of related features of democratic practice, along with systematic consequences of this pattern.

 | Democratic Practice in Action

I. Introduction

At its core this is a book about the cross-national difference in how democracy is understood and practiced in two countries that had been extremely similar in numerous ways before their divergent roads to democracy in the 1970s. In this chapter we turn to the essence of the matter—democratic practice itself—to examine evidence about the large difference between the cases in the inclusion of social and political "outsiders" within the system's institutionally central "conversation." The central claim is that much of what goes on in politics follows a logic that is not written down in the formal rules of official institutions and that cannot even be discerned in the tacit yet firm set of rules and sanctions of informal institutions (Helmke and Levitsky, 2006). The forms of democratic practice that we examine here are instead rooted in quite general assumptions about democratic politics that shape countless forms of conduct, including those manifested in circumstances that actors had never expected to encounter. Indeed, the way in which political actors understand and make use of democratic freedoms, and the form taken by their interactions with others so engaged, hold relevance for an extraordinarily wide array of political behaviors and outcomes. Unlike the clear rules of institutions, the cultural orientations shaping predominant forms of democratic practice are rather general. Lacking the enforcement sanctions of clearly established rules, their effect may be somewhat less constant—with some exceptions to general patterns as a result of this absence and as a reflection of the repertoire-like range of cultural "matter" that shapes conduct—but the scope of their relevance is broader and more all-encompassing than in the case of explicit rules with their clear boundaries of applicability.

Before we turn to the substance of this chapter's claims about democratic practice in action, a brief explanatory note is in order for readers appropriately concerned with social science methodology.[1] What follows in this chapter is, from a strictly methodological standpoint, a theory that makes several interrelated and broad claims about the underlying understandings and the related conduct of the political actors "populating" Spanish and Portuguese democracy. As a theory, it is intended to facilitate explanations, predictions, and efforts to "make sense out of" empirical realities extending well beyond the research observations directly used to formulate it. However, there are many types of theories in the social sciences, and this is one based on lengthy empirical work and on a process of theorization that has involved induction. Like many theories that are based on extensive empirical research (Stinchcombe, 1968), the argument on democratic practice presented here is the result of a lengthy and wide-ranging program of empirical investigation used to stitch together the basis for formulating the theoretical claims advanced. The overall theoretical reach of the claims made in this book involves a constellation of factors so broad that it would have been impossible to subject all elements of the argument to rigorous testing before reaching full closure on it. I did, of course, adjust the argument when new findings from my work led me to see earlier assumptions as faulty.[2] I offer several partial tests of the book's central theoretical claims in chapters 4, 5, and 6.

Over the course of several decades of post-transition political life, the forms of democratic practice to which we now turn have shown their ability to orient political interaction and outcomes under constantly changing circumstances. In examining—and illustrating—democratic practice in the two countries, I rely primarily on actual examples of political conduct as well as declarations of political actors about their conduct and that of others. Insofar as it has been possible to do so, I make use of instances of democratic practice that provide us with evidence on the two cases or with evidence that can be "matched up" with a discussion of more or less parallel circumstances and actions in the other national case. I also draw on survey data to provide crucial information of a systematic nature on underlying perspectives of actors in the Spanish case. None of the cases or incidents that I recount would be sufficient, standing on its own, to establish the validity of my claims on the cross-national contrast in democratic practice and political inclusion. However, taken as a whole, the collection of evidence presented in this chapter builds a very strong case, making use of numerous types of evidence and sources. Ultimately it is only through tests or efforts at replication by others that the theory can be fully assessed. However, I do offer several partial tests in the following three chapters. For now I focus on presenting the theory and building the case for its plausibility. We begin the discussion of the cases with a rather stark example of the contrast, indeed one that is so stark that its initial impact on some readers may be to lead them to "recoil" intellectually much as, historically, many white Americans initially "recoiled" in tacit denial when they first encountered visual evidence of the brutal treatment long experienced by many African Americans. This first example helps to establish the way in which political conduct can be marked by nationally specific logics that are more reflective of cognitive frames of reference than institutional rules.

II. The Incident at the Border: June 2002

Just over twenty-five years after Spain's regime-inaugurating democratic elections of June 15, 1977, and twenty-eight years after Portugal's liberation from dictatorship on April 25, 1974, a small yet dramatic incident took place on the border separating the two countries. By late June 2002, when the events in question took place, the border had become virtually invisible. Europe's Schengen accord on travel and border control had eliminated border checkpoints at most frontiers between sovereign states in the European Union and on January 1, 2002, the entry into circulation of Euro notes (Fishman and Messina, 2006)—accompanied by the elimination of national currencies within the large Euro-zone—had put an end to the need to change currency when crossing the border. Borders such as the Iberian frontier between Spain and Portugal lived on in two ways: in the territorially based legal structures and actions of sovereign states, and in the broader population's cognitive frameworks, cultural constructions, and related forms of conduct that continue to treat national borders as very real demarcations.[3]

On a weekend late in June 2002 over two hundred Portuguese protesters organized by the Bloco de Esquerda (BE) set out for the Spanish city of Seville, intending to participate in a demonstration being held in that city during the European Union (EU) summit, which would mark the end of Spain's EU presidency—a status that rotates among EU member states. Francisco Louçã, a member of the parliament representing the BE, was among the Portuguese citizens traveling toward Seville. Despite the absence of border checkpoints between the two countries, on this instance Spanish police stationed near the border attempted to block the entry into Spain of vehicles carrying would-be demonstrators. Citing considerations of "national security," these Spanish authorities refused entry into their country. Louçã got off the chartered bus in which he was riding and insisted that the police allow the demonstrators to proceed, noting that they were all European citizens with rights of movement across national borders. What followed was captured by video cameras and was shown repeatedly on Portuguese television in the days that followed. The parliamentary deputy was physically beaten by Spanish police, who succeeded in preventing the Portuguese from traveling onward to Seville and their planned demonstration there.

This incident at the border was extensively covered in Portugal, where it quickly became a topic of political discussion in newspapers, television, Internet fora, the parliament, and beyond. The presiding officer of Portugal's parliament, the President of the Assembly of the Republic (AR)—a member of the country's principal right-of-center party, the Partido Social Democrata (PSD)—announced plans to cancel a scheduled official trip to Spain as a way of protesting what had happened. In Spain the public response to the incident was almost non-existent. The Socialist Party (PSOE) and smaller parties in opposition to the conservative government of the Partido Popular (PP) never chose to raise the issue. Although it might have been useful to do so from a purely electoral standpoint concerned with competitive advantage in future trips to the polls—to say nothing of the principles at stake— none of the opposition parties sought to make these events into a matter of genuine public debate. One of the very few lengthy newspaper articles discussing the incident in Spain was an op-ed piece in Barcelona's establishment newspaper, *La Vanguardia*, authored by Mário Soares—former Prime Minister and President of Portugal.[4] Early in July of the same year the European Parliament voted to condemn the Spanish police action, but the reprimand was only weakly noted in Spain, where the country's largest circulation newspaper, the Socialist-leaning *El País*, devoted only one paragraph to the parliamentary condemnation—placing the story on page 20 in the print edition.[5] Spain's Foreign Minister at the time, Josep Piqué, ultimately issued an official apology to the Portuguese but that statement, from one of Spain's few right-of-center politicians who had earlier been active in the left opposition to Francoism, was an exception to the broader pattern of seeming indifference within Spain. Many politically active Spaniards remained totally unaware of the incident at the border.[6]

When I interviewed Louçã four years after the incident, he underscored the enormity of the difference in response between political forces in the two countries.[7] Within half an hour of the police action, Louçã received a telephone call from the chief of staff of Portugal's President, Jorge Sampaio, expressing support and offering to immediately contact Spain's Ambassador in Lisbon. Soon afterward, João Bosco Mota Amaral, the right-of-center President of Portugal's AR, called Louçã to express his solidarity. Mota

Amaral quickly put the wheels in motion to hold a vote of the parliamentary body condemning the Spanish police action—and the vote was unanimously in favor of the condemnation. All parties present in the representative body voted in support of the demonstrators' rights. Sometime after the incident, after a long wait, Louçã ultimately received a communication from the President of Spain's parliament, the Congress of Deputies in Madrid, but he reports that the message offered justification rather than condemnation for the police action.[8]

One could construct two somewhat different readings of the incident at the border and of the way it was discussed—or ignored—in the neighboring Iberian Peninsula democracies. One might attribute the stark cross-national difference in the public treatment of the incident by the news media, political leaders, and the general public to what could be called the blinders of national identity. By this logic, both the communications media and major political forces in the two countries would have simply evidenced concern for their own nationals and a profound disinterest in the nationals of their Iberian neighbor. Even if we accepted this interpretation as reflective of the only dynamic at work—leaving aside the inconvenient matter of inappropriate police behavior—it would still, in a sense, represent evidence of nationally specific forms of democratic practice. The interest of multiple Portuguese actors in the incident, and the disinterest of their Spanish counterparts in what happened—in events that, after all, took place in Spanish territory and involved highly questionable actions by the Spanish police at the scene—cannot be attributed to legal constraints, institutional imperatives, or material incentives of any easily discernible sort. The vast cross-national contrast in how Portuguese and Spanish actors treated an unfortunate incident on their border can only be explained by invoking cognitively embedded cultural factors leading those actors to see the incident in different ways and—as a result—either to respond to it with concern or ignore it. Thus even the "national blinders" interpretation of this case assumes that the political decision to bring the incident into the public sphere, or ignore it, is rooted in cultural understandings and forms of practice that vary by country. However, there is another "democratic practice" interpretation of this case that relies much less heavily on national identity and the blinders that it can sometimes put in place. This view sees Portuguese democratic practice as far more oriented than its Spanish counterpart to the rights and actions of demonstrators—understanding them to constitute an important component of democratic public life.

I rely on various types of evidence—including survey data, newspaper and television coverage, qualitative interviews, relevant documents and secondary literature, and sustained observational research—to delineate overarching patterns of democratic practice in the two countries. On the basis of this broad array of evidence as well as the substance of this June 2002 case, I argue that the national contrast in the political handling of the incident at the border is, in fact, connected to just such a general differentiation between the neighboring countries in their predominant form of democratic practice, one that is historically rooted in their pathways to democracy. Portugal's post-revolutionary democratic practice is highly inclusionary in multiple ways—providing a hearing and a place in the political system's principal "conversation"[9] for actors of little power, be they low-income and socially marginal sectors, relatively small parties, or others located in positions conventionally seen as subordinate, and crucially, understanding the legitimate political arena to encompass protest in the streets as well as the official doings of representative institutions. In contrast, Spain's predominant form of democratic practice is institutionally and hierarchically segmented in ways that limit interactions and "conversation" between institutional office holders and the system's long list of political "outsiders" including demonstrators, low-income or socially marginal sectors, and peripheral nationalists especially in Catalonia and the Basque Country.[10]

Indeed, I argue that in the Spanish case the understandings and forms of practice that limit such interactions assume, for many actors, the existence of a sharp line of demarcation between the system's formal institutional core and political action located elsewhere. For reasons rooted in the history of the country's pathway from dictatorship to democracy, Spanish mainstream political actors tend to take for granted a sharp political boundary separating what goes on inside official institutions from the expression of popular sentiments outside the bounds of such official bodies. In mirror image form, for many actors outside the institutional core of greatest power, those inside the core seem distant and unapproachable. At the same time, mainstream Spanish actors tend to see their own political world in hierarchical terms, validating as appropriate the considerably greater power of those at the top of institutional structures.

Despite the efforts of some inside the PSOE, and other parties or movements on the left to forge connections between social protest and institutional power, the perspective of many powerful actors, even on the left, and virtually all actors further to the right, has taken as a given the desirability of maintaining a sharp separation between the politics of the streets and the doings of official institutions. As a result, in practice demonstrators are typically kept at a distance from institutional power in Spain but are understood to form part of the core of democratic politics in Portugal. Moreover, in a matching relational logic, many activists involved in Spanish protest movements seek to maintain a considerable distance from institutional power (Flesher Fominaya, 2007) instead of trying to engage it in "conversation"—whether through direct dialogue or an indirect exchange of public statements intended to engage the other conversational party (Fishman and Everson, 2016). Even though Spain is a world leader in public protest (Fishman, 2004: 10–15; Jiménez, 2011), when demonstrations have a tangible effect on politics, that tends to reflect either their impact on mass-level public opinion (Jiménez, 2007: 414–417) or their capacity for disruption (Fishman and Everson, 2016). The two worlds of politics—in the streets and inside representative institutions—have been kept almost entirely separate from one another. Both those engaged in social protests and power holders inside institutions tend to assume the existence of sharp lines of demarcation between their worlds. Those who try to push politics in other directions—by promoting dialogue and "conversation" between the largely separate worlds of Spanish politics—tend to encounter strong cultural resistance to their efforts. As much evidence to be discussed in this chapter shows, the cross-national contrast revealed by the incident at the border is, in fact, reflective of a very broad difference between the two countries in how political actors view the connection—or separation—between demonstrations and institutionalized political life, a constraint that is parallel to the broader difference in the treatment of social and political outsiders.

The Portuguese demonstrators who were blocked entry into Spain were located politically well to the left of the country's major institutional forces; the deputy who was beaten was a leader of a then small party that held only three seats in the country's parliament. Nonetheless, the demonstrators' rights were taken to be a matter of political significance by actors across Portugal's ideological spectrum. In contrast, in Spain, their rights—and the coercive conduct of the police—were seen as largely irrelevant by major political actors, even on the political left. Police efforts to disperse or restrain demonstrators, and the use of official force in such matters, are hardly shocking to Spanish political actors even though on occasion they may complain of it. In contrast, in Portugal, demonstrations are widely understood to be a normal component of politics as usual. The incident at the border revealed a deep and wide difference between the neighboring countries in unwritten understandings about democratic politics and in forms of conduct linked to those understandings. Those differences are clearly visible in the relationship between protest demonstrations and institutional power in the two political systems but are not limited to that matter. The differences are broader than that, holding wide-ranging consequences for democratic depth.

III. Demonstrations in the Two Political Systems

Demonstrations are quite a common form of political expression—and participation—in both countries. However, the interconnection of protest demonstrations with the politics that goes on inside official institutions takes on very different forms in the two Iberian Peninsula cases, as does the capacity of protest in the streets to reshape political outcomes. The cross-national contrast between the neighboring democracies in the nexus between social protest in the streets and officially constituted centers of power is manifested in the conduct of multiple actors and the interactions among them. Nationwide political elites, lower-level leaders, rank-and-file activists, and actors inside at least two secondary institutions—the news media and schools—all provide evidence of the broad pattern of difference between the two cases. These differences are to be found in both the words and actions of those involved. Perhaps the most direct and powerful evidence is that of the very tangible matter of the spatial destination of demonstrations in the two countries. Whereas many Portuguese protest marches end at the steps of the parliament building—on occasion taking their demands inside for a hearing from representatives of the parties present in the AR—in Spain demonstrators are officially prohibited from doing so. The original Spanish prohibition on such conduct is incorporated in Article 77 of the country's Constitution; further legal elaborations have solidified this exclusion. When demonstrators have managed to bring their demands to the steps of the parliament building in Madrid, that has involved moving beyond police barriers.[11] In the Spanish case, formal institutional rules have served to reflect and reinforce the cultural understandings generative of the country's predominant form of democratic practice.

In the Portuguese case abundant evidence reaffirms the democracy's predominant assumption that demonstrations and the Parliament are complementary forms of political expression that together—and along with other forms of participation to be discussed later—constitute the country's democratic life. The Portuguese political elite's mainstream conception of public protest and of its place in democratic politics was quite effectively conveyed by an official exhibit organized by the AR in April 2006 to commemorate the thirtieth anniversary of the Constitution. In that exhibit, and in the accompanying book-length catalog published by the AR at the time, the constitutional text itself was featured along with photographs of relevant political actions including, quite prominently, protest demonstrations. Many of the featured protesters engaged in critiquing government policies of one sort or another were, by some standards, socially marginal or relatively powerless actors. The protesters celebrated by the official exhibit in the parliament included university students opposing tuition charges and changes in the curricular plan of their universities, workers opposing plans to privatize companies, gay rights activists calling for changes in the official definition of families, retirees denouncing the pension system as insufficient, and children demonstrating against the use of child labor. All of these types of protest were celebrated officially by the country's parliament and were presented as being intrinsically linked to the Constitution. Nothing equivalent has taken place in post-Franco Spain, where political elites have instead tended to promote a sharp demarcation between the official work of representative bodies and the expression of citizen disapproval in the streets. When demonstrators attempt to take their grievances to the doors of the country's parliament, the Congress of Deputies in Madrid, or to the regional parliaments of the country's autonomous communities, the end result has often involved violent clashes between demonstrators and police engaged in protecting the strict separation between those two worlds of politics. Political elites in Spain have called and led large demonstrations against terrorism but when political representatives inside institutions have been the target of demonstrators, the official response has been thoroughly different from that of Portuguese authorities.

Spanish protest movements have increasingly attempted to challenge this strict separation, especially after the May 2011 occupation of public squares in Madrid, Barcelona, and other large cities by the 15-M movement. However, the demarcation has been maintained. In the fall of 2012, in the midst of the period of severe austerity analyzed in chapter 5, demonstrators attempted to take their grievances to the proximity of the Spanish parliament on at least four occasions. An initial declaration of the government promised to prohibit such attempts, declaring that it was "illegal to demonstrate near the parliament."[12] However, this initial position of the government's Madrid delegate Cristina Cifuentes was soon modified to a somewhat more conciliatory approach allowing demonstrators to mass on a major avenue and plaza located just one and a half short city blocks below the parliament building.[13] The street on which the parliament is directly located was to be blocked off by the police. However, when the demonstration took place on September 25, clashes between the police and protesters led to sixty-four injuries and thirty-five arrests. The police ultimately moved below the barrier intended to separate the parliament from the protesters, and proceeded to clear the Plaza where protest activity had been authorized. Rubber bullets were used in this operation.[14] When the country's budget was subject to parliamentary debate in October of that year, the demonstrators returned—attempting again to get close to the parliamentary building. The PP President of the Madrid regional government (later indicted on corruption charges, in the spring of 2017) declared, "It is unacceptable to intimidate the parliament."[15] Some deputies on the left replied that they felt no intimidation. Indeed, parliamentary deputy Gaspar Llamazares, then leader of Izquierda Unida (IU), left the parliament to join the demonstration, but in his gesture of support he was not accompanied by parliamentarians of the more establishment-oriented PSOE.[16] I return to the issues posed by these events in chapters 5 and 7.

On unusual occasions clashes between police and protesters have also occurred in Portugal,[17] but such events have been infrequent in the smaller Iberian Peninsula case and, as we will see later, they stand in clear tension with predominant understandings among Portuguese political actors about how democracy should operate. The broadly shared Portuguese understanding of demonstrations as a normal component of public life—seeing them as fully compatible with public order and with the smooth functioning of democratic institutions—is captured by another occurrence from 2012. In September of that year, in one of many anti-austerity demonstrations that took place in Lisbon, a young demonstrator was famously photographed warmly embracing a policeman who was charged with ensuring order during the protest. When questioned later about her gesture of affection toward the policeman, the young protester responded that surely she "was not the first person in the world to hug a policeman."[18] This remark transmits as a taken-for-granted assumption the absence of a dangerous line of demarcation between the police and demonstrators. Portugal's post-revolutionary democracy has managed to either eliminate or at least reduce the magnitude of a series of interrelated demarcations that culturally segment public life in Spain. It is important to note that the sharp separation between public protest and representative institutions in the Spanish case is not limited to Madrid and can be found also in some contexts[19] within the country's plurinational periphery. In Barcelona a related incident took place on June 15, 2011—roughly three weeks after the Catalan autonomous police had used considerable force to clear the city's central plaza where demonstrators, involved in the *indignados* movement, were camped out. On June 15 militant demonstrators massed outside the Catalan autonomous parliament as deputies prepared to enter the building. A confrontation took place, and several months later, on October 3, twenty-two of the demonstrators who had participated in the June protest outside the Catalan parliament were arrested, charged with a crime against state institutions.[20] The fact that the predominant Spanish form of democratic practice has shaped a great deal of public life in the Catalan context holds theoretical relevance to be discussed in chapter 6 and in the conclusion.

Declarations of prominent political leaders and of political parties as such help to establish the clear cross-national contrast between Portugal and the Spanish pattern. . As Mário Soares—the single most important political leader of Portugal's post-revolutionary democracy—put the matter in 2008, "In Portugal the right to indignation exists." He explained that in his view representative democracy "is compatible with participatory democracy and I am in favor of citizens expressing their demands in the streets."[21] In 2002, Jorge Sampaio, then President of the Republic issued a call for "democratic agitation" while he was on a presidential visit to the town of Beja in the Alentejo in June of that year.[22] Politicians of the center-right, as well, have issued calls for public participation and have articulated an expansive, inclusionary sense of democracy. On the anniversary of April 25 in 2007 the local leader of the center-right PSD in Maia, a municipality north of Porto, remarked, "Democracy only really exists when it assures everyone, without exception, the possibility to exercise in absolute fullness, their rights and duties . . . the best way to commemorate and respect the spirit of April 25 is creating mechanisms to consolidate a truly participatory democracy."[23] Portugal's inclusionary approach to democratic practice is not limited to parties and political actions located on the left of the country's political spectrum.

The declarations and actions of Spain's political leaders—especially those located to the right of the country's political center—have been quite different. Indeed, many right-wing politicians have sought to place in question the legitimacy of political forces and forms of action tied to social protest in the streets. In one of the clearest examples of this general tendency, the Madrid PP leader, Esperanza Aguirre, suggested in 2011 that the large-scale 15-M movement of indignados should be seen as "precursors of totalitarianism."[24] In this instance a large-scale movement of peaceful social protest that helped to shape the emergence shortly afterward of the Occupy Wall Street movement in the United States (Romanos, 2016a, 2016b) was denounced by a mainstream politician as dangerously associated with totalitarianism. A similar effort to delegitimate public protest was clearly reflected in February 2012 by the declarations of the police chief of Valencia, a city ruled at the time by the PP, when he referred to student protesters as "the enemy."[25] This characterization of protest, and the underlying view of politics to which it is linked, have also led to efforts to diminish opportunities for the expression of protest: In March 2011 the PP asked judges to prevent a planned demonstration against corruption from taking place in Valencia.

The PP complained that the demonstration, which intended to call for the resignation of the President of the Valencian Autonomous Community, was guilty of grave insults "against the authority exercising its position of power."[26] Subsequently, official investigations of corruption in the Valencian Community led to numerous arrests and trials. Although Spanish conservatives sometimes make use of public demonstrations for their own purposes, the general hostility of many on the center-right to popular voices of protest in the streets has strongly conditioned the practice of democracy in Spain. However, the sharp demarcation between public protest and the official world of representative institutions is a broader feature of Spain's post-Franco democracy; it is not limited to the worldview of the country's political right. We turn now to evidence provided by two paired comparisons of protest and discontent in the two countries, first taking up cases that involve housing and second focusing on the protests of truckers in the face of rising fuel costs.

IV. Discontent and Protest over Housing and Regarding Fuel Costs: Paired Comparison

The metropolitan areas of both Lisbon and Madrid are the sites of large concentrations of formally illegal housing in areas close to the municipal limits of the two capital cities. Thousands of people, most of them immigrants from Africa, Latin America, or eastern Europe, live in informal structures erected without official sanction or permission on land owned by others. These structures and their residents are concentrated in neighborhoods such as "Cova da Moura" in the municipality of Amadora outside Lisbon and, in Greater Madrid, in the large area of the "Cañada Real" spanning territory in the municipalities of Coslada, Rivas, and an edge of Madrid itself. The formal illegality of the dwellings involved, many of them "shanties" but others more structurally impressive, has led to various official efforts at demolition in both countries. Residents of these informal neighborhoods have been faced with either the reality or at least the implicit threat of the loss of their homes in both Portugal and Spain. They have faced this challenge as political outsiders with limited economic means, many of them lacking citizenship in their country of residence. Among those involved, many are members of racial and/or religious minorities. We now turn to evidence about their struggles and their place in the two political systems, before briefly taking up other cases of housing-related movements and protest.

In late January 2006, just as the Portuguese public was assimilating the results of the presidential election held two days earlier, an important incident occurred on the morning of January 24 in the municipality of Amadora. That morning all three national television networks suddenly broke away from their regular programs and offered viewers on the scene coverage of events then taking place in a poor neighborhood of Amadora.[27] Accompanied by a few outside supporters, residents of informal dwellings slated for demolition, mostly immigrants of African origin, were resisting the destruction of their houses. The reporters covering these events interviewed those involved, allowing them to calmly present their case to the nationwide television audience. A small immigrants' rights organization, Solidariedade Imigrante, helped to mobilize support for those involved, framing the issue at stake as the basic right to housing. The immigrant rights organization took the case of the Amadora residents to the country's parliament in a protest march held several weeks later. At the AR, the demonstrators asked all parliamentary groups present for a hearing and received it. Even the parliamentarians located on the right of the political spectrum took these immigrants, and the demonstrators supporting their cause, to be legitimate participants in the country's political system, deserving a hearing from elected representatives in the AR. The immigrant rights organization also took the case of those affected by demolition plans to municipal governments and court houses. Despite the relatively small numbers of Solidariedade Imigrante members, and the limited resources of those facing the loss of their homes, the economically disadvantaged immigrants living in informal dwellings were treated by both parliamentary deputies and news reporters as legitimate members of the country's public "conversation" on politics. Neither the generally quite useful "power resources" approach to political explanation (Korpi and Shalev, 1979; Huber and Stephens, 2012; Stephens, 1979) nor other approaches lacking our current emphasis on democratic practice would predict the reception received by these demonstrators (Fishman, 2017).

Much more can be said on the willingness of Portuguese office holders to take up the needs and concerns of housing protesters, but before we turn to such evidence it is useful to first examine the experience of the Madrid-area counterparts of the Amadora immigrants: In 2008, residents of the Cañada Real and their supporters sought a hearing from governmental office holders, hoping to arrange for either an end to demolitions or at a minimum replacement housing capable of meeting the needs of those affected by the destruction of their informal housing. However, the left-Catholic priest Javier Baeza and others involved in efforts to support those faced with the loss of their Cañada homes were repeatedly frustrated in their efforts to speak with elected office holders and find solutions for those involved. A substantial group of immigrant families who had lost their homes in the Cañada Real had no alternative but to live for more than a month inside the parish church of Baeza.[28] The immigrant residents of informal dwellings in Amadora and elsewhere in greater Lisbon were far more fortunate. In 2008 Portugal's chief of national housing policy, João Ferrão, initiated efforts to improve the life and living conditions of residents in Cova da Moura and other "critical neighborhoods."[29] These efforts included a plan to formalize the status of residents, securing for them official ownership rights to their dwellings. Although that objective was not ultimately obtained, many improvements in the neighborhood occurred and the residents of the dwellings in question were treated by Ferrão and other government officials as full participants in the process.[30]

The cross-national difference in the treatment of the concerns and protests of immigrants dwelling in informal housing are paralleled by other experiences of housing-related movements in the two countries. Residents of the Lisbon neighborhood of Amendoeiras who lived in housing occupied during the revolution (Ramos Pinto, 2013: 220) suffered a loss of control over their housing in 2005 with a legal change that they interpreted as a landlord-oriented privatization of the dwellings' ownership status. They responded with a campaign of protests. Their concerns were attended to in negotiations with all political parties present in the parliament, and in conversations with João Ferrão. A unanimous vote in the parliament, and the initiatives of Ferrão, led to the return of the dwellings to a status allowing the residents both greater control over the houses and the option to buy them at an acceptable price. These housing protests led to concessions by elected representatives and a return of the dwellings in question to a status more like the one that the residents had initially obtained during revolutionary-era occupations.[31] Whereas Portuguese housing protesters sought out interchange and "conversation" (Fishman and Everson, 2016) with elected representatives—hoping to achieve significant concessions in the process—Spanish housing protesters, far more skeptical of the possibility of winning a hearing and actual concessions from power holders, tended to focus their campaigns more on public opinion and civil society than on elected institutions. Leaders of the emblematic Barcelona-based movement V de Vivienda (in English, H for Housing) achieved much support for their efforts in favor of housing affordability in the midst of a real estate bubble in 2006 and 2007, but were at the time reluctant to seek out and sustain negotiations with elected office holders.[32]

As the experience of V de Vivienda suggests, the predominant Spanish model of democratic practice, with its demarcation and distance between the worlds of social protest and governmental power, has often predominated even in Catalonia with its nationally distinct identity and political history. The strikingly different experiences of the Okupas movement in the Catalan capital, Barcelona, and Lisbon also confirm the strong relevance of the predominant Spanish model for much political life in Catalonia and the fundamental difference with post-revolutionary Portugal. In Barcelona the relations between the Okupas movement and municipal authorities—in a city where the political left has tended to control the municipal administration—have been characterized by a relative paucity of negotiated understandings and by pitched battles between the police and those engaged in the occupations.[33] In contrast, in Lisbon, the Okupas movement and municipal authorities typically expect to resolve points of disagreement by negotiation and accommodation. When in August 2002 the Portuguese capital's Okupas were dislodged from an occupied building, they complained that this action violated their negotiated understanding with city authorities. Municipal power holders offered a different version, but both parties to the dispute oriented their claims to the expectation of reaching an understanding through conversation.[34] It should be emphasized that the history of the Okupas and other movements dealing with housing clearly shows that the Spanish pattern of democratic practice is not restricted to elites. Both institutional elites and their adversaries in protest movements see their two worlds of politics as sharply separated from one another. In Spain, the tendency to segment democratic practice institutionally has not been limited to elites.

The clear pattern of cross-national difference in the interactions—or lack thereof—between housing protesters and office holders, has a thematically distant "echo" in the politics surrounding a very different type of protest that touched both countries in June 2008. In the face of a rapid run-up in fuel costs that year, truckers engaged in protest campaigns in both countries, seeking to disrupt commercial transportation as a way of pressuring governments to take steps to lessen the economic impact of the increased costs on their own pocketbooks. These protests may have been difficult to place on a conventional left-right spectrum, but they expressed the genuine economic concerns of those involved. The truckers were engaged in efforts to use pressures "from below" to change public policies. In both countries the protests tragically led to one death—remarkably on the same day in June—but that similarity was not paralleled by the response of elected political leaders to the events. When on June 10, 2008, a Portuguese truck driver who was participating in a picketing effort to halt transportation was struck and killed by another vehicle, Prime Minister José Socrates immediately expressed his regrets, lamenting the loss of life by the protester. Earlier, he had issued a statement indicating that the government would attempt to take steps to ameliorate the economic impact of the increase in fuel costs on truckers and related enterprises.[35] On the very same day, June 10, a trucker who was participating in a picket line in Granada, Spain, was killed by a vehicle attempting to move through the line of strikers. In both countries and on the very same day a striking truck driver was killed while participating in picketing in support of the strike. Despite the similarity of circumstances, the response of public authorities—at the time Socialists in both countries— was quite different.

Whereas the Portuguese Prime Minister publicly expressed his regret over the loss of life, Spanish authorities responded to the situation with declarations more focused on the question of public order as such. Instead of singling out for special regrets the loss of life by one striking worker, Spanish authorities spoke to the broader set of confrontational encounters between picketers and non-strikers. The conservative PP accused the Socialist government of Prime Minister Zapatero of being "passive" and of "abandoning its functions" ("dejación de funciones"). Prime Minister Zapatero, arguably the country's most left-oriented chief executive since the 1930s, declared that the state's security forces would act with "more means and firmness" and with "zero tolerance" toward picketers engaged in protests. The Minister of the Interior and prominent Socialist leader Alfredo Pérez Rubalcaba offered assurances that Spanish highways were "completely clean."[36] A right-of-center online newspaper, *El Confidencial*, reported at the time that a leader of the striking truckers responded to the Interior Minister's handling of the protest with a lament that official treatment of the strikers was "worse than the Franco era."[37] This episode underscores how even the PSOE is at times subject to a tendency to frame protest events in a way that sees them more as a threat to public order than a contribution to democracy.

V. Survey Evidence on the Segmented Perspectives of the Spanish Left on Democratic Practice

Our analysis of qualitative evidence on democratic practice in Portugal and Spain has provided strong grounds to argue for the existence of major differences between the two national cases, but evidence of this nature necessarily leaves some important questions unanswered. Qualitative evidence can provide us with crucial insights into causal processes and mechanisms—evidence of a sort that is very difficult to extract from what Brady, Collier, and Seawright call "data set observations" (2010). Qualitative evidence can also offer decisive information on theoretically relevant phenomena, cases, and questions, but evidence of this nature cannot answer questions about the distribution of characteristics within a population (Small, 2009; Brady, Collier, and Seawright, 2010; Spillman, 2014). For the purposes of concept and theory formation, qualitative evidence can often prove more deeply useful than standard quantitative evidence, but quantitative data from sample surveys and other sources remains completely essential for the overall social scientific enterprise. Our examination of a wide range of qualitative sources has shown much evidence of the tendency of Spanish rightists to minimize the legitimacy and the role of public protest in democracy. We have also encountered some evidence of a tendency of (at least some) Spanish Socialists in the PSOE to treat protest in the streets more as an unfortunate form of "disorder" than as a welcome and legitimate complement to the work that goes on inside representative institutions. The evidence that we have provided on other forces in the Spanish Left is more limited, but it has suggested the existence of perspectives quite different from those that predominate in the large mainstream political forces, the PP and the PSOE. Given the existence of qualitative evidence on divisions within the Spanish Left on fundamental perspectives concerning normal forms of democratic practice, there is clearly much to be gained by examining survey evidence on this question.

Fortunately, a survey of local leaders in industrial working-class communities in several Spanish regions provides highly relevant evidence. The survey was carried out in 1990–1991, interviewing party, union, and reputational leaders in forty-nine predominantly industrial municipalities with populations above 25,000 people (Fishman, 2004). I designed the survey as part of a research effort focused theoretically on the contribution of working-class linked political or union organizations to the quality of Spanish democracy. By theoretical design, the study was limited to the main organizations and leaders on the left, at that time—the PSOE, Izquierda Unida, Comisiones Obreras (CCOO) and the Unión General de Trabajadores (UGT). It should be added that many of the union and reputational elites interviewed were also party members. The individuals interviewed were included in the sample either on the basis of their institutional leadership position in parties or unions or because their names were mentioned in a "snowball" extension of the sample designed to include other recognized leaders in the communities in question. Although the primary purpose of the survey was to identify socio-political determinants of local leaders' tendency to frame local interests in generalizing or "globalizing" discourses capable of engaging large extra-local publics, the questionnaire, which I designed primarily for that objective, also included one item that serves our current purposes rather well. Respondents were offered six possible answers to the following question:

> Many times in the labor movement—just as in other social sectors, such as the employers for example—actions which to some extent are illegal are considered and carried out. These actions can include unauthorized demonstrations, the non-observance of legislation on labor matters, encierros (shut-ins), etc., and may at times include holding a boss hostage. I would like to ask you about your opinions on what the state can do to respond to illegal actions of the labor movement. If the state arrests those involved and places them on trial, does this seem reasonable to you?

Those interviewed were then provided with a list of possible responses, each of which was included on a printed card shown to the respondents and also read out loud to them. This point is crucial, and it underscores a crucial advantage of the closed-ended format for survey interviews: It allows us to be certain that the answers chosen were actually preferred over the other alternatives listed—given that those interviewed both heard and read all of the alternatives. With open-ended responses one can never be certain whether a given response is actually preferred to theoretical alternatives or instead was articulated simply because it came to mind more quickly than theoretical alternatives. The text of the six responses that were provided to those interviewed as possible answers is as follows:

1. Yes it is reasonable because the state has the right and the duty to do so; if not the laws make no sense.
2. As long as we are talking about a democracy it is reasonable.
3. In theory it is reasonable, but in reality many times the state enforces the law when it runs against our interests and does not enforce it when it runs against the interests of capital. So we have the right to insist that the law be enforced in a just manner.
4. It is reasonable only if we are talking about something very serious, such as holding a boss hostage, for example.
5. It may be that the state has the right to do so, but I am not interested in the rights of the state but rather in the interests of the workers.
6. It is not reasonable. What the state ought to do is respond to the needs and interests of workers and not arrest them.

The responses of those interviewed provide crucial insights into the segmented foundation for democratic practice in post-Franco Spain. As the data presented in Table 3.1 show, the perspectives of interviewed PSOE members were remarkably different from those of other interviewed leaders in the forty-nine sampled municipalities. These other respondents were local working-class leaders who were members of other parties or no party. For our current purposes, the question can be understood to capture the way in which respondents weigh the relative merit and significance of the legal claim made by the state versus demands pressed "from below" by labor militants. In quite general terms the responses fit into three large categories. The first two responses strongly prioritize the legal claim of the state to enforce the law, making no effort to find ways to acknowledge the complementary legitimacy of pressures from below while also reaffirming the principle of law enforcement. The second two responses seek to draw some sort of balance, accepting the principle of law enforcement by the state while attempting to complement that principle with a sensitivity to the concerns and actions of those applying "pressure from below." The final two responses manifest a complete disinterest in, or hostility toward, the state's claim to enforce laws, conceptualizing the defense of workers' interests as fundamentally inconsistent with acceptance of the state's Weberian legitimacy. From a very general perspective, the placement of the respondents in these three broad

TABLE 3.1 Perspectives of local working-class readers in industrial towns in Spain—attitudes toward the use of State power to enforce laws broken by the labor movement

	SOCIALIST PARTY MEMBERS (%)	OTHER WORKING-CLASS LEADERS (%)
Always justified	26.3	2.6
Justified as long as under democracy	18.4	3.7
Justified if law is fairly enforced for business, too	22.8	51.3
Justified only in extreme cases	19.3	13.6
Respondent interested only in labor activists, not in State	2.6	6.3
Unjustified in principle	7.0	19.9
Other answer; no answer	3.5	2.6
N	114	191

SOURCE: Robert M. Fishman (2004), *Democracy's Voices: Social Ties and the Quality of Public Life in Spain* (Ithaca, NY: Cornell University Press).

groupings highlights the segmentation of the Spanish Left into three important categories: a large segment of the PSOE that sees no need to search out complementarities between the concerns of labor militants and the principle of state power, thoroughly prioritizing the statist view; a substantial segment of the labor leadership pool located outside the PSOE (and, given the milieu of the interviews, located clearly to its left) that thoroughly rejects the principle of state legitimacy, prioritizing only social pressure from below; and an intermediate group seeking to find complementarities between the two principals involved.

These responses clearly suggest that the underlying basis in the internalized commitments and understandings of the sampled leaders—and the broader political universe that they represent—is not favorable to the construction of a national democratic "conversation" between protest in the streets and the political power wielded by elected office holders. The responses chosen by a large sector of the interviewed PSOE members are strongly congruent with what I have described as the predominant form of democratic practice in Spain—with its insistence on a sharp and hierarchically ordered demarcation between the expression of discontent in the streets and the official workings of representative institutions. The single most widely chosen answer by the PSOE respondents fully prioritizes the enforcement of the legal order by the state—arresting and placing on trial labor activists who have broken a law of some sort—without even insisting, as is stipulated in the second response, that this principle should be contingent on the democratic status of the system. Considering the fact that the survey was carried out less than fifteen years after the end of authoritarian repression and the restoration of democratic rights in 1977, this failure to choose the available answer that limits the normative principle of state legitimacy to democratic systems, is quite noteworthy. Over one quarter of the sampled PSOE leaders, 26.3% to be precise, thus chose an answer reflective of a strong identification with state power irrespective of the political system's status as a democracy—or an anti-democratic regime. If this had been the most common answer of a right-wing party the choice might be expected, but absent any data on the perspectives of PP members on this question we are left with the fact that the highly state-oriented view is held by a large segment of the PSOE. The 18.3% of PSOE respondents who insist on the priority of law enforcement, but make that principle contingent on the existence of democracy, increase the weight within the PSOE of those who clearly prioritize state power over an interest in social pressure from below. Others in the PSOE and many of the other respondents do attempt to draw a balance between some sort of sympathy toward social pressures from below and a simultaneous acceptance of the principle of state legitimacy in enforcing the law. At times this more inclusionary tendency has proved dominant in the PSOE, but the survey suggests just how easily those who search for such a synthesis may encounter culturally based resistance—even within their own party—from leaders who hold a narrow and exclusionary conception of democratic politics. We also encounter in the survey data the cultural basis for a mirror-image resistance to that very same type of synthesis within organizations to the left of the PSOE. In this case the resistance comes from those inclined to thoroughly reject state legitimacy—a view congruent with the effort of some Spanish movement activists to avoid any contact or dialogue with those holding positions of political power. The segmented nature of Spanish democratic practice has strong cultural roots.

Our analysis of predominant forms of democratic practice in Portugal and Spain has focused thus far primarily on cross-national differences in two elements of variation: the interactions between institutional office holders and those expressing discontent "from below"—especially in the form of protest demonstrations—and the perspectives of political actors on such pressures from below. We have been able to examine those perspectives in a variety of ways including public declarations of political actors, material from qualitative interviews, responses to a systematic survey of local leaders, and cultural displays such as the Portuguese parliament's commemoration of the thirtieth anniversary of their Constitution's approval in 1976. We now turn to new types of evidence including the record of participatory institutional initiatives in the two countries, the perspectives of parliamentary elites and the mass public in Spain, and evidence about practice inside two crucial secondary institutions: the communications media and the educational system.

VI. *Politics within Institutions: Participatory Budgeting and Evidence on Parliamentary Elites*

Participatory budgeting (PB) and other participatory or deliberative institutional innovations have captured the imagination—and the hopes—of many political actors and students of politics in the Iberian Peninsula cases, and in a very long list of other countries. The early successes of PB in Porto Alegre, Brazil (Baiocchi, 2005), served as a source of inspiration to political actors in both Portugal and Spain. In various ways PB and similar initiatives can be seen to hold many things in common with demonstration-based forms of social pressure from below. Admittedly, some analysts of participatory and deliberative initiatives see them as serving more often as a tool of control or co-optation than as a genuine instrument for popular power that extends beyond what is generated by standard elections for representative bodies (Lee, 2015). But for scholarly students of democratic depth and for many political actors, participatory platforms such as PB seem to offer an institutional instrument for capturing the concerns expressed by social pressure from below, and for turning that pressure into meaningful outcomes on matters of material importance—such as the fixing of budgetary priorities. Indeed, some of the declarations of prominent Portuguese political leaders mentioned in this chapter actually articulated the case for building complementarities between representative and participatory forms of democracy. It should be emphasized that a crucial argument in favor of participatory approaches such as PB focuses quite directly on the inclusion of low-income actors in decision-making, a point strongly emphasized in Baiocchi (2005). Moreover, the literature on democratic depth is operationally split between works that focus on participatory institutional initiatives such as PB and others that center their attention on protest movements. From a number of perspectives, it makes sense to examine the record of participatory institutions in Portugal and Spain, checking to see if what we find adds in any useful way to this chapter's characterization of predominant forms of democratic practice in the two countries.

Participatory budgeting initiatives were introduced in both Iberian Peninsula cases shortly after the turn of the millennium in 2000, but the experience of such initiatives has been quite different in the two cases. In both countries, advocates of PB saw the new approach to budgeting as a way to enhance the involvement of ordinary citizens in decisions that affect their lives and as an instrument potentially capable of moving contemporary representative democracy toward the classical ideal of government by the people. The first major Iberian Peninsula initiative took place in Spain in the Andalusian city of Córdoba beginning in 2001 (Baiocchi and Ganuza, 2017). In their important analysis of this and other initiatives, Baiocchi and Ganuza—both major scholarly experts on PB—underscore how Córdoba quickly became a fundamental point of reference for advocates of enhanced citizen participation in Spain and elsewhere in Europe. From many perspectives, Córdoba can be seen as an especially promising context for a PB experiment. The municipality was governed by a political formation ideologically predisposed to favor such initiatives, the post-communist coalition IU, which held the mayor's office at the time when PB was introduced. IU remained in that position of municipal leadership until after PB was abandoned. Moreover, the regional government of Andalucia has been consistently led by the center-left PSOE throughout the post-Franco period. The ideological and institutional context would, at least superficially, appear to be more favorable to PB in Córdoba than in many other Spanish cities. Nonetheless, the experience was relatively short-lived. By 2007 the experiment in increased citizen participation had been abandoned for reasons carefully analyzed by Baiocchi and Ganuza.

Baiocchi and Ganuza show how neighborhood associations, bureaucrats, and other actors accustomed to pre-existing ways of reaching decisions at the municipal level, first reduced the scope for effective grassroots participation and then ultimately succeeded in closing down the PB initiative in 2007 (2017: 90–97). Neighborhood associations played an especially important role, defending the conventional model of representative democracy against this new effort to expand citizen participation, and power, during the long expanses of time between elections. As Baiocchi and Ganuza formulate the perspective of these actors: "Associations claimed that traditional politics required representatives who rule and make decisions. It was these representatives' responsibility to monitor the political agenda and oversee its implementation. After these decisions were made, citizens would elect the most effective politicians" (2017: 96). In a city ruled at the time by the post-communists of IU, neighborhood associations long active in defending the interests of urban residents actively opposed efforts to fuse traditional representative democracy with new participatory mechanisms intended to incorporate "voices from below" in decision-making. The city council offered support to the concerns of the neighborhood associations. In the practice of municipal-level politics, actors located on the left managed to halt the implementation of a participatory approach to budgeting that was intended to empower ordinary citizens. The internalized assumptions of these actors about normal political life defeated the initiative.

How generalizable is the experience of Córdoba? Numerous other Spanish municipalities have implemented participatory experiments of one type or another, and new efforts continue to emerge. Future research will continue to focus on this important question. But one important piece of research by political scientists Joan Font and Clemente Navarro offers potentially rather troubling findings. Font and Navarro (2013) find that in Spain those citizens who have actually participated in such institutions have a more critical view of their functioning than their counterparts in the Spanish citizenry who lack such experience. Comparative and theoretical work tends to assume that citizens' enthusiasm for participation will increase with actual experience, but the systematic examination of available data by Font and Navarro leads them to rather different conclusions for the Spanish case. Of course, Spain is a moderately sized and quite varied country; exceptions to many broad country-wide patterns can be found. But on average, something about the day-to-day functioning of would-be participatory institutions seems to dampen the enthusiasm of most participants in Spain. The implications of the research of Font and Clemente seem quite congruent with the analysis of Baiocchi and Ganuza.

The Portuguese case has also been the site of many PB initiatives, some of which failed, at least temporarily. However, over time PB experiments have grown more common and more successful in Portugal. In their important analysis of Portuguese experiences with PB, Lopes Alves and Allegretti (2012) emphasize the analytical importance of identifying and explaining instances of instability in PB initiatives. They take note of several shortfalls in the overall Portuguese record with PB—including the initially top-down nature of many initiatives and the absence of internally generated regulating documents capable of defining the scope and behaviors of PB instruments or institutions. Yet their analysis also specifies important positive components of the Portuguese record. Those PB initiatives that obtain a co-decisional status—providing the new participatory bodies with genuine decisional functions—have tended to gain consolidation, in some instances in major cities such as Lisbon. But perhaps even more importantly, in the Portuguese case a change in the party of government at the municipal level has exerted no significant effect on the continuity of pre-existing participatory initiatives. Although studies on other countries have often hypothesized a major impact of partisan change in control over municipal government on the discontinuation of PB initiatives, their analysis of data for Portugal shows no such effect. Indeed they observe, "A large number of PB experiences are promoted by local authorities governed by conservative majorities" (2012: 7). In the Portuguese case, the introduction of reasonably robust forms of PB has been treated as politically normal by political actors left to right. Numerous politicians and citizens across the ideological spectrum have welcomed this type of democratic deepening as thoroughly congruent with their conception of democracy. The Spanish experience to date appears much less promising.

In Portugal, the growth and consolidation of PB initiatives in many cities and towns, often with significant decisional powers, has been complemented by the development of participatory budgeting at the national level. Citizens are invited to offer proposals and vote on the alternatives either through the national PB website or in local meetings. In September 2017 the first national participatory vote awarded public funds to thirty-eight projects, among them one that was dubbed "Culture for Everyone." The initiators of this project, members of a cultural association based in the small town of Óbidos, had proposed offering "culture checks" to eighteen-year-olds and book vouchers to those who donate used books to public libraries. The victory of their project in the nationwide participatory voting was widely reported in the national press and publicized online at the government's website.[38] The Portuguese conception of democratic practice has favored the development of initiatives that incorporate ordinary citizens into budgetary decision-making and has quite explicitly linked this tendency to an inclusionary approach to the cultural sphere.

At the same time in Spain new survey evidence confirms elements of this book's assessment of the country's predominant way of understanding and "doing democracy." An important source on the perspectives of Spanish institutional power holders is to be found in the large program of survey work on parliamentary elites led by sociologist Xavier Coller with the collaboration of Antonio Jaime, Fabiola Mota, Guillermo Cordero and others (Coller, Jaime, and Mota, 2016; Cordero, Jaime-Castillo, and Coller, 2016). Although in some respects their view of the country's elites is a relatively positive one, they take note of both hierarchical and non-inclusionary tendencies in the recruitment of candidates for parliamentary positions and in the internal relations of parliamentary groups. In a summary of their most important findings (Coller, Jaime, and Mota, 2018, 10) they highlight among other points the extremely pronounced levels of party discipline within parliamentary groups and the character of candidate recruitment, which "tends to be at the same time decentralized and non-inclusive." Thus even decentralizing initiatives have tended to leave political power in the hands of relatively exclusionary and hierarchically oriented elites.

Survey evidence also proves to be helpful in elucidating how ordinary citizens perceive the interest of elites in the voices of the citizenry. Bonet, Martín, and Montero find that in the period from 1999 through 2002 Spain was a laggard within Europe in the extent to which citizens felt that governmental office holders were inclined to act in response to their concerns (2006: 121). Only Russia generated a lower level of citizen efficacy in the indicator examined by these scholars. Thus survey data at both the elite and the mass level is supportive of the argument made here.

VII. *Practice inside Two Secondary Institutions: The News Media and Schools*

We now turn to evidence on practice within two secondary institutions that hold special theoretical relevance for the concerns of this book. Those institutions are the news media and the educational system, especially at the high school level. These institutions hold special relevance for us for two quite different reasons. First, both the communications media and the school system hold immense implications for the fulfillment of democracy's manifold promises. High quality and inclusionary news coverage is essential if citizens are to fully inform themselves about public issues as a precondition for active civic involvement. The public educational system also has a vital role to play in democracy; only an active commitment of schools and teachers to building students' civic capacities can create a broadly competent and engaged citizenry. Families and voluntary organizations can activate the civic potential of many citizens, but active schools, committed to citizenship capacity-building, are essential for citizenship competence to reach those individuals and groups left relatively untouched by these other sources of political activation. But if these two secondary institutions have a vital role to play in facilitating an inclusionary form of democratic practice in the polity writ large, they are also the scene of their own internal forms of practice. I argue that it is those educational and journalistic entities in which internal institutional practices are most participatory and anti-hierarchical that contribute most strongly to political inclusion in the larger polity. In other words, these two secondary institutions are both key contexts within which the cross-national Iberian divide in democratic practice is manifested—and reproduced.

In *The Civil Sphere*, the distinguished cultural sociologist Jeffrey Alexander quite persuasively articulated the case for the significance of the news media: "The fact that protest movements take place does not, in itself, guarantee that they will be represented publicly in the mass media, much less that they will be represented in a civil manner that elicits audience sympathy for the movement and possible identification with it" (2006: 296). In other words, the full inclusion of protest movements into a democratic polity is contingent on the practice of both journalists and political officeholders. Very much in keeping with the rest of Portugal's post-revolutionary and inclusive democratic practice, Portuguese journalists have been committed to reporting the voices of all democratic actors, including those of limited economic means or political power. As the Portuguese journalist and scholar Estrela Serrano put the matter, "It is legitimate for the 'common citizen' to feel that the freedom of expression and right to information must involve, also, their own access to the media. In fact, on the balance and variety of voices expressed in the media depends, also the quality of democracy" (2006: 193). The dual commitment to inclusiveness and impartiality is common among Portuguese journalists, thereby helping to explain the coverage obtained by immigrants fighting to save their informal dwellings and other protesters of relatively limited power resources. However, in Spain news coverage often fails to meet this rigorous Portuguese standard, tending at times to limit the reporting of voices of discontent.

The important scholarship of Victor Sampedro on the journalistic coverage in Spain of movements such as the Galician environmentalists in Nunca Mais, the anti-war *insumisos* who resisted military conscription—and others—finds that the treatment of these protesters in the press has been uneven and often surprisingly limited, providing information on disruptive tactics of the movements but often not on their concerns and demands (Sampedro, 1997, 2004). The analysis of Jaume Asens of press coverage of Barcelona's Okupas movement produced quite similar findings (Asens, 2004). Enric Bastardes, a leader in Spain's federation of journalists unions, explained that the disinterest of news executives in the voices of protest, and the unwillingness of most rank-and-file reporters to challenge those executives, together produced the sort of coverage that demonstrations have received in Spain.[39] Some journalists have reported pressures to manipulate or limit coverage of the news. They complain of hierarchical demands from the directors of their newspapers or television stations.[40] Portuguese journalists, in contrast, report the news in a relatively non-partisan and inclusionary way as suggested earlier. What accounts for this difference?

I interviewed both rank-and-file journalists and news executives in Portugal to address that question,[41] and they all told essentially the same story. Journalists feel free to report the news the way they see fit and insist on their right to do so. Media directors regularly solicit the opinions of rank-and-file journalists and yield to their instincts as reporters. This pattern of participatory, unhierarchical practice within Portugal's media outlets is congruent with the institutional structure of the media where journalists elect representatives to editorial councils within each news reporting entity. However, practice itself is even more participatory and inclusionary than dictated by the formal institutional rules. The elected editorial councils officially only hold consultation functions. However, even where such councils do not exist—as in the case of Radio Renasença, where Arsenio Reis, a radio journalist I interviewed in collaboration with Manuel Villaverde Cabral, had worked prior to moving to TSF radio—journalists insist on the right to decide how to report the news.

The journalists whom I interviewed in Portugal pointed out that this practice of de facto reporter control over the full content of news stories began during the revolution—and has lived on. When I interviewed José Manuel Fernandes, at the time the Editor-in-Chief of the Portuguese *Publico*, the country's principal newspaper of record, he emphasized that journalists at his paper felt fully comfortable disagreeing operationally with individuals such as himself in positions of authority. He added that it is important for journalists to "listen to people of little power" and report the news accordingly.[42] In accounting for the generally inclusionary and politically independent approach of news reporting at RTP, the Portuguese state-owned network, Luis Marinho, at the time Director of News and Information, attributed these qualities to pressures from journalists and the public.[43] In contrast, Spanish journalists often have more limited autonomy in practice than in theory. In some media entities elective editorial committees meant to represent journalists have gone empty due to the unwillingness of journalists to stand for election to such posts.[44] The difference between the two countries in journalistic practice is greater than the contrast between them in the formal structure of institutions meant to safeguard the professionality and autonomy of reporters. Thus the actual conduct of journalists and their superiors inside the news media provides strong evidence of the Iberian divide in democratic practice and at the same time contributes to sustaining it.

Institutional practice inside the two countries' public schools also varies considerably in ways that exceed what one might expect based on a strict reading of current formal institutional regulations in the two cases (Fishman and Lizardo, 2013). In the most theoretically elaborate and holistic analysis to date of the Portuguese educational system, sociologist of education Stephen Stoer has argued that the revolution left in place inside the schools a participatory ethos influencing teachers, students, and administrators and "a radical pedagogy which tried to encourage the personal freedom and autonomy of students" (1982: 17). A leading Spanish sociologist of education whose work focuses on practice within schools has argued that in Spain relatively hierarchical practices and understandings were reinforced by the country's democratization scenario (Fernández Enguita, 1987, 1993). Indeed, in the formulation of Fernández Enguita, in Spanish schools "as in the army, the principle of authority at times presents itself as more important than the content of its exercise" (1993: 87). His research and that of other sociologists (Doz Orrit, 1995; Morgenstern de Finkel, 1995; O'Malley, 1995) has argued that even when official institutional reforms have intended to promote innovative and capacity-building pedagogy, actual practice inside the schools has substantially lagged such reform initiatives. Once again, practice within a crucial secondary institution confirms the broader arguments of this book.

My interviews inside Spanish and Portuguese schools strongly confirmed the contrast noted in the literature. Luis Costa, a high school instructor of both civics education and physical education in the Portuguese town of Quelluz outside Lisbon, reflected on the functioning of elective bodies inside the schools, "there is a lot of discussion, a lot of disagreement, a lot of hours. It takes a lot of time to reach consensus; we try to reach consensus."[45] He also related that he would explain to students their rights and "ways to demonstrate to defend their rights." He also would inform students of demonstrations programmed to take place in Lisbon.[46] An expansive conception of democratic practice was intrinsic to his educational practice. The understanding of education as an innovative capacity-building endeavor is widely shared by Portuguese teachers. Speaking of her students, Sara, a high school teacher of philosophy, explained "We try to open their minds so that they think by themselves, not like their parents. The teacher is someone who tries to develop the abilities of students and doesn't just transmit information."[47] Many Spanish teachers also feel a call to play such a role—as my interviews showed—but others have a more traditional content-centered conception of their responsibilities as teachers. But most importantly, even the Spanish teachers who would like to activate students' capacities in creative ways may encounter resistance from colleagues or administrators making such practice difficult to sustain. Elvira, a Madrid teacher committed to innovative efforts to awaken student capacities, reported that she was able to pursue that objective successfully in one school where she had taught, thanks to support from colleagues, but not in another school where such support was lacking.[48] In a more discouraging case, a would-be innovative teacher, in the most prestigious public school in a provincial capital, lamented that both hierarchical attitudes and professional rigidities by some teachers and administrators got in the way of innovative attempts at cultural capacity building for students.[49] None of the Portuguese teachers I interviewed reported such impediments or discouragement.

Other types of evidence point in the same direction. Survey research on teachers offers systematic confirmation of fundamental contrasts between the two cases in the practice of schools. TALIS, a cross-national survey of teachers sponsored by the Organization for Economic Cooperation and Development (OECD), finds a large difference in the way teachers are evaluated. Portuguese teachers were far more likely than their Spanish counterparts to report that feedback from students (82.7% in Portugal vs. 54.9% in Spain) and from parents (73.3% vs. 59.7%) played a significant role in their professional evaluations. The Portuguese inclination to listen carefully to the voices of students has not been limited to the formal evaluations of teachers. In November 2016, the Portuguese Minister of Education, Tiago Brandão Rodrigues, held a large discussion-oriented meeting with students in Leiria, a city in central Portugal. Calling the listening session "The Voice of the Students," the Minister later promised to repeat the experience regularly and received encouragement from the OECD on this matter.[50] The possible impact of this inclusionary practice on at least some of the students involved is highlighted by the words of a student present at the Leiria assembly, as related by the Minister: "We don't want formatted citizens, we want citizens of the world."[51]

Institutional practice inside both schools and media entities has been more participatory, un-hierarchical, and inclusionary in Portugal than in Spain. This pattern of contrast is in part a reflection of the highly dissimilar pathways to democracy in the two cases as discussed in chapter 2. But this contrast between the school systems and the news media of the two countries clearly exercises "feedback" effects on the two democratic systems, tending to reinforce and reproduce the broader pattern of cross-national difference. The legacies of the two pathways to democracy are not limited to formal institutional contrasts; they are reflected in actual practice within formal institutions. The difference between the two countries in their predominant form of democratic practice is not limited to politics in the narrowest sense of that term but is reflected and experienced in a broader range of societal settings. What goes on inside schools, news organizations, and other secondary institutions or venues holds the ability to impinge on and influence the meaning, practice, and inclusionary scope of democracy in the two countries.

However, it is not sufficient to establish the large difference between the neighboring countries in the conduct and understandings of key actors. It is also crucial to turn to the consequences of the Iberian divide in democratic practice for actual public policy and societal outcomes. We do so in the next chapter, examining employment, distributional outcomes, public expenditures, individual level civic practices, and cultural tastes. The contrast in predominant forms of democratic practice proves to exert an impact on numerous important societal outcomes.

CHAPTER 4 | *How* Democratic Practice Matters

I. Introduction

The large differences that I identify between Portugal and Spain in the ways that actors understand democracy, make use of its freedoms, and interact with others involved in political action would be a shallow and relatively insignificant addition to our study of democracy if we failed to find evidence that such contrasts actually matter for many other outcomes of importance. In this chapter we turn to a consideration of a number of arenas of "impact," showing how democratic practice matters for a wide range of outcomes. We focus here on outcomes identifiable long after the end of the transition and consolidation period, but before a major exogenous shock—the "great recession" of 2007–2009 and the Euro crisis initiated by that recession—raised new questions about the nature of democracy in the Iberian Peninsula cases and the rest of southern Europe. The impact of the Iberian divide in democratic practice on the politics of crisis is the theme of chapter 5; chapter 6 examines the impact of Spanish democratic practice on the Catalan crisis. Here we turn to unemployment, economic inequality, social spending, housing, civic practice, and cultural tastes. All of these are matters on which hard data exist, making it possible for us to examine the nature of differences between the countries and search for explanations consistent with the available data. We also take up and analyze possible objections to the argument advanced here. On two of the themes discussed in this chapter—cultural tastes and citizenship practice—I carried out research in full collaboration with scholarly experts in the area in question. In this chapter I discuss those collaborations and the main conclusions they produced.

II. *The Iberian Employment Paradox*

The cross-national difference between the Iberian Peninsula cases that has attracted the widest scholarly interest is, without question, the Iberian employment paradox. Unemployment has been higher in Spain than in Portugal throughout virtually the entire post-authoritarian period. Only for a short time in late 2006 and early 2007—during a period of unsustainable outperformance of Spain's economy in the context of a dangerous real estate and construction bubble (Fishman, 2012b; Royo, 2013; Buendía, 2018)—did the relative position of the two countries reverse, but that exceptional state of affairs proved to be very brief indeed. During the following year Portuguese unemployment actually fell while Spanish unemployment began a swift ascent to levels well above 20%. As the data reported in Figure 4.1 show, Portugal's advantage in employment has been consistent and typically quite large. Indeed, the starting point of the disparity lies further back than the coverage provided by the Eurostat data reported here.

This pattern of sustained and large difference in the unemployment rate is obviously a matter of great significance. After all, the positive impact of employment is not limited to the remuneration provided by a job—or to the linkage between employment rates and favorable aggregate economic performance. Work can provide the employed with some measure of fulfillment, dignity, and social integration. Moreover, prolonged high unemployment—as in the Spanish case—can produce lasting structural damage for an economy (Dutt and Ros, 2007). Despite the numerous similarities between the two countries, during the post-transition period, Portugal has on occasion actually

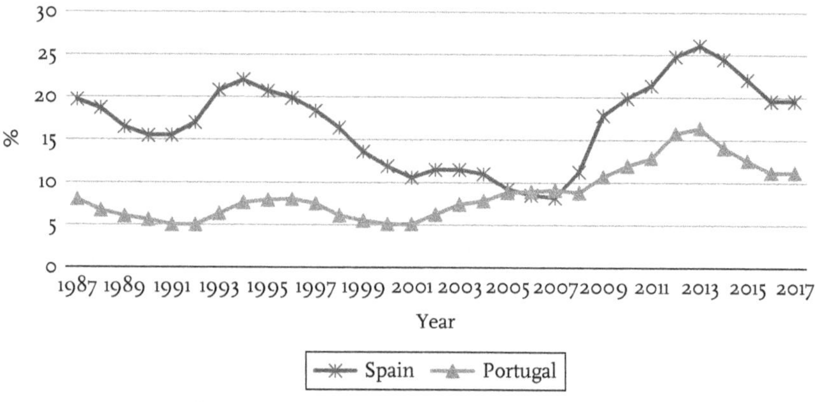

FIGURE 4.1 Unemployment—Spain, Portugal—1987–2017 (% of labor force)
SOURCE: EUROSTAT—Data base—Employment and Unemployment—une_rt_a. Date extracted: 05.05.2018: http://ec.europa.eu/eurostat/web/lfs/data/main-tables.

boasted one of Europe's lowest unemployment rates, whereas Spain's unemployment has been consistently high except for a brief period of time at the end of the unsustainable bubble economy. The large construction bubble of the years immediately preceding the Great Recession essentially masked underlying problems in Spain's economy (Fishman, 2012b). There is ample basis for the widespread scholarly interest in explaining this puzzle. Well-known economists (Blanchard and Jimeno, 1995; Bover, García-Perea, and Portugal, 2000; and Silva Lopes, 2003) along with sociologists and political scientists (Bermeo, 1998; Cameron, 2001; Esping-Andersen, 2000; Fishman, 2010; Glatzer, 2000) have been attracted to the analysis of the Iberian employment puzzle. The economists contributing to this literature have searched for explanations focused on labor costs and unemployment compensation payments, which were higher in more economically developed Spain than in Portugal—especially prior to the 1990s. One version of the economists' argument also took Spanish unions to be stronger than their Portuguese counterparts—despite lower membership numbers—thereby supposedly producing disincentives for employers to create jobs. However, the most distinguished team of economists to have written on the topic, that of Blanchard and Jimeno, acknowledged that their approach could not account fully for much of the cross-case contrast between Portugal and Spain.

The difficulties with the orthodox economic explanation, and its assumption that high Spanish unemployment is primarily attributable to labor costs or labor market "rigidities," are considerable. In Spain, the highest employment regions, the Basque Country and Navarra, have the strongest unions and some of the highest salaries in all of Spain along with a legal labor market regime that is exactly the same as the rest of the country. Nonetheless, their unemployment rates fall far below the rest of the country and have often stood close to the level of Portugal.[1] Comparative research on the impact of labor market regulation on employment has raised considerable questions about the alleged existence of a large negative effect of legal rights protecting against worker dismissals without adequate cause (Esping-Andersen and Regini, 2000). Moreover, the disparity in unemployment levels between the neighboring countries has proved to be surprisingly resilient over long periods of time even as cross-case variation in some alleged explanatory factors has diminished significantly in magnitude. Indeed, in the twenty-nine years elapsed between 1970 and 1999—when the two countries were incorporated into the Euro and lost their monetary autonomy—living standards as measured by private per capita consumption adjusting for purchasing power parity advanced in Portugal from 55.2% of the average for the EU15[2] to 74.4% of the average for the EU15, whereas in

Spain during the same period of time the advance in living standards was far smaller, extending from 77.0% of the average for the EU15 in 1970 to 79.2% in 1999 (Barreto et al., 2000: 372). Even with the near approximation of living standards in the two countries in 1999, unemployment remained more than twice as high in Spain in that year. Moreover, despite a long series of aggressively liberalizing labor market reforms in Spain, and ample possibilities for workers to be hired on temporary contracts lacking the supposed rigidities of permanent contracts, unemployment has remained stubbornly high in Spain. The contrast with unemployment rates in Portugal has been quite durable—suggesting the need for some type of socio-political explanation that looks beyond the narrow focus on relative labor costs or labor contract guarantees.

I argue that the cross-case disparity in unemployment is an example of a long list of outcomes that reflect the two countries' difference in the relative openness of institutional power holders to social pressure from below. I suggest that the contrast between the two cases in their predominant form of democratic practice has tended to influence a long series of policy-making decisions with effects that on average have been more favorable to workers and the potentially unemployed in Portugal than in Spain. The disparity between the cases began during the transition period itself, when—faced by very challenging economic circumstances in both countries—economic policy-makers quite openly placed greater emphasis on fighting inflation in the Spanish case (Perez, 1997; Royo, 2000; Ban, 2016) and greater weight on efforts to maintain employment in Portugal (Constancio, 2008). Both countries were faced with the employment-destroying effects of a worldwide recession, rising inflation, and an intensification of both phenomena as a function of the political regime transitions. The oil shock of 1973–1974 had contributed to both inflation and recession on a global scale, and the effects were at least to some degree aggravated in the Iberian Peninsula cases by uncertainties linked to regime change. However, in the following years the neighboring countries developed divergent policy responses that reflected the underlying contrast between them in political sensibilities. Faced with strong social pressures from below and perceiving the need to respond in some economically viable way to those pressures, Portuguese policy makers had strong reason to cultivate their professional contacts with the best American neo-Keynesians. It was Portugal that suffered the higher inflation rate, especially in 1974, but the country's policy makers prioritized employment over inflation control. Perhaps the most important Portuguese economist of the period, the mainstream neo-Keynesian José da Silva Lopes, who served as both a government Minister and Governor of the Bank of Portugal, underscored in an important interview with journalist Sónia Lourenço both the significance of the social pressure from below during this period and the operational importance of his repeated efforts to seek and obtain expert advice from American neo-Keynesians, especially at MIT (Silva et al., 2006: 41–62).

The recurring interchanges between Portuguese economists such as Silva Lopes and another prominent neo-Keynesian, Vitor Constancio, and American Keynesians such as Robert Solow, Paul Krugman, and others have strongly influenced the policy recommendations and professional self-confidence of many Portuguese policy makers. In contrast, the economists working in the research department of the Bank of Spain were oriented toward more orthodox neo-classical and monetarist paradigms,[3] an approach that influenced policymaking in both Spanish major parties (Perez, 1997; Ban 2016). The strong orientation of Spanish economic policy makers toward German ordo-liberalism had strong roots in Spanish history (Ban, 2016). Thus even though inflation was higher in Portugal than in Spain during the transition period, Portuguese policy makers elected to prioritize the fight against rising unemployment, whereas Spanish policy makers tended to emphasize the effort to contain inflation—even if doing so accentuated the employment destruction of the economic crisis. The economic impact of this point of contrast became apparent with the new economic crisis induced by the 1979 oil shock. In both countries policy makers believed they were serving their countries' long-term interests, but they did so in very different ways and by 1980 Spanish unemployment was significantly higher than that of Portugal, initiating the Iberian employment puzzle.

Whereas most prominent policy-oriented economists in Spain assumed that an increasing reliance on market mechanisms—such as those put in place by a deregulated labor market—would ultimately resolve the country's economic challenges,[4] many Portuguese policy makers were convinced of the benefits of actively searching out forms of state intervention and stimulus capable of promoting employment and growth. In both national cases, the perspectives of the policymaking community were congruent not only with their scientific epistemic community but also with the inclination of political leaders to search for ways to address—or, alternatively, largely ignore—social demands expressed "from below." One large structural contrast requires emphasis—especially for the early years of the employment paradox: Portuguese policy makers had at their disposal a large resource-base that policy makers in most Western economies, including that of Spain, lacked. The nationalizations of the revolutionary period had produced a large state-owned sector of the economy and a Constitutional commitment to the construction of a socialist economy. Reprivatization was explicitly prohibited until the Constitution was amended in 1989 to make that possible. The state-owned sector included the entire Portuguese finance system and much industry as well. As Nancy Bermeo has emphasized, the Portuguese state was able to use its control of nationalized firms to maintain employment levels in much of the economy during the late 1970s and early 1980s (2001: 333–334). The fully state-owned finance sector was also energetically used to expand credit to firms in crisis in order to stimulate the economy and limit the increase in unemployment.

The aggressive use of credit-expansion to keep firms in business and minimize any possible employee dismissals during the economic crisis was, in fact, a major element of intervention by the Portuguese state during the revolution and in its aftermath (Mateus, 1998: 110). The heavy initial reliance on this approach was obviously in large measure made possible by the state's full control over the finance sector—a structural position that the state maintained until the revolutionary-era nationalizations were returned to private hands after the Constitution was amended to permit that in 1989. The revolution structurally enabled the state to intervene in market dynamics in ways that were largely unavailable to Spanish policy makers. As a general matter, the pursuit of economic expansion, or at a minimum stability, through credit expansion was better suited to exceptional circumstances—that actors could expect to soon overcome—than to ordinary times, but for certain more carefully targeted purposes, such as addressing the needs and growth aspirations of small and medium enterprises (SMEs), the use of credit to promote development was of continuing interest to some well-placed policy makers in Portugal. Their focus was reflective of a view common among development scholars, many of whom have argued that national financial systems exert a significant influence on the growth and employment rates of countries in part as a function of their greater or lesser tendency to address the credit aspirations of SMEs (Stallings, 2006). Indeed, when one of Portugal's leading economic policy makers, Silva Lopes, was named to a leadership position at the European Bank for Reconstruction and Development in 1991, he advocated the use of bank loans with state guarantees to SMEs in countries then in transition in eastern Europe, a recommendation that ran counter to the more conventional instincts of others in leadership positions in the London-based bank (Silva et al., 2006: 59–60). His instincts, and those of other Portuguese policy makers, ran counter to the free-market thinking of neo-liberal economists, who assumed that relatively unregulated market competition—rather than state intervention in markets—would generate optimal economic outcomes such as robust rates of growth and employment.

Portugal's policy makers, predisposed by social pressures from below to search for ways to actively promote employment, were institutionally enabled by features of the country's banking system. For nearly fifteen years the entire finance system was state-owned, but even after the 1989–1990 privatizations, the country's largest bank, the Caixa Geral de Depositos (CGD) remained in public hands, facilitating its use (or that of its subsidiary, the Banco Ultramarino) to meet the credit needs of SMEs. Emilio Rui Vilar, President of the CGD group from 1989–1995—just when the privatization of the rest of the finance sector increased the importance of the CGD for innovative pro-employment policy making—pointed to the significance of one of the large bank's principal subsidiaries: "We tried to specialize the Banco Ultramarino in credits to medium and small businesses."[5] Rui Vilar understood that in order to be effective in this strategy, the CGD and its more specialized subsidiary would have to develop special competences: "Banks need to know better the way small companies are managed, their real situation. [We were] eager to find useful ways of ascertaining the credit worthiness of small firms. We trained young people to be more able to gain accurate information from the companies."[6] At roughly the same time as this Portuguese effort to use a large publicly owned bank to address credit needs of SMEs, Spain's Socialist government chose to reprivatize two banks that had been nationalized as a temporary emergency measure. In Spain, policy makers tended to trust the country's large banks to handle credit needs as a direct function of market logics; the Socialists maintained close relations with the large (private) banks (Perez, 1997).

The contrasts between Portuguese and Spanish policy makers in their handling of the banking system obviously raise the question of whether this cross-national point of difference is in any way reflected in the experience of SMEs. Fortunately Eurostat data on precisely this point is available for the mid-1990s. In 1996–1997 the "internal funds ratio" for small manufacturing firms was 21.2% in Portugal and 67.2% in Spain, and the European Union (EU) median was 40.9% (Eurostat, 2001: 161). This means that Spain's small manufacturing firms were forced to rely on internally generated funds for 67.2% of their needs whereas the equivalent firms in Portugal only needed to cover 21.2% of their financing needs internally—and could rely on external funding sources such as bank credits for the remaining 78.8%. Portugal and Spain were both outliers in the EU context, but they were located at opposite ends of the Europe-wide distribution. The predisposition of Portuguese policy makers and finance institutions to address the specific financing needs of small firms, instead of relying on unregulated markets and private banks to handle such matters "automatically," was strongly reflected in this data. It is not surprising that Spanish SMEs have frequently complained that banks tend to be insensitive to their legitimate credit needs—with real consequences for their economic activity.[7]

Given the major contribution of SMEs to employment creation, the large contrast between the Iberian Peninsula cases in policy-maker and finance sector orientations toward the credit needs of such firms appears likely related to Portugal's superior record in the field of employment. Portuguese policy makers in both major parties took other measures, as well, to aid SMEs—viewing the matter as an employment-friendly active labor market policy. The use of EU structural funds played a major role in their strategy. As Paulo Pedroso, a former Labor Minister of the Portuguese Socialist Party (PS), put the matter, "We put structural funds into national labor market policy. They [the Spaniards] did not."[8] Pedroso explained that governments of both the PS and the Partido Social Democrata (PSD) had used structural funds to provide either direct grants or loans to small firms. This policy operated primarily through the Ministry of the Economy and of Innovation and was seen as a way to pursue the goal of employment creation.[9] Spanish policy makers' preference to use structural funds for ends such as public infrastructure had its virtues—as emphasized in Boix's (1998) discussion of gross domestic capital formation in the form of public infrastructure— but in the two approaches' impact on employment, the Portuguese "model" appears to have been far more effective.

Direct state intervention in economic dynamics—whether through credit policies, the management of state-owned enterprises, or other means— became at least somewhat more difficult for the Portuguese after the 1989–1990 reprivatizations, but the large-scale shift that I conceptualize in chapter 2 as the "coda" of the Portuguese transition proved to be the take-off point for a new phase of Portuguese social policy, one that focused on the construction of an active and redistributive welfare state. In this objective, as well as in the management of the state's direct role in the economy, the country's policy makers attempted to pursue employment-friendly policies. Before turning to a discussion of Portugal's welfare state and how its redistributive goals have been influenced by the country's inclusionary democratic practice, we will first examine the partially related question of how gender dynamics contributed to Portugal's superior record of employment creation.

The work of Gosta Esping-Andersen on employment in post-industrial economies (Esping-Andersen, 1999) provides the theoretical basis for understanding how Portugal's rapid incorporation of women into the labor force after April 25 helped produce the country's superior performance in employment creation. Esping-Andersen argues that in post-industrial economies a high employment equilibrium requires the externalization of a great deal of traditionally unpaid work from the family to the broader economy. With high levels of employment by women, households have more funds but less time than available in the traditional male breadwinner model of employment. Numerous tasks such as child and family care, meal preparation, and many others can be handled externally as part of the service economy or within the family—depending on the operative "model." For this reason, an increase in the employment of women generates a large multiplier effect, adding more new jobs than those that are "taken" by the new entrants into the labor force. Esping-Andersen offers ample empirical support to show that cross-national differences in aggregate employment and in the presence of women in the labor force are fully congruent with the theory. Two forms of high employment equilibrium are possible in his analysis: a welfare-state-based model with significant public sector employment of welfare-state-linked care givers, or a market model in which the relevant service sector employment is all provided by the private market.

Crucially, Portugal's social revolutionary road to democracy quickly generated a major increase in the participation of women in the labor force. Spain's regime-led transition to democracy produced no such effect. OECD data published in 2000 shows that the average level of female participation in the labor force from 1970 to 1973, just prior to the transitions, was 24.8% of the total labor force in Spain, 26.0% of the total in Portugal, and an average of 33.3% in the countries that would ultimately form the EU15 (OECD, 2000: 37). During the next time segment covered by the OECD data, 1974–1979, Portugal's level of female presence in the labor force had increased greatly to 38.6%, whereas Spain's level had increased only slightly to 27.9% and the average level for the EU15 had grown to 35.7%. With the revolutionary passage from authoritarianism to democracy, Portugal had quickly moved from being a relative laggard on this important indicator to a new position located above the average level for the EU15. Portugal was alone in southern Europe in surpassing the average European level at that early date. On this key measure, linked by Esping-Andersen to national success in employment creation, Portugal—unlike neighboring Spain—had become a European leader.

Some scholars have tended to assume that this shift was generated above all by a substitution effect driven by the engagement of Portuguese males in the colonial wars in Africa,[10] but the available data—as reported here—seem more consistent with the claim that the revolution itself was the prime driver of the sharp and rapid increase in labor force participation by women. The work of Virginia Ferreira (1998) helps explain why the revolution would generate this effect. Social demands by women that emerged in the context of revolution led to new legal guarantees for women workers. The social gains of the revolution—reflecting the ability of previously subordinate actors to gain a hearing from power holders—led to measures that tended to facilitate the compatibility of work and family, much as Scandinavian social democracy sought to do through a variety of welfare state measures (Esping-Andersen, 1999). Moreover, the revolution quickly created a surge in domestic demand due to large wage increases instituted in 1974 and a freeze in prices, all of which must have created much new economic demand for precisely the sort of externalized services emphasized by Esping-Andersen's argument. Thus the rapid increase of women in the labor force with democratic transition in Portugal, but not in Spain, provides another explanation of how the cross-national difference in historical pathways to democracy contributed to the employment paradox (Fishman, 2010). By 2017, after a wait of more than forty years, the two countries had finally converged on this indicator,[11] following a long process of improvement in the rate of female labor market participation in Spain. However, the strong economic argument of Dutt and Ros (2007) on the enduring structural damage inflicted by a long period of unresolved high unemployment suggests that Spain's early inability to match Portugal's success on this indicator may have contributed significantly to the initial Portuguese advantage in employment creation and—as a result—to lasting effects of a now structural nature.

From the standpoint of our concern here with societal consequences of the cross-national difference in democratic practice, one major conclusion is merited. Worker and union concerns over job creation—and employment protection—were treated as a major priority by Portuguese policy makers; in contrast, from an early date Spanish policy makers instead placed greater priority on fighting inflation. As noted above, this difference in turn led Portuguese economic policy-makers to cultivate ongoing connections with technically distinguished and relatively pro-labor American neo-Keynesians, while Spanish policy makers looked instead to more orthodox and neoliberal paradigms for guidance. Luís Angel Rojo, a distinguished Spanish economic policy-maker who served as Governor of the Bank of Spain for eight years, expressed the dominant thinking in Spanish policy circles quite succinctly when in 2010 he boasted that his country's economic trajectory showed the benefits of sustained reliance on increasing deregulation, market liberalization, and European integration (Rojo, 2010). At that time, whereas some countries were recovering from the Great Recession, Spain was initiating a deep descent into a massively job-destroying extension of the

Great Recession. Even under governments of the Socialist Party (PSOE), neo-liberal economic thinking played a large role in decision-making, leading to growing tensions between the PSOE and the country's unions (Royo, 2000; Astudillo, 2001; Burgess, 2004; Hamann, 2012). Indeed, in Spain a recurring policymaking reliance on wave after wave of labor market liberalization emerged as a matter of relative bipartisan consensus. An anomaly of Spanish economic policymaking is the recurring recourse to labor market deregulation despite the failure of this approach to resolve the country's poor record of employment creation and the related failure of the economy to produce adequate gains in productivity (Fishman, 2012b).

In contrast, in Portugal, as the important work of Miguel Glatzer (2000) has shown, for the period of a decade and a half that he studied, liberalizing proposals for labor market deregulation tended to be ultimately abandoned by political elites in response to pressure from the unions. Glatzer's findings—on the tendency of Portuguese policy makers to abandon efforts at market-oriented deregulation of labor markets while Spanish policy-makers pressed ahead with such initiatives—are strongly congruent with the argument of this book on democratic practice. After all, unions strongly opposed such efforts at neo-liberal deregulation in both countries but their opposition was far more successful in Portugal than in Spain. More recently, Jorge Sola (2013) has done important research on explanations for Spain's repeated liberalizing labor market reforms. Sola notes that from the standpoint of the theoretical expectations of the power resources approach, one would not have expected such reforms under PSOE governments, but they occurred nonetheless. This would have a certain logic if the Spanish approach, promoting pro-market remedies for the country's employment deficit, had proved to be successful, but given the country's stubborn status as an unsuccessful outlier in the area of unemployment, the repeated tendency of policy makers to ignore pressures from below and press ahead with deregulation appears anomalous (Fishman, 2012b). As a general matter, there can be no guarantee that pressures from below will always lead to successful policy decisions, but in the Iberian Peninsula cases and in the specific field of employment policy, the Portuguese record of often heeding social pressures from below (while seeking out technically distinguished advice about how to do so) has yielded far greater success than the Spanish tendency to disregard such pressures. In the field of employment outcomes, Portugal's historically rooted tendency toward political inclusion has yielded a far better record than the much less inclusionary tendencies of Spain's democracy.

An interesting perspective on related matters is offered by the political economy analysis of Sebastian Etchemendy (2011). In his comparative study of the politics of economic liberalization in several Latin American cases as well as Spain and Portugal, Etchemendy argues that national approaches to liberalization followed quite different patterns in the two Iberian Peninsula cases. Spain—in his analysis—has been characterized by state- and government-directed adjustments whereas Portugal has been characterized by a more neo-corporatist reliance on concertation that has incorporated unions into the policymaking arena. From my perspective, Etchemendy's fundamental point of contrast between the cases is best explained by the overarching Portuguese tendency toward "conversation" in the political sphere juxtaposed against the lesser Spanish inclination to adopt that practice. Clearly, some concertation also took place in Spain in certain critical contexts (Fishman, 1990b; Royo, 2002; Hamann, 2012) but the greater systemic reliance on conversations between unions and the government that Etchemendy documents for Portugal fits the broader pattern identified in this book. A point of differentiation that manifests itself in the political economic arena is thoroughly congruent with the Iberian divide in political inclusion, a fundamentally cultural phenomenon.

III. Democracy in Iberia and Welfare State Development

One underlying and somewhat persistent difference between the Iberian cases is of relevance to the construction of the welfare state: Spain has enjoyed a somewhat higher level of economic development than Portugal throughout the time covered by our analysis—and well prior to that as well (Prados de la Escosura, 2017; , Freire Costa, Lains, and Miranda, 2016). The difference is not a large one when juxtaposed against the global range of distribution in GDP per capita and it decreased in magnitude for much of the period of democratic political life after the transitions—especially until the two countries lost their monetary policymaking autonomy with incorporation into the Euro in 1999. Nonetheless, holding everything else constant, this variable ought to produce a somewhat more robust welfare state in Spain given the well-demonstrated average tendency of economic development to promote welfare state growth.[12]

There are strong theoretical and comparative reasons to expect democracy to have encouraged welfare state development in both Iberian Peninsula cases, and the data clearly show such an effect, although the historical pattern of growth has been a complex one. The comparative literature on this theme provides some reasons to expect such a pattern. The important book by Huber and Stephens on democracy, power constellations, and inequality in Latin America and the Iberian Peninsula finds that the significant effect of democracy on economic distribution is clearly discernible only after a lag of approximately twenty years (Huber and Stephens, 2012). In my analysis, some effects emerged quite quickly after democratic transition but others have taken time to be fully manifested for reasons to be discussed later. The initial impact of democratization itself was stronger in Portugal than in Spain, according to the comparative analysis of Esping-Andersen (1994), but, after the first rapid increase in social spending in revolutionary Portugal, that pattern quickly reversed. During the 1980s social spending grew more quickly in Spain and the country surpassed Portugal in the dimensions and effects of its welfare state (Maravall, 1993; Guillen et al., 2003).

It is not difficult to see why welfare state growth was more robust in Spain during the 1980s. During this period of time a great deal of Portuguese social policy was focused on state intervention in the economy through the large nationalized sector—explicitly linked to the ideological goal of building socialism (de Sousa Santos, 1990). This ambitious project presented policy makers with numerous challenges. Welfare state development, a matter that was largely separate from the effort to make the economy work successfully with a large and recently nationalized state sector, did not attract the full attention that it would later receive. With the bipartisan PS–PSD consensus of the late 1980s in favor of both reprivatizing the large nationalized sector and turning toward the construction of an enlarged welfare state, the social commitments of the revolution were transposed from the arena of enterprise ownership and direct intervention in the economy to the more conventional sphere of welfare state development (Fishman, 2010) This major shift in the focus of the political system's social commitments soon produced predictable effects.

During the 1990s Portuguese social expenditures through the welfare state increased rapidly under governments of both the center-left PS and the center-right PSD. In Spain welfare state social expenditures continued to grow in the early 1990s but then stagnated under governments of both the center-left PSOE and the right-wing Partido Popular (PP). During the decade of the 1990s social expenditures grew substantially more in Portugal than in Spain. Taking the 1990 level of expenditures in each country as a base and controlling for changes in price levels, by 1998 social expenditures had increased by 89% in Portugal and 22% in Spain. With the new (and essentially "post-socialist") political emphasis on pursuing social objectives through the development of the welfare state, the smaller Iberian country was on its way to the creation of a more robust and more redistributive welfare state than that of Spain. This cross-national difference is manifested in a number of relevant indicators.

A useful first step in comparing the political commitment to social expenditures in the two cases is to examine the percentage of GDP collected in total tax receipts. This indicator is relevant for several closely interrelated reasons: As should be obvious, the capacity of states to deliver redistributive social spending in a sustained way is delimited by their tax collections. The political capacity of governments to collect monies from individuals and organizations that have available resources sets the limits of their capacity to provide resources to those who lack them. Thus the political will of governments to collect taxes can be seen in part as reflective of their social attentiveness to low-income and socially marginal sectors. Huber and Stephens (2012: 66–68) offer clear empirical evidence and strong reasoning for the proposition that even non-redistributive taxation offers the potential for significantly redistributive effects through the impact of social spending. Thus there are good reasons to treat this indicator as one of real importance. We rely on Eurostat data on total general government tax receipts—the broadest available measure—in order to include taxes collected by regional and local entities. As the data reported in Figure 4.2 show, for the twenty years elapsed between 1995 and 2015, tax receipts represent on average a

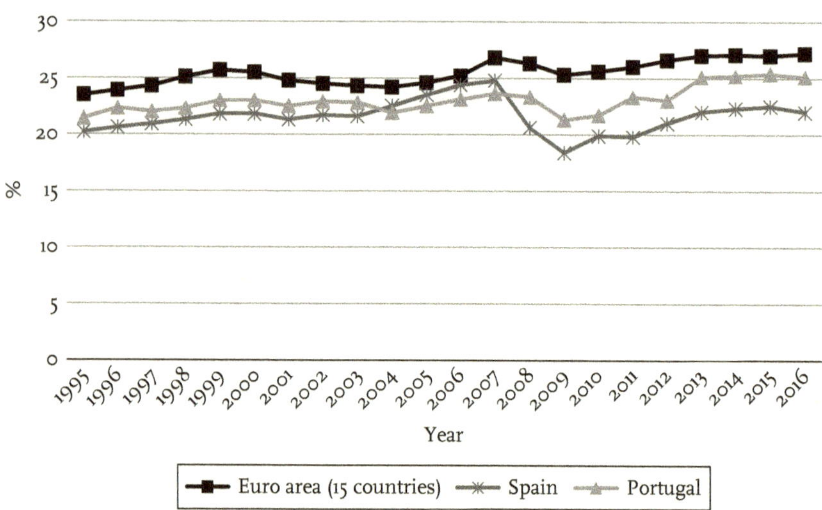

FIGURE 4.2 Total tax receipts—general government—EU15, Spain, Portugal—1995–2016 (% of GDP)

SOURCE: EUROSTAT—Data base—Tax revenue statistic—gov_10a_taxag. Date extracted: 05.05.2018: http://ec.europa.eu/eurostat/web/government-finance-statistics/data/database.

higher percentage of GDP in Portugal than in Spain. The pattern has been reasonably consistent during the twenty-one years covered by these data. As a percentage of GDP, Spanish taxation exceeded that of Portugal for only four out of those twenty-one years; the four years of Spanish outperformance coincide with the country's unsustainable construction bubble and—as a result—an above-trend increase in economic growth accompanied by a temporary decline in Spain's chronically high unemployment. Tax receipts in Spain were temporarily higher than normal during the height of the bubble, but that state of affairs proved unsustainable.

Once the crisis brought Spain's bubble economy to an end in 2008 (Royo, 2013) Portugal's advantage in tax collection reasserted itself. In most years from 2008 onward the smaller country collected somewhere between 2% and 3% more of GDP in taxes than Spain. This aggregate difference is manifested in the level of specific taxes. As of this writing the value added tax is higher in Portugal than in Spain and the income tax rate on the highest incomes is also more elevated in Portugal. We return to this theme in the next chapter in the context of our analysis of the politics of economic crisis in the two countries, but for now the crucial point is that the Portuguese advantage in tax collection existed both before and after the height of Spain's bubble economy. The cross-national difference on this indicator is not a huge one, but it does provide the Portuguese welfare state with a somewhat stronger foundation than its Spanish counterpart. It is also important to note that Portugal's advantage over Spain in taxation does not appear to be contingent on the party in power in either country; the predominant pattern of cross-national difference is found under governments of both the left and the right in both countries.

The available data on government expenditures on social protection measures—the core of the welfare state—are even more relevant for our purposes. However, the analysis of this indicator presents researchers with several complex decisions to be made. Social expenditure totals can be calculated either with or without unemployment compensation, and with or without other components such as public expenditures on education. Unemployment compensation is clearly a crucially important form of social protection, and for that reason seems to merit inclusion in aggregate measures of how much social protection any one given national welfare state provides. However, the amount spent on unemployment compensation in a given year is as much a function of economic circumstances as of underlying policy preferences. Moreover, states that succeed in policy efforts to diminish unemployment obviously reduce their unemployment compensation expenditures. That reduction in expenditures is reflective of policymaking success in lowering unemployment and does not signify a lack of political commitment to address the needs of workers. Thus there is also a strong rationale for excluding unemployment compensation from aggregate measures of social spending. We will examine the data both ways. There are other similarly complex choices involved in configuring the basis for cross-national comparisons in social spending. Eurostat data presents education funding as a separate matter—not included in aggregate measures of social spending. However, Huber and Stephens (2012) make a strong case for the claim that education spending is a centrally important policy tool of governments that seek to remedy social inequality. We will examine data on education spending immediately after our consideration of Eurostat indicators on social protection.

As the data reported in Figure 4.3 show, when we include unemployment compensation in aggregate measures of social protection, for the years examined the Spanish welfare state was initially somewhat more generous, but Portuguese expenditures converged with those of Spain in the late 1990s, and by 2001 the two welfare states were essentially equal in the percentage of GDP devoted to social protection. By 2003, under then right-wing governments in both countries, the Portuguese welfare state emerged

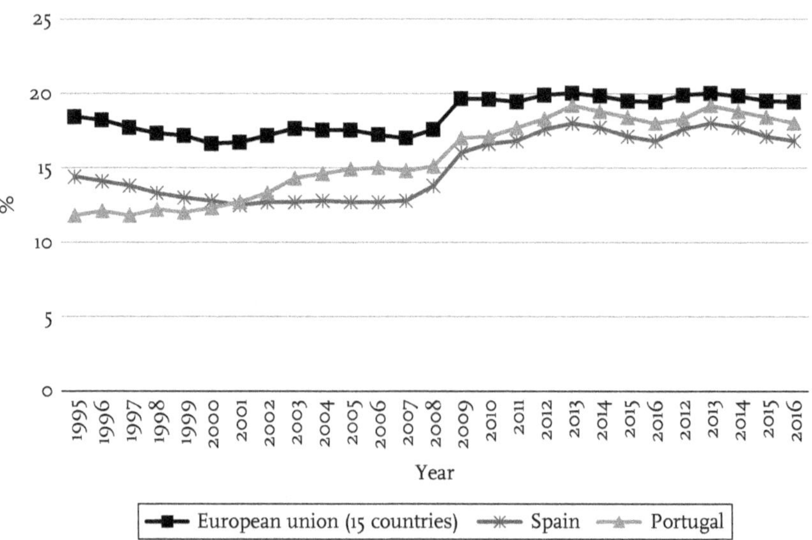

FIGURE 4.3 General government expenditures on social protection (with unemployment)—EU15, Spain, Portugal—1995–2016 (% of GDP)

SOURCE: EUROSTAT—Data base—Government expenditures by function—gov_10a_exp. Date extracted: 05.05.2018: http://ec.europa.eu/eurostat/web/government-finance-statistics/data/database. NOTE: The information on the EU15 for the years 2006 until 2016 is not indicated separately in the statistics. The calculated average of the fifteen member states is used.

as somewhat more generous in its provision of social protection. Subsequent to that date Portugal either sustained its advantage in social spending or at worst maintained parity with the Spanish welfare state; for several years during the economic crisis, Spain's higher level of unemployment generated a larger Spanish expenditure on unemployment compensation—raising Spain to parity with Portugal in total spending on social protections. However, as the data presented in Figure 4.4 show, when we exclude unemployment compensation from our measure of social protection, Portugal's advantage in other forms of social spending emerges quite clearly. On this indicator, excluding unemployment payments, Portugal's welfare state had asserted its greater strength by 2001 and maintained the advantage in spending as a percentage of GDP from then onward. This advantage—manifested under widely divergent economic and political circumstances, including times of growth and of economic contraction—typically represented just over 2% of annual GDP.

Thus for the past fifteen years Portugal's state expenditures on social protection outside the area of unemployment compensation have represented a consistently higher percentage of GDP than Spain's expenditures on such forms of social protection. If, as some scholars are inclined to do, we conceptualize state education spending as a social expense linked to the general

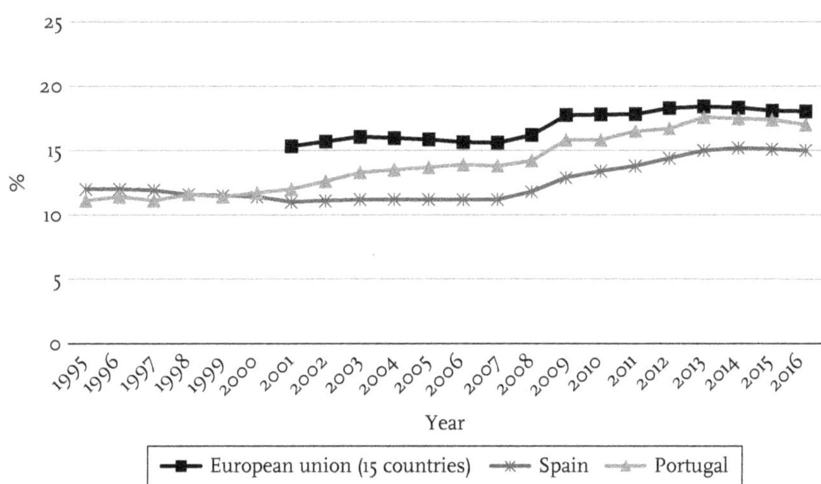

FIGURE 4.4 General government expenditures on social protection (without unemployment)—EU15, Spain, Portugal—1995–2016 (% of GDP)

SOURCE: EUROSTAT—Data base—Government expenditures by function—gov_10a_exp. Date extracted: 05.05.2018: http://ec.europa.eu/eurostat/web/government-finance-statistics/data/database. NOTE: The graph reflects the results of the share of government expenditures on social protection with unemployment minus the share of Government expenditures on unemployment.

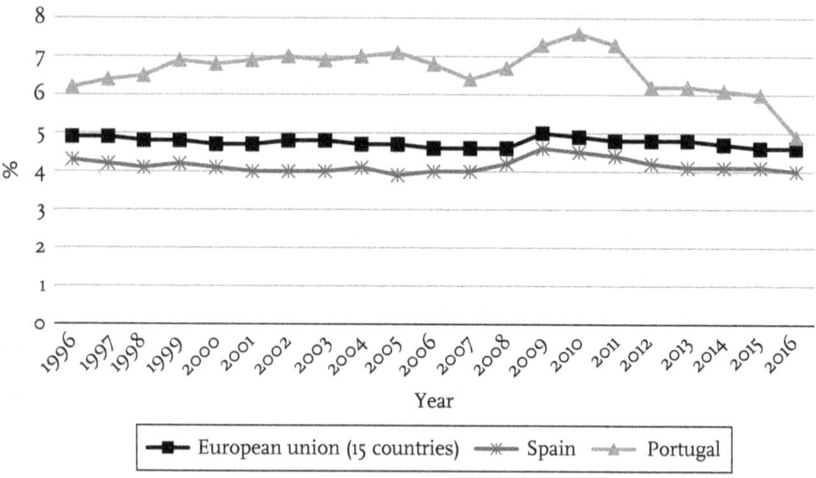

FIGURE 4.5 General government expenditures on education—EU15, Spain, Portugal—1995–2016 (% of GDP)

SOURCE: EUROSTAT—Data base—Government expenditures by function—gov_10a_exp. Date extracted: 05.05.2018: http://ec.europa.eu/eurostat/web/government-finance-statistics/data/database.

concerns of the welfare state, Portugal's advantage over Spain grows considerably in magnitude. As the data reported in Figure 4.5 show, Portugal has consistently devoted a significantly higher percentage of GDP to education spending than Spain. For most years the cross-national difference in education spending represents at least 2% of GDP. When we add Portugal's advantage in education spending to its higher level of social spending on matters other than unemployment compensation, it becomes clear that once Portuguese political leaders focused their attention on welfare state construction—after the 1989–1990 reprivatizations—they did in fact build a welfare state that is more robust than its Spanish counterpart.

The obvious question raised by these data on expenditures is whether the effects of public spending have really been advantageous for low income and socially marginal sectors of Portuguese society. There are various ways to address that centrally important question, but the most basic one is to examine Eurostat data on the percentage of the population at risk of poverty in both countries after government transfers, the theme addressed by the data reported in Figure 4.6. At the beginning of the period covered by these Eurostat data, poverty was more common in Portugal than in Spain—even after government transfers. We will later turn to a consideration of why that was the case when we discuss the long-lasting consequences of Portugal's historically delayed introduction of universal access to education in the 1950s

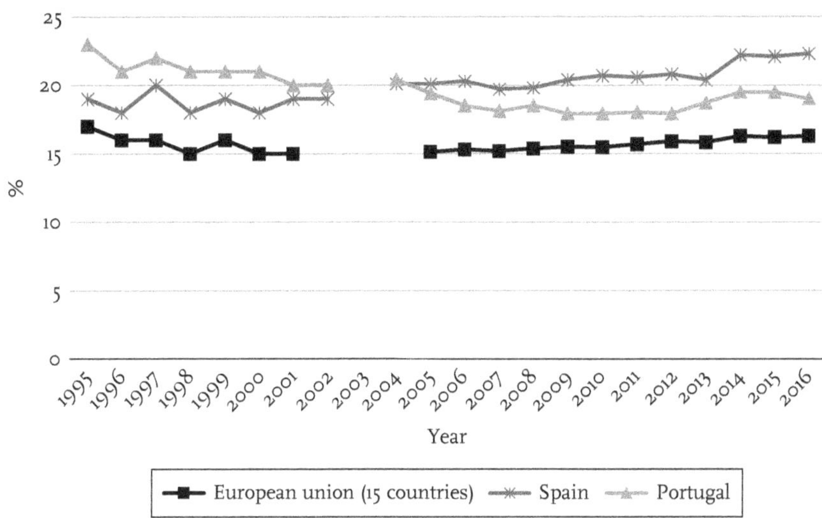

FIGURE 4.6 At risk of poverty—after social transfers—EU15, Spain, Portugal—1995–2016 (% of population)

SOURCE: EUROSTAT—Data base—Income distribution statistics—ilc_li02. Date extracted: 05.05.2018: http://ec.europa.eu/eurostat/web/income-and-living-conditions/data/database. NOTE: The information on the EU15 for the years 2006 until 2016 is not indicated separately in the statistics. The calculated average of the fifteen member states is used.

(Candeias et al., 2007). But during the second half of the 1990s Portugal initiated new efforts to address the problem of severely low incomes, reducing its after-transfers poverty rate through social expenditures. By 2005 Portugal had managed to reduce its poverty rate after transfers to a level lower than found in Spain. This success in poverty reduction has been sustained in comparative terms—when the country is compared to other cases such as that of Spain—although Portugal did experience an increase in its after-transfers poverty rate in 2013 and 2014 under the combined influence of economic crisis and externally imposed austerity.

Portugal's success in reducing poverty from the mid-1990s onward was initially put in motion by an income support program launched by the Socialist government elected in October 1995 and then modified by later governments. A robust program of poverty relief was fully embraced by the Socialists and parties to their left. Moreover, for the most part, parties to the right of the Portuguese center accepted the goal of poverty relief through income support payments. Portuguese parties disagreed over various specific elements of this policy approach—for example with regard to work requirements and the total budgetary outlay dedicated to such matters—but in the broadest possible terms parties agreed that the state should devote resources to income support for the poor. In Portugal's post-revolutionary democracy, the goal of poverty relief through public expenditures received broader political support than in neighboring Spain, and the data in Figure 4.6 show the effects of this point of contrast.

Thus for more than a full decade, and under economically rather diverse circumstances, the Portuguese welfare state has shown a greater ability than its Spanish counterpart to reduce poverty. The cross-national difference in actual effects is not a huge one, but it is large enough to be consistently discernible. One important point to which we will return later deserves mention: For almost the entire period of Portugal's clear advantage in poverty reduction the two countries were governed by parties similarly located on the left-right dimension of variation. The PSOE governed in Spain from 2004 through late 2011, when it was replaced by a government of the right-wing PP; the PP remained in government beyond the end of 2016, when our data terminate. In Portugal the PS won power in an election held in late February 2005 and then lost power to a right-wing coalition of the PSD and the Partido do Centro Democrático Social (CDS) in mid-2011, the same year when the Spanish Socialists lost power. The Portuguese PS then recovered governmental power in Lisbon in November 2015, following elections held in early October of that year, but this change occurred just one year before the termination of the data examined here. The two countries were ruled by the same side of the partisan political divide for just over ten years out of the twelve-year period in which Portugal manifested a superior record in the reduction of poverty. The neighboring countries were ruled by opposite sides of the political spectrum for just under two of those twelve years. Despite the considerable explanatory power of the power constellations approach of Huber and Stephens (2012)—with its prominent focus on the ideological placement of parties in power—these findings clearly suggest that other factors, such as those emphasized here, also contribute to differences in outcome between Portugal and Spain. In the concluding chapter I discuss ways to combine this book's explanatory approach with more conventional frameworks.

Important as the findings on the reduction of poverty are, it is useful to look beyond efforts to reduce economic inequality or poverty as such. Many of the political demands made by low-income or socially marginal sectors in a democracy are not directly related to income but instead deal with other matters—such as housing, for example. I argue that at the periphery of welfare state politics, a variety of social concerns other than income levels also attracted greater interest from policy makers in Portugal than in Spain. As the material discussed in chapter 3 suggests, this is especially true in the area of housing policies and regulations. Evidence of the greater attentiveness of

Portuguese policy makers to the housing needs of low-income and socially marginal actors is not limited to the specific cases mentioned in the previous chapter. Much of the housing found in Lisbon and Oporto—the country's two historically largest cities—has been devoted to publicly owned low-rent units. Rent controls in privately owned housing have also been stricter than in Spain and when proposals to reduce rent controls have emerged, the country's national renters' association has been included in top-level policy negotiations.[13] In contrast in Spain, as the scholarship of José Adelantado and Ricard Gomà has documented, governments of both major political parties have produced policies more oriented toward promoting ownership and the construction of new units than offering low-rent options in response to social demands for it (Adelantado and Gomà, 2000). These scholars note that by the end of the 1990s Spain had the EU's lowest level of public spending on housing but its highest level of private home ownership (346). Portugal's more social approach to the housing question had an impact on the financial burden faced by households: In 2010, Eurostat data on the distribution of household expenses among numerous items reveal that Portuguese households spent 15.6% of their overall expenditures on housing. That figure was 8.0% below the average for the complete universe of EU member states and 4.6% lower than in Spain.[14]

Clearly, then, the greater social sensibilities of Portuguese policy makers are not limited to matters that directly shape the distribution of income. Indeed, the impact of the Iberian divide in democratic practice on societal outcomes is manifested in terrains relatively far removed from the distribution of material resources—as we will shortly see—but before we turn our attention to such matters it is appropriate that we first examine possible objections to the argument advanced thus far. Despite all the evidence presented, there are elements of empirical reality and scholarly arguments that could be seen to raise questions about the claims advanced here, and we now turn to a consideration of such possible objections.

IV. Counterpoints: Possible Objections to the Argument Advanced Here

Empirical reality is invariably at least somewhat more complex than the clear lines of argumentation provided by theories that seek to identify and conceptualize the main lines of causation primarily responsible for societal outcomes. That is the theoretical and methodological assumption of the Weberian approach to social science, to which I fully subscribe (Fishman,

2007). Needless to say, the matters taken up by this book are not an exception to this general proposition: It is possible to find Spanish triumphs and Portuguese shortfalls in matters of wide social concern. The goal of theories such as the one presented in this book should be to identify and explain probabilistic regularities. If exceptions to the probabilistically predicted patterns can be found, they do not necessarily invalidate a theory, but empirical "counterpoints" do need to be weighed alongside more supportive evidence in order to assess a theory. In this section I seek to identify the main possible objections that I believe readers should be able to consider in their evaluation of this book's argument.

The most important qualification to be introduced concerns the very real achievements of Spain's welfare state. As the important comparative analysis of Huber and Stephens (2012) clearly establishes, Spain's post-Franco success in containing income inequality and addressing many basic social needs has been quite substantial. Indeed, both Iberian Peninsula cases addressed social needs—and pursued redistributive objectives—more thoroughly and successfully than the Latin American cases to which Huber and Stephens compare Spain and Portugal. For at least some periods of time, Spain managed to reduce inequality as measured by the Gini coefficient more than Portugal and the Spanish public health system is often seen as a global point of reference. The success of the Spanish Socialists in achieving such goals clearly reflects at least some concern of that party for the sort of social objectives pursued by most social democratic or labor parties.

Moreover, as the excellent analysis of Chhibber and Torcal (1997) persuasively establishes, where the PSOE managed to govern at the Autonomous Community level, they enacted policies that addressed workers' social interests and as a result the party was strongly supported by class voting on the part of workers. In those regional contexts in which the Socialists failed to gain power, class voting was lower. However, if certain conventional concerns of Spanish workers were addressed by Socialist governments, other grievances were not treated with receptivity. The predominant Spanish model of democratic practice limited governmental attentiveness to public voices of discontent of all sorts, and that left poorly organized or socially marginal sectors at a special disadvantage. Thus the institutional dynamics highlighted by power resources and power constellations theory—with their emphasis on left party and union strength—did provide a strong basis for many socially oriented and redistributive policies not only in Portugal but also in Spain. Yet it remains the case that many concerns of low-income and socially marginal sectors were more fully admitted into the public agenda of Portugal than that of Spain. Organizational resources—particularly those of workers, the poor, immigrants, and other socially "subordinate" sectors—went further in Portugal than in Spain. Both cases have had their triumphs, but on balance, the incorporation of demands articulated by low-income or relatively powerless sectors has been considerably greater in Portugal, as the data and evidence presented in this chapter clearly suggest.

The very real achievements of the Spanish welfare state may be seen to offer a partial qualification to the main argument of this book, one that does not invalidate the argument but instead refines it in a way that clearly acknowledges the existence of meaningful social accomplishments in this case. There is however, at least one possible objection that might be seen to introduce significant questions about the central argument of this book. Data on inequality, and concretely on the Gini coefficient, is less consistently available for Portugal than for Spain, but data for the years immediately after the turn of the millennium in 2000 point to rising inequality in the Portuguese case and to a Gini coefficient higher than for Spain—indicating the existence of more inequality for those years in the smaller Iberian case. Indeed, in their important broadly cross-national examination of the social costs of inequality, Wilkinson and Pickett (2010) identify Portugal as a case of relatively high inequality. This raises the very reasonable question of how a country with a political system that is relatively attentive to the demands of low-income and socially marginal sectors could experience an increase of inequality at least during the years just after the turn of the millennium. The magnitude of the increase is still open to debate, given the paucity of available data and the tendency of more recent data to show a very different pattern, to be discussed in the next chapter. Nonetheless, the paradox is a real one and it merits our attention.

I offer two main explanations for the increase of inequality in the first years after the turn of the millennium. The first and most important one is related to the connection between educational and income inequality. In their comprehensive analysis of inequality in Latin America and the Iberian Peninsula cases, Huber and Stephens (2012) examine both of these forms of inequality. Their empirical concern with educational inequality follows from their emphasis on how educationally based inequalities in human capital strongly condition the level of income inequality within a society. They note the highly pronounced inequality of Portugal in the year 2000 in the distribution of human capital and educational attainment (Huber and Stephens, 2012: 128–132). What should be added to this important observation concerns a critical antecedent variable: The underlying problem was directly traceable to the very late date of the introduction of universal access to education in the 1950s under the authoritarian Estado Novo (Candeias et al., 2007). The pattern of inequality in educational attainment was essentially a legacy of the authoritarian period. Moreover, the expansion of broad-based post-primary education came even later than the 1950s (Vieira, 2007). Widespread access to education was a much later development in Portugal than in Spain, and in the year 2000 many older Portuguese citizens were still constrained by that old historical legacy—dating back to the authoritarian period. The post-revolutionary expansion in education strongly marked those born after 1974, but among those born under authoritarian rule access to education was very weakly and unevenly distributed. Thus the effort to pursue relative income inequality in Portugal involved sailing against rather strong "headwinds" generated by the historically late introduction of broad-based access to education. Paradoxically, the revolution's strong emphasis on educational improvement initially introduced the basis for a new type of inequality, especially along generational lines. The dynamic involved is that of the Kuznets curve: At certain levels of development, societal growth and improvement can increase inequality because improvements reach some sectors of the population before others, but that infelicitous relationship between development and inequality is later reversed as development progresses further. With generational replacement this old historical legacy will ultimately be fully overcome, and more recent assessments of Portugal's educational performance have been strongly positive.[15]

A second paradoxical explanation for Portugal's post 2000 difficulties with income inequality as measured by the Gini coefficient also deserves our attention. Esping-Andersen (2007) has shown that where both men and women participate in the labor force in high numbers, household income inequality can increase as a result of marital or couple "homogamy." That is to say that the joining of two relatively high incomes in one household and two relatively low incomes in another household generates more household income inequality than would exist with only one earner in each household. Given that Portugal long enjoyed a higher rate of female participation in the labor force than Spain, this factor may have contributed somewhat to Portuguese difficulties in lowering the country's Gini coefficient. With the recent increase in the presence of women in the Spanish labor force this sociological basis for cross-national difference has finally virtually disappeared. Thus there are historically delimited explanations for Portugal's temporary difficulties with the reduction of income inequality. If those difficulties were to reappear or persist in the future there would then be reason to search for explanations rooted in the country's policymaking and political-economy institutions. We will turn to the latest data on income inequality when, in the next chapter, we examine the politics of economic crisis.

We now turn to a recent scholarly argument on contrasts between Portugal and Spain that proposes an interpretation fundamentally different from the one presented in this book. In a book titled *The Left Divided: The Development and Transformation of Advanced Welfare States*, political scientist Sara Watson has argued that Portugal's political economy—and the development of its welfare state—should be seen as an example of "liberal welfare capitalism," whereas the Spanish case in her analysis is an example of "protective welfare capitalism." She argues that the basis for this contrast lies in the early structure of the party systems in the two cases and relatedly in the nature of competition within the labor movement; in her analysis the presence of a strong Communist Left in Portugal and its close linkage to the union movement provided the Socialists with incentives to move toward the center of the political spectrum, whereas the weaker status of the Communists in Spain channeled the system's competitive dynamics into a search by both the center-right and the moderate left for the electoral support of workers. *The Left Divided* places its central explanatory and theoretical emphasis on alleged consequences of the extent to which the political space to the left of the Socialists is occupied or remains vacant, and related competitive dynamics among unions in the labor relations system: "When the labor movement is divided, and a substantial part of it is closely linked to a far-left party, it is likely to push a country's political center-of-gravity to the right" (Watson, 2015: 37). Watson argues that as a consequence the Portuguese developed political economy and welfare institutions that subjected workers to a rather strong dose of market forces, whereas the Spaniards developed institutions and policies that tended to protect workers from the effects of market forces.

Watson's claims have been taken up in a lengthy scholarly review by Portuguese political scientist Rui Branco in the journal *Analise Social* (Branco, 2017) In evaluating the argument, Branco emphasizes the relevance of two indexes of labor protection: The OECD index on labor protection from dismissal shows Portugal to be on average much more protective of permanent workers than Spain for the period 1985–2000. Portugal's average score for that time period is 4.74, whereas Spain's average is 3.10 (Branco, 2017: 208). For workers with temporary contracts, Portugal is on average slightly less protective than Spain—3.23 versus 3.56—but this average difference, again for the period from 1985–2000—is much smaller than for permanent workers. On balance the Portuguese system of legal guarantees has been more protective than that of Spain, not less so. Moreover, as Branco notes, over time the Spanish system was increasingly inclined to adopt liberalizing market-oriented changes. Branco also examines another index, the Allard (2005) measure of job security. This is the index that Watson uses in *The Left*

Divided to assess the applicability of that book's theory to other cases outside the Iberian Peninsula. This index is somewhat more favorable to the argument of *The Left Divided* than the OECD index, but it still fails to confirm the claim that the Portuguese system has been less protective of workers than the Spanish system. Portugal's average score on the Allard index for 1975–1990 is 3.58, whereas Spain's average is 3.46 (Branco, 2017: 209) Thus on this second index Portugal was, on average, slightly more protective of workers than Spain; Portugal was less protective than Spain according to the Allard index for only a brief period immediately after the transitions. The relationship between the two cases then reversed direction (209). Thus on the available measures of employment protection, the argument that Portugal is more market oriented and Spain more protective of workers appears to lack empirical support.

To Branco's very useful review of relevant evidence I add one centrally important theoretical point. In the early years of Portugal's post-revolutionary democracy many of the social objectives that actors pursued were politically channeled through the management of the large state-owned sector of the economy that had been nationalized during the revolution. The idea of socialism was very much alive in the Portuguese Left during those years and was enshrined in the Constitution—along with a wide range of social guarantees that established it as the most socially oriented constitution in the democratic world (Magalhaes, 2013; Vieira and da Silva, 2010). Distributional objectives along with macro-economic performance targets could all be pursued in part through the political management of strategic state economic assets. Of course, managing the large state sector and pursuing positive macro-economic performance in a national economy of these characteristics presented policy makers and other political actors with significant challenges. This in turn helps to explain political efforts to restrain wage demands in order to improve the viability of an economy with a large socialized sector. At various places in the text Watson's analysis acknowledges such points, yet the argument fails to incorporate those observations into its overarching theorization of the case. From my perspective, it is untenable to characterize as "liberal," and in that sense heavily market-oriented, a political economy with a large recently nationalized state sector and in which the idea of socialism helped to structure the political management of the state's economic assets. The social objectives of the Portuguese Left in that initial post-revolutionary period were pursued through an approach that was more fundamentally opposed to market-oriented economic liberalism than welfare state social democracy is.

This is not to argue that all of Watson's claims are misplaced. *The Left Divided* does make valid points such as the fact that unemployment compensation was initially significantly more generous in Spain than in Portugal—before the cases moved toward convergence on that matter. However, as an overarching interpretation of differences between the two Iberian Peninsula cases, that book's central claims run up against a great deal of evidence that on balance state interventions in the economy in defense of social objectives have been stronger, more pervasive, and more historically persistent in Portugal than in Spain. No theory can be expected to account for absolutely all elements of empirical reality, but theories should be assessed on the breadth of explanatory coverage that they provide—the range of outcomes and of historical circumstances for which they prove useful. On that standard, the ability of this book's theory of democratic practice to account for a wide range of differential outcomes in Portugal and Spain—from the early post-transition years when Portugal had a large nationalized sector through the years of welfare state construction and economic crisis—seems to place this book's theory on very strong grounds. It bears repetition that one important example of the cross-national difference is the greater tendency of Portuguese economic policy makers to prioritize employment as an economic goal. In this and other ways Portuguese office holders have shown a much greater tendency than their Spanish counterparts to acknowledge and address social demands from workers and socially marginal sectors. Social spending is higher in Portugal; the difference is especially clear if we include education expenditures as a measure intended to generate social benefits. As a result Portugal has been more successful than Spain in reducing poverty and, as we will see in the next chapter, the broader trend in inequality in the two countries now follows this same pattern. Before we examine the performance of the two systems during the Great Recession and the Euro crisis in chapter 5 we turn to an examination of two non-economic outcomes of significance.

V. Activating Cultural Capacities and Civic Practice: The Broad Impact of Democratic Practice

I argue that the impact of the Iberian divide in democratic practice on important societal outcomes is not limited to matters involving the distribution of material resources or economic opportunities—such as holding a job—but also encompasses the formation of cultural and civic capacities among citizens. Democratic theory is concerned with the processes that generate the capacity for agency among citizens (O'Donnell, 2010)—their ability to critically evaluate political circumstances and act on that basis—and which can provide for effective equality among citizens on this practice-oriented dimension (Somers, 2008). If citizens are to genuinely influence crucial political dynamics—such as the processes of agenda setting, policymaking, and opinion formation—that unfold in the long intervals between election campaigns, they require well-developed civic and cultural capacities. Here we encounter the possibility of large-scale positive and negative feedback loops: If inclusionary democratic practice such as found in Portugal encourages the formation of citizen capacities, partly through the intermediating role of practice inside secondary institutions such as the school system, as a consequence the inclusionary tendencies of national democratic practice are likely reinforced and strengthened by those enlivened citizen capacities. Fortunately, both cultural and civic capacities can be systematically studied through the use of survey data and other sources. The theoretical importance of this theme is matched by the methodological feasibility of its study with existing data sources.

I turned to collaborative work with scholarly experts on these two themes to ascertain whether the processes theorized in this book had helped to shape the outlines of civic and cultural capacities in democratic Spain and Portugal. The joint research projects with Omar Lizardo on cultural tastes and with Manuel Villaverde Cabral on citizenship practice led to co-authored articles and to conclusions that hold important implications for the questions posed by this book. Both collaborations were based on strong complementarities. Lizardo, a leading theorist in the field of cultural sociology, had been carrying out research on the "omnivore" phenomenon characterized by the "consumption" of widely differentiated cultural products such as highly dissimilar musical genres. Cultural "omnivores" have broadly inclusionary tastes that lead them to make use of a wide array of cultural products instead of concentrating their "consumption" on a small set of highly preferred items or activities. In his research on that phenomenon, Lizardo had noted unexpected patterns in the data on Spain and Portugal, patterns that existing theories could not easily explain. Villaverde Cabral, one of Portugal's most accomplished social scientists, had led numerous surveys in that country as part of international research networks and had developed a long line of research studies on citizenship and civic practice (Cabral, 2003, 2006; Cabral, da Silva, and Saraiva, 2008) while also serving as the Director of the country's National Library. His empirical data showed areas of great strength in Portuguese civic practice that had not been theorized or explained in existing work. In both instances, our early conversations on the theoretical and empirical issues that my collaborators had been researching and on the historically oriented argument that I had been developing led to the quick realization that we had the basis for fruitful collaborative work.

Both projects (Fishman and Lizardo, 2013; Fishman and Villaverde Cabral, 2016) produced strong evidence about the long-term effects of forms of institutional practice rooted in pathways to democracy in the 1970s. The two studies are quite different in numerous ways—including the identity of the dependent variables being analyzed and the selection of cases for comparison. However, there is a common core in the findings of the two studies, and those shared conclusions merit discussion along with a few of the principal findings of these two collaborations. At the most basic level, the two research efforts coincide in showing greater signs of civic and cultural vitality in Portugal than one might expect to find there. At the time that the two data sets were collected[16] Portugal was the least economically developed country in western Europe. Nonetheless, among Portuguese youth, cultural "omnivores"—typically associated with high levels of development, education, and political tolerance—were approximately as common as in the most successful societies of Nordic Europe. Portugal also stood out in the research on citizenship practices, in this case thanks to its high levels of engagement in the electronic public sphere and also a surprisingly high predisposition, in some population segments, to discuss politics with others in the hope of influencing their preferences. The explanation for these points of strength—not shared by Spain—is what makes these two studies strongly relevant for this book's concerns.

The two studies share an important methodological point in common: In both instances we examined the impact of generational experiences on the dependent variables of interest. The participation of citizens in political life is often shaped at least in part by phenomena that vary by age cohort (van Deth, Montero, and Westholm, 2007), and the political dispositions of young people offer special interest for a number of reasons (García-Albacete, 2014). Our findings show how important it is to differentiate age cohorts through a coding strategy that allows researchers to capture the effects of major historical processes of change on outcomes of interest. When we did so we found that the effects of Portugal's revolutionary pathway to democracy are manifested especially strongly among young people born and educated under democracy in a school system that shows the continuing effects of the country's distinctive road to political freedom. Before we turn to the effects of Portugal's post-revolutionary educational practice on citizenship and cultural tastes, it is useful to take up one additional point of evidence on the difference between the two Iberian Peninsula school systems. In chapter 3 we considered contrasts between the neighboring countries in institutional practice within the school systems, but that dimension of differentiation raises an obvious question: Do the two school systems actually differ in what students are taught? A Europe-wide study of history students in the ninth grade that was carried out in the mid-1990s (Machado Pais, 1999) provides valuable systematic evidence on this point. In a question that asked whether class discussions covered "different explanations about what happened in the past," Portuguese students were the most likely to agree and Spanish ninth graders the least likely to agree in the multi-country study (43). The inclusionary approach of Portugal's post-revolutionary educational practice shaped not only the social relations of the school system but also the content of the educational experience.

The two collaborative studies make use of completely separate and independent data sets, in both instances sample surveys carried out in a number of countries after the turn of the millennium and before the onset of economic crisis in 2007–2008. Both investigations clearly show that Portuguese young people born and educated under democracy are in certain respects different from their Portuguese elders and from their same-age counterparts in other countries such as Spain. As the data reported in Table 4.1 show, when—in the study of musical tastes among Spanish and Portuguese respondents—we model predictors of the number of musical genres "consumed" by respondents, we find that the country of the respondents is a significant predictive variable only for those born after the democratization of both countries had been achieved in 1977. Portuguese young people were systematically different—and more "omnivorous" in their

TABLE 4.1 Robust Poisson regression coefficient estimates of the country effect on the number of genres chosen

	BEFORE 1947	1947 TO 1962	1963 TO 1976	AFTER 1977
Country—Portugal	.0537	.123	.145	.375*
	(.48)	(1.48)	(1.78)	(4.58)
Model Log Likelihood	−848.7	−700.4	−1016.0	−737.1
Model BIC	1723.3	1425.0	2057.3	1498.0
N	634	424	552	390

Note: Models hold constant responders' education, gender, marital status, urban residence, and frequency of music listening. t-statistics are in parentheses.

*$p < .05$ (two-tailed tests)

Source: Robert M. Fishman and Omar Lizardo (2013), "How Macro-Historical Change Shapes Cultural Taste: Legacies of Democratization in Spain and Portugal," *American Sociological Review* 78(2): 213–239.

musical tastes—than Spaniards of the same generation. But Portuguese respondents of earlier age cohorts were found to be statistically indistinguishable from their Spanish counterparts. The pre-democratization baseline of cultural tastes in the two countries showed no sign of systematic and significant cross-national differentiation among those who were socialized and educated before the transitions of the 1970s. Democratization through polar opposite processes put in place just such a difference for those born after 1977—producing higher levels of omnivorous acceptance of cultural diversity among Portuguese young people educated in the post-revolutionary school system.

The study of citizenship practice also found strong age effects that appear to operate through the Portuguese high school system. In the level of citizen involvement in political discussions intended to influence others, the Portuguese data show a considerable advantage of young high school graduates over the general population, an advantage that was not duplicated in any of the other twenty countries included in the study[17] (Fishman and Villaverde Cabral, 2016: 542–543). The graduates of Portuguese high schools in the post-transition period are substantially more likely than the general Portuguese population to engage in conversational efforts to politically influence fellow citizens. The prevalence and liveliness of informal political conversations among citizens is a clear marker of a lively democracy, and in the Portuguese case we found that young people educated in high schools under democracy contributed significantly to this outcome. On one other type of citizenship practice—namely participation in the electronic public sphere—we found a Portuguese advantage that was not limited to young people born under democracy. This generalized Portuguese advantage is thoroughly congruent with the inclusionary nature of both the political system and the handling of the news in the communications media. Thus survey evidence shows strong indications of Portugal's historically based activation of cultural and citizenship capacities.

My collaborators and I found strong evidence that social practice in secondary institutions strongly shaped by Portugal's revolutionary path to democracy can largely account for patterns observed in the survey data. The relatively non-hierarchical and inclusionary nature of Portugal's post-revolutionary democratic practice is reflected in institutional practice within both the school system and the news media, with significant effects for the formation of cultural and civic dispositions. The non-hierarchical forms of practice that we encountered in in-depth interviews contribute to the inclusionary character of Portugal's democracy through both direct and indirect means not matched in the Spanish case. The activation of cultural and civic capacities by the Portuguese high school system provides the country with more active citizens than it would otherwise have. And the inclusionary reporting of the news by journalists who work in relatively non-hierarchical media outlets contributes to producing a public sphere that includes multiple voices and perspectives. The cross-national Iberian contrast in forms of practice rooted in history continues to produce a wide range of societal consequences, some of them mediated by practice within crucial secondary institutions. We now turn to evidence on the politics of crisis in the neighboring countries.

 How the Cultural Frameworks
Underpinning Democratic Practice
Shaped the Politics of Crisis

Testing the Argument in the Age of Austerity

I. Introduction

The external imposition of harsh austerity measures on the democracies
of southern Europe just when much of the world was struggling to recover from the Great Recession was the type of exogenous shock that social scientists often look for when they try to account for shifts in long-term
patterns. When contagion from Greece's severe crisis strongly affected the
standing of Portugal and Spain in international bond markets in the spring
of 2010, leading to powerful external pressures on the two countries to adopt
austerity measures, one might have expected this major external disturbance
to the political economies of the Iberian Peninsula cases to erase existing
differences between the two countries. There is at least an element of truth
to such thinking: The imposition of austerity did present the democracies of
southern Europe with severe limitations on their autonomy to develop and
carry out policies of their choosing. Pressures from the weakly regulated
international bond market (Fishman, 2011b, 2014) and from supranational
institutions (Sánchez-Cuenca, 2014b) produced that effect. Democracies
were substantially constrained from pursuing policies that many in the
mass public and among elected representatives believed appropriate for the
circumstances—with supporting advice in many cases from quite distinguished economists. However, despite the presence of some shared effects
in Portugal, Spain, and other Euro-periphery countries, I argue in the analysis that follows that the handling of the crisis and its effects in these two

countries followed substantially different paths, confirming the usefulness of the theoretical approach introduced here even under these extreme circumstances.

This chapter provides clear evidence that the potentially regressive[1] effects of crisis were muted in Portugal by the inclusionary qualities of that political system, an effect not shared by the Spanish case. However, the available evidence also shows significantly negative effects of the imposition of austerity in both cases. The exogenous disturbance in the normal functioning of national-level democracy was quite real, even though the magnitude of the effect was limited in the Portuguese case by factors discussed in this chapter. Crucially, our analysis here also allows us to focus on the mechanisms that can account for the impact of the Iberian divide in democratic practice on distributional outcomes. As the discussion that follows shows, social pressure in the streets proved to be decisively important in the Portuguese case, closing off a regressively redistributive pathway of adjustment that the pro-austerity government in power in 2012 had tried to implement. Elected political leaders in the two cases reacted quite differently to pressures from actors external to the institutional political system. Whereas Spanish actors on both the left and right were highly sensitive to pressures from economically powerful actors but remained relatively closed to influence from social actors defending the interests of workers, low-income sectors, and small business owners, in Portugal the pattern was quite different. In the Portuguese case, social pressure in the streets proved to be relevant for the decision-making of governmental elites—even under a right-wing government committed to austerity. Formal institutional matters also exerted an effect, as we shall see, but in Portugal crisis-era distributional outcomes were decisively constrained by the country's predominant form of democratic practice.

Along with the rest of the world, the countries of southern Europe had been experiencing the effects of the Great Recession for roughly two years prior to the intensification of the crisis in the Eurozone's southern fringe just when much of the globe was finally recovering. The broadly comparative question of how this global economic downturn reshaped political realities has attracted a great deal of interest (Bermeo and Bartels, 2014); the experiences of Spain and Portugal during that initial period of globally shared economic crisis deserve attention before we focus on consequences of the more regionally delimited imposition of austerity in 2010. With Socialist parties in power in both Iberian Peninsula cases when the crisis first hit, it should be no surprise that the first inclination of both the Socrates government in Lisbon and the Zapatero government in Madrid was to launch counter-cyclical Keynesian stimulus plans. This initial effort at counter-cyclical stimulus was more successful than is often appreciated (Fernandez-Albertos, 2012; Sánchez-Cuenca, 2012); it was exogenous pressures rather than endogenous failures of stimulus that later led to a reversal of Spanish and Portuguese policies. Nonetheless, the two Iberian efforts at Keynesian crisis management were not identical. The Zapatero government's Plan E emphasized "shovel ready" public works (Fernández-Albertos 2012), whereas the Socrates government's anti-crisis plan prominently included measures designed to address social needs, especially those of economically marginal sectors (Castro Caldas, 2013). In the initial period of the crisis, before the onset of austerity, the Portuguese approach included increases in anti-poverty income supports and several other types of social measures intended to simultaneously stimulate the economy and meet significant needs of families and individuals. The provision of credit to small and medium enterprises (SMEs) was another priority in the anti-crisis package of the Portuguese government (Castro Caldas, 2013). The road to crisis had also been strikingly different in the two cases; the historically simultaneous imposition of austerity on the neighboring countries in 2010 should not be taken as evidence that their economic challenges were strictly parallel at the time (Blyth, 2013).

II. *Managing Finance during the Crisis: Political Dimensions*

The early crisis era efforts of the two governments to actively intervene in economic processes were not limited to Keynesian fiscal policies. In the Portuguese case the long-standing national practice of seeking to stimulate the economy during times of crisis by ensuring a steady flow of bank credits to SMEs was kept in place even after the Socialists lost power to a right-of-center alliance in the elections held in June 2011. In late September 2011, several months after the Right had taken the reins of government, one of the top office holders in the Ministry of the Economy emphasized the importance of governmental support for the financing of firms and promised measures designed to help SMEs.[2] Just one month earlier, one of the Portuguese state's most reliable instruments for pursuing that end, the large state-owned Caixa Geral de Depositos—the country's largest bank—had declared its commitment to keep loans flowing to firms.[3] In the Spanish case, private firms, especially small and medium-sized ones, insisted strongly on their frustration over the drying up of access to credit during the crisis,[4] a matter that led to the public airing of divisions within the Socialist government. In a long meeting between top-level members of the government and leaders of the banking sector, Spain's Prime Minister Zapatero asked bankers to make an "additional effort" in extending credit during the crisis, but leading bankers, defending their own record, insisted that difficulties in the credit markets were a consequence of the deterioration in macro-economic conditions and not an independent cause.

From the pro-market perspective of many private bankers, the difficulty experienced by many firms in obtaining credit was a logical result of market conditions, the consequences of which should not be substituted by government intervention. However, from the standpoint of proponents of government efforts to facilitate access to credit, both the lending decisions of private banks and those of publicly owned entities are socially embedded in institutional or cultural structures in ways that are in no sense "natural," or automatically dictated by market dynamics. As the important recent analysis of Cornel Ban (2016) has shown, theoretical disagreements such as this one were reproduced within the policy circles of the Zapatero government itself. In this context Miguel Sebastian, Minister of Industry and Commerce, declared publicly, "the Government's patience with the banks is running out," a statement that proved disturbing to leading members of the banking community. Two senior members of the Socialist Party (PSOE), influential in its policy circles, quickly responded to Sebastian, offering assurances to the bankers. The Party's deputy secretary general, José Blanco, remarked, "the PSOE has unlimited patience with the financial entities" while Pedro Solbes, Deputy Prime Minister and Minister of Economics, spoke to the matter during a trip to London, reaffirming his patience with the banks and faith in them.[5] External pressure on the government from economically powerful actors led to a quick and generally sympathetic response from some of the government's major "heavy hitters." Their conception of democratic practice was quite amenable to addressing the concerns and sensibilities of powerful actors in the economy. Governmental pressure on the private banking system was not to assume a major role in Spain's response to economic crisis. The advocates of orthodox policies ultimately won the internal battles within the Zapatero government, in large measure because pressures from economically powerful actors were treated as more decisively important than pressures from workers, low-income sectors, and their supporters.

The large semi-public savings bank system—the *cajas de ahorro*, which were largely subject to control by local political and social actors—could have formed an alternative instrument for funneling credits to SMEs in need of crisis financing. Instead, in most of Spain, these financial institutions proved to be part of the problem instead of a solution to it; their lending efforts focused heavily on the real estate and construction sectors where many bubble-era loans went bad, leading to a need to restructure the sector. A top-level veteran of the savings bank system, Antoni Serra Ramoneda, who served as President of the large Caixa Catalunya for two decades, has published a revealing critical analysis of how the cajas operated (Serra Ramoneda, 2011). He quite explicitly laments the poor record of the cajas in providing loans to SMEs outside the real estate or construction sectors. The one major exception that Serra Ramoneda identifies is that of the Basque *Kutxas*, the most unambiguously politically controlled savings banks in all of Spain (Serra Ramoneda, 2011: 147). These Basque savings banks oriented their credit policy toward the financing needs of SMEs, many of them industrial concerns. In this respect, the lending practices of the Kutxas were congruent with policy preferences of Basque political authorities with their commitment to various forms of public–private coordination in the economy (Royo, 2008: 145–179). Within Spain, only in the Basque Country did the political system successfully address the concerns of SMEs by motivating publicly controlled financial institutions to attend to their credit needs. What was taken for granted in Portugal—the use of a publicly owned financial institution to address the credit needs of SMEs—was an exception in Spain even during an economic crisis when the need for such measures seems to have been especially acute. In 2014, several years after the severe contraction of credit that helped to produce economic crisis, a survey of mostly small and medium-sized Spanish firms showed that 75% of the companies surveyed had experienced no improvement in their access to financing.[6] This problem plagued SMEs under governments of both the PSOE and the Partido Popular (PP).

III. *Contagion from the Greek Crisis*

The first major pressures for the Iberian Peninsula countries to adopt stern austerity measures were felt in May of 2010 as a consequence of contagion from the Greek crisis. Greece's economic and debt problems had been long in the making, but they were largely covered over by government and financial sector elites who had prepared and reported official data that made the country's financial situation appear quite substantially better than it really was. The Socialist Party (PASOK) government of Georges Papandreou, elected in October 2009, made public the country's previously hidden financial situation shortly after replacing the conservatives of New Democracy (ND) in government in Athens. The magnitude of the country's true level of accumulated debt proved to be substantially higher than in the rest of the Eurozone, a state of affairs that was of acute significance because of the then-existing need for Keynesian-inspired deficit spending to combat the effects of the broadly international Great Recession. Once the magnitude of the country's accumulated debt was publicly revealed, assurances of some sort were needed to facilitate financing new debt on the international credit markets. This in turn led the Greek government to initiate a series of austerity measures. By the spring of 2010 Greece faced severe problems financing its debt in the international bond markets and sought a bailout from European Union (EU) and international institutions. This introduced pressures for intensified austerity, a recipe that proved to be counter-productive. Market participants that had underestimated the risks posed by holding Greece's sovereign debt quickly began to reassess the creditworthiness of Euro-zone sovereign debt—not only in Greece but also elsewhere. The standing of Portuguese and Spanish sovereign debt in the international bond markets then deteriorated quickly as the international rating agencies and large institutional investors sought to recalculate the risk of default in the bonds issued by these countries.

Although in the initial years of Europe's new common currency the large financial players had treated the threat of default by Euro-zone countries as virtually nil—thus providing all Euro-zone countries with interest rates on their sovereign debt that were only marginally higher than that paid by Germany—the Greek crisis raised questions about this assumption. With the introduction of serious concerns about the risk of default on sovereign debt, Spain and Portugal were quickly subject to strong pressures from the markets, and from large supranational and transnational institutional actors, to sharply curtail public spending—in the midst of efforts by these countries to recover from the financial crisis of 2007–2008. In this context, the same market actors that had previously underestimated the risks posed by Greece's sovereign debt shifted their concern and quickly began to search for other sovereign states whose creditworthiness could—or should—be critically reassessed. Private credit rating agencies, which have had a clear record of miscalculating systemic risk, and large banking and investment institutions with large sums at stake, were major participants in the shifting dynamics of the international bond market. In this new context, the often unpredictable directionality and magnitude of market movements came to exert a political role. Most governments are unable to engage in deficit spending without access to the international bond market and for that reason the shift in sentiment within the bond markets essentially closed off a reasonable policy response—that of counter-cyclical Keynesian stimulus.

One would expect most analysts and decision makers in the credit rating agencies and large financial sector investment banks to be more oriented toward orthodox economic analysis, friendly to the market-enhancing recommendations of neo-liberalism, than the neo-Keynesian formulations favorable to counter-cyclical fiscal policy and other forms of state intervention in market dynamics. Such orthodox views unquestionably play a large role in the functioning of contemporary economies and in the debates that underpin electoral competition in democracies. However, orthodox and neo-liberal economic thinking is obviously not uncontested in the world of policy-relevant ideas. Keynesian strategies to pursue economic recovery clearly called for significant deficit spending in the effort to restore economic growth and also suggested the usefulness of other types of state intervention in the operation of markets, such as Portugal's recurring emphasis on maintaining the availability of adequate financing for employment-creating SMEs. With the growing salience of the international bond market in the politics of economic crisis in 2010, the danger emerged that unelected market participants could end up introducing politically asymmetric constraints into the operation of democracies at the national level. After all, a government that cannot successfully sell newly issued bonds in the credit markets cannot engage in Keynesian deficit spending as a counter-cyclical tool intended to promote economic reactivation. In effect, politically unaccountable actors in the bond market imposed significant new constraints on the options available to governments.

At the time of this major episode of market contagion, both Portugal and Spain were governed by center-left Socialist prime ministers, but their responses were significantly different. The Spanish government of Jose Luis Rodriguez Zapatero, the most left-oriented Spanish prime minister since the Republic of the 1930s, responded with a massive shift in government policy, abandoning efforts at counter-cyclical Keynesian stimulus and curtailing public sector salaries as well as public expenditures of all sorts (Sánchez-Cuenca, 2012; Ban, 2016). The large-scale move to adopt austerity measures was quickly met with enthusiastic praise from former Socialist Prime Minister Felipe González, who famously messaged Zapatero to the effect that "governing is this, making tough decisions."[7] For Spanish office holders whose cultural framework for understanding political life led them to view governing as isolating themselves from pressures from below, both the message of González and the magnitude of the government's change in direction must have held considerable logic. Their cognitive framework, with its strong congruence to the predominant Spanish approach to democratic practice helped to shape Spain's response to changing circumstances.

Yet in Portugal, where government office holders understood governing to involve efforts to *heed* pressures from below and voices of discontent, the initial response in May 2010 was far more limited. The Portuguese government of José Socrates was steadily pushed to move closer to the austerity perspective, which had been rapidly adopted by their Spanish counterparts in May 2010, but the process was a long one in which Socrates and much of his government resisted what may be thought of as "pressures from above" or perhaps better, as external pressures. In April 2011 the Socrates government was ultimately forced to seek a bailout, but even in that context it attempted to influence the negotiation of the bailout memorandum in a way that was hoped to preserve some elements of the Portuguese approach to political economy (Rodrigues and Adao e Silva, 2015). Ultimately both Iberian Peninsula Socialist governments were forced to accept harsh austerity measures, and both lost power in elections held in 2011, but in the road to that outcome and in the experience under austerity, the Iberian divergence reasserted itself.

A common argument in favor of the approach followed by Spain's Socialist government in May 2010, that is, the rapid adoption of deep austerity measures, emphasizes the fact that Portugal was forced to seek an external bailout package just under one year later whereas Spain avoided that outcome. More than two years after the May 2010 U-turn of the Zapatero government, the conservative government of the PP sought and received a more limited bailout package focused on the Spanish banking sector, but under the Socialists' "watch" no bailout was sought or received in Spain. It is true that Spain's rapid shift to austerity was more favorably viewed by the private rating agencies and credit markets than Portugal's more reluctant and slower shift in the same direction, but that does not necessarily mean that the decisions of Spain's Socialist government produced better long-term outcomes than those of the Portuguese Socialists under Socrates. It is quite debatable whether Portugal genuinely needed a bailout in 2011. Although some observers assumed that the crisis was produced by a failure of Portuguese policies and institutions, a careful review of the evidence at the time reached a different conclusion (Fishman, 2011b).

If the European Central Bank had been willing to purchase the country's sovereign debt at levels sufficient to dissuade financial speculators from pushing up interest rates on Portuguese bonds, it is likely that the crisis could have been weathered without the turn toward deep austerity imposed in the terms of the bailout (Fishman, 2011b). Ultimately the International Monetary Fund (IMF), a major institutional player in the transnational pressure in favor of austerity, admitted that its calculations had been faulty. The

IMF recognized that the severe austerity plan it recommended along with its Troika partners had most likely worsened Portugal's budgetary and economic situation instead of improving it.[8] Given how international markets operate, it may well have been almost inevitable that the political system shaped by an inclusionary form of democratic practice would be treated especially harshly by bond market analysts and traders. Just over one year later, when in 2012 Lisbon's right-wing pro-austerity government yielded to the pressure of crowds in the streets and abandoned an especially regressive element of its policy package, two major rating agencies noted with concern the impact of social pressure and suggested that the country might well be forced to ask for a second bailout. [9] That warning proved to be unnecessarily pessimistic and it also missed the strong advantages of the Portuguese sensitivity to social pressure in the streets—as discussed in this chapter. When all is said and done, one can identify significant advantages of the Portuguese approach in handling the crisis.

IV. Government by the Right

In both Spain and Portugal the Socialists were reduced to roughly 28% of the national vote in the crisis-era elections of 2011. The incoming governments of the center-right obtained an absolute majority of parliamentary seats in both countries, allowing them considerable leeway to follow their own instincts in policymaking. However other factors—including the divergent willingness of these new governments to be influenced by popular mobilizations in the streets—showed the mark of the remarkably different forms of democratic practice shaping political action in the two cases. The response of the right-wing pro-austerity governments to pressures from below—expressed in massive street demonstrations—provides some of the strongest evidence of how dissimilar cultural frameworks and the related forms of democratic practice shaped societal outcomes in the two cases. Indeed, the cross-national difference in governmental response to pressures from below has played a large role in producing a substantial contrast in the distributional impact of austerity. The "conversation" between the streets and the halls of power constrained the politics of austerity more strongly in Portugal than in Spain.

This is not to say that this component of democratic practice born in the two countries' virtually polar opposite pathways to democracy can fully explain the cross-border contrast in the distributional effects of austerity. Other factors, some of them also legacies of the 1970s democratization scenarios, helped to shape the precise form taken by austerity in each case. One major institutional legacy of the 1970s transitions, the social components of the two Constitutions and, largely as a result, the decisions made by the two countries' Constitutional Courts, also tended to tie the hands of Portugal's pro-austerity government more than those of its Spanish counterpart. After all, the Portuguese Constitution stands out in comparative quantitative analysis as more strongly focused on the provision of social guarantees than most democratic constitutions (Magalhaes, 2013, 2003). On several occasions Portugal's Constitutional Court ruled major elements of the governments' austerity policies to be unconstitutional. This important point has been stressed by analysts such as Fernandes (2017) and others. But the single greatest "parting of the ways" between the two countries during the harshest period of austerity was reflective of the far greater capacity of Portuguese protest movements to reshape government policies. In both countries stringent austerity measures proposed by the right-wing governments were met by massive protests in 2012, but it was only in Portugal that those protests attained a major success.

During the summer of 2012 Portugal's Constitutional Court ruled unconstitutional a major element of government policy that proposed to cut state expenditures substantially through large reductions in the remuneration of public sector workers. The Court ruled that this approach violated the constitutional guarantee of equal treatment for all—discriminating unfairly against public employees. The government responded by attempting to effectively cut the pay of *all* wage and salary earners—transferring resources from labor to capital. The proposal introduced by the government in early September 2012 would have increased all social security (TSU) payroll taxes deducted from workers' pay by 7% while reducing the employer-paid payroll tax. This major pro-business switch in the operation of the country's TSU would have reduced pay for all employees—public and private—by a full 7%. The distributional impact of this change would have been quite large and clearly regressive—shifting a large portion of national income from workers to employers. The government presented the proposed change as an employment-creating initiative allegedly needed at a time of austerity-induced economic contraction, but the response of the public was rapid and strongly negative.

Large-scale demonstrations swept the country during the month of September, culminating in a major protest outside the Presidential Palace in Lisbon, where center-right President Cavaco Silva was meeting with the Council of State to assess the situation and offer advice to pro-austerity Prime Minister Passos Coelho. The crowd implored the President to act with the chant, "Cavaco Escuta, O povo esta em luta" ("Cavaco, listen—the people are struggling"). Both Cavaco and Passos Coelho responded in ways that acknowledged the legitimacy of the grievances articulated by protesters—and the importance of listening to them.[10] They withdrew the proposed change, citing the protests and public opinion as the reason for this change in direction. A massive effort to redistribute resources from workers to business was defeated by the mobilization and chants of crowds in the streets—and by the culturally rooted inclination of office holders, including those unmistakably to the right of the political center, to listen to such protests and adjust their policies in response. What would have been a major regressive redistribution of resources to business was prevented by large-scale protests in the streets and the willingness of elected political leaders—even on the right of the political spectrum—to listen to the voices of protest in the streets and modify their policy decisions in response.

The linkage of this crucial turn of events to Portugal's revolutionary road to democracy was evident to at least one leading member of the country's political elite. Mário Soares, the founder of the country's Socialist Party and a former prime minister and president offered remarks favorable to the demonstrators who had forced a change in government policy. In an explicit reference to the words of "Grandola," the emblematic song of the April 25 Revolution, Soares stated, just after the right-wing government's decision to withdraw its regressive proposal, that "it is the people who best order things [*o povo é quem mais ordena*, in the original words of the José Afonso song, often translated into English as 'it is the people who lead']. I always believed that after April 25 and even before [April 25] I believed it."[11] The country's cultural inheritance from the Carnation Revolution had saved it from an especially regressive austerity measure.

The fall of 2012 was also a time of massive protests in Spain, but their ability to reorient government policies was essentially nil. Instead, Spain's governing PP responded with efforts to delegitimize protesters and ultimately with new legislation that criminalized various forms of protest through the so-called Ley Mordaza. The government also acted to criminalize various forms of conduct by picketing strikers (Julia López, 2017). In Spain protest during the crisis led to increasingly harsh treatment of those involved but not to a switch in governmental policies. A social movement–induced change in the national conversation was able to reshape material outcomes in one case but not in the other despite cross-case similarities in the structural nature of the problems being faced and in the magnitude of protest. Yet if the process of crisis-era policymaking was clearly different in the two cases, what of the actual material effects of austerity? We turn now to evidence on that question.

V. The Distributional Effects of Austerity in Spain and Portugal

It is now possible to assess the distributional impact of austerity measures in the Iberian Peninsula cases and the rest of southern Europe through two approaches: simulations of the effects of tax and spending changes and the analysis of aggregate outcome data published by Eurostat. The findings generated by both approaches clearly show that the Iberian contrast in forms of political practice and in the openness of political elites to protest is fully matched by material outcomes. The economists Matsaganis and Leventi (2014) used micro-simulations of the expected effects of austerity-era measures on inequality in southern Europe and found strong evidence that Portugal's austerity program was the most equality-friendly of the region. Their methodology focuses on concrete measures approved by governments and quantifies their expected distributional effects. At times Portugal's austerity measures actually reduced inequality, but even when that was not the case, their impact on distributional outcomes was less regressive than in the other cases—and contrasted strongly with the clearly inequality-augmenting record of Spanish austerity. This is not to suggest that Portugal's austerity policies aided the poor or other low-income sectors. That was not the case, and in fact the poor were victims of some austerity-era cutbacks. But even when policies harmed the poor, their overall distributional impact was less regressive than in other cases. The Eurofound data published by Eurostat reports actual distributional outcomes by country during the period 2005–2014 and the findings are consistent with those of the Matsaganis and Leventi simulational study.

As the data presented in Table 5.1 show, the Gini coefficient of income inequality for Portugal fell by 7.4% between 2005 and 2014, indicating a trend toward reduced inequality in incomes. During the same ten-year period, the Gini coefficient of income inequality increased by 10.5% in Spain. Portugal's performance was more favorable to the pursuit of income inequality in both the first and second halves of this period of time. Granted, Portugal started off in 2005 with more income inequality as measured by the Gini coefficient than Spain and ended up in 2014 with only slightly less income inequality than Spain on that measure. However, if we focus instead on the ratio between the income of the top two deciles of the distributional structure and the bottom two deciles, the conclusions are still more favorable to Portugal (do Matias and Carmo, 2015: 450). But in the difficult years of economic crisis when hard decisions had to be made under strong external pressures for austerity, the Portuguese political system took those decisions in ways that treated low-income citizens as full members of the polity, tending to weigh their interests

TABLE 5.1 Household disposable income inequality across countries (Gini indices and percent)

	2005	2006	2007	2008	2009	2010	2011	2012	2013	2014	CHANGE 2005–2014 (%)	CHANGE 2005–2009 (%)	CHANGE 2009–2014 (%)
Portugal	0.376	0.372	0.366	0.356	0.352	0.333	0.339	0.340	0.344	0.348	−7.4	−6.2	−1.3
Spain	0.320	0.309	0.310	0.310	0.319	0.329	0.335	0.342	0.341	0.353	10.5	−0.1	10.6
EU	0.355	0.344	0.343	0.337	0.330	0.333	0.333	0.333	0.334	0.336	−5.4	−7.1	1.9

SOURCE: Eurofund (2017), *Income inequalities and employment patterns in Europe before and after the Great Recession* (Luxembourg: Publications Office of the European Union).

as seriously as those of other citizens. In the Spanish case, inequality clearly increased during the period of austerity. The partisan identity of governments in the two countries was quite similar, but the reigning form of democratic practice was not. Cross-national variation in the way that southern European countries distributed the impact of austerity measures strongly confirms the magnitude of the contrast between Portugal and Spain in political inclusion. The historically rooted cultural frameworks that shape how institutional office holders and protest movements relate to one another have strong material consequences.

One might be tempted to surmise that the negative distributional consequences of the economic crisis in Spain were simply an indirect effect of the country's severe rise in unemployment during the period of economic contraction. However, the available data suggest that serious economic insecurity was experienced not only by the unemployed but also by many Spaniards with jobs. OECD data from 2015 show that Spain is the European country with the highest poverty rate among the employed. Whereas 14.8% of working households live in poverty in Spain, in Portugal the figure is 9%.[12] The evidence that the effects of public policy are more favorable to low-income sectors in Portugal than in Spain seems quite clear, both before and after the economic crisis.

This is not to argue that the external imposition of austerity was without consequences in Portugal. As noted earlier, the IMF itself has recognized that the austerity recipe was excessively harsh and therefore counterproductive.[13] Recent research by Cardoso and Branco (2017) shows that the bailout package and the external pressures associated with it fundamentally altered how the Portuguese political system dealt with the issue of labor market regulation. A major liberalizing deregulation of employment rights and guarantees was introduced as a result of the new conditions. On this point, external pressure and the exigencies of the bailout package outweighed the voices of social protest. Welfare state benefits for the poor were also cut as part of the broad-ranging and deep turn toward austerity. Yet when Portugal's experience is juxtaposed with that of Spain, the cross-case differences are quite marked. Austerity had negative consequences throughout southern Europe, but the effects were less regressive in Portugal than elsewhere.

VI. *Effects on the Iberian Peninsula Party Systems and on Protest Itself*

Another large effect of the cross-national difference in democratic practice is visible in variation between Portugal and Spain in the impact of economic crisis on major political parties, the pre-existing party system, and other types of political expression. Although the classic Huntingtonian approach to political institutions such as parties suggests that their strength is in considerable measure a function of their *independence* from social pressures (Huntington, 1968), the Iberian experience offers evidence that strongly undercuts that assumption. The cultural framework conditioning democratic politics in Portugal exposes political party elites and the organizations they lead to pressures from below, whereas post-transition democratic practice in Spain has tended to isolate that country's political elites from such pressures—affording them with far greater autonomy than their Portuguese counterparts. In direct contrast to the expectations of the Huntingtonian hypothesis, the Portuguese/Spanish comparison shows that openness to social pressures from below and an inclination toward inclusion can be a source of institutional strength, whereas the insulation of elites from social pressures can bring about institutional weakness and decline. By 2015, when elections were held in both countries, the difference between the cases in the effect of economic crisis on parties and the party system had become quite clear.

In the December 2015 elections, roughly 34% of the Spanish electorate voted for alternative parties that had not competed nationally four years earlier, in 2011. Support for the country's Socialists declined from the 28% registered in 2011 to only 22%—even as votes for the right-wing PP also plummeted, making it quite difficult for either major party to form a new government. The third-ranking party in number of deputies in the country's parliament, Podemos, had not even come into existence until well after the previous elections. Although some within the Spanish political elite have congratulated crisis-era governments for essentially ignoring pressures from below, "making tough decisions," in the words of Felipe González, many voters did not see things the same way, and the pre-crisis party system was badly weakened. This effect is most visible in declining support for the PSOE. In contrast in Portugal, where political elites saw their democratic world in a very different way, no new party emerged as a major player in the elections held in 2015 and the Socialists increased in support from the 28% recorded in 2011 to 34%. The cross-border contrast in support for the Socialists was essentially non-existent in 2011—in perhaps the most difficult moment of the crisis—but by 2015 there was a cross-border difference in support for the Socialists of 12%. The crisis-era reluctance of the Portuguese socialists to radically alter their policy approach in the face of external pressures to adopt austerity measures was at least minimally rewarded by voters, whereas the approach followed by the Spanish Socialists from May 2010 until they left office late in 2011 was punished by many of their former supporters.

In another reflection of the effects of dissimilar cultural frameworks on crisis-related outcomes, the Socialist Parties of the two countries handled the election results of 2015 in quite different ways. In both countries the governing parties of the center-right or Right had lost both votes and seats after four years of crisis-era austerity, but in both cases they maintained a plurality in votes and seats. The two conservative governments claimed victory, arguing that they should continue governing since their electoral lists had won more votes than any one specific alternative. However in both countries the political forces in opposition to those governments had won significantly more votes and parliamentary seats than the incumbent right-wing governments. The elections had not resolved the question of who would govern. That decision had to be made by the political forces present in the parliamentary chambers of Madrid and Lisbon. The challenge for the forces in opposition was to find a formula for coordination—or even coalition—in support of an alternative to government by the Right. The challenge for the governments of Spain and Portugal was to persuade the Socialist Parties to abstain in a parliamentary vote of investiture or even to join a "grand coalition."

Some differences between the two cases deserve mention. In the Portuguese case the center-right bloc of two governing parties had run a joint electoral list whereas the three parties of the Left—the Socialists, the Communists of the PCP, and the Bloco de Esquerda (BE)—had run separately. Although the rightist coalition won a plurality of votes and seats, together the three parties to their left had won 12% more votes and a clear majority of seats in the Assembly of the Republic. Formally the country's President—directly elected by the voters—had to decide whom to call on to form a government, but given that governments required parliamentary support to remain in office, in practical terms the decision about who would govern had to be made by the Socialists, unless the President, Cavaco Silva, chose to dissolve parliament and call new elections.

In the Spanish case the governing PP, although still the largest single party in parliament, had fallen fifty-three seats short of an absolute majority of seats with the support of just under 29% of the voters. Taken in their totality, the election results in Spain seemed to give the Socialists greater chances to govern than the PP. Ciudadanos, a party that presented itself as centrist but that most observers placed on the right of the political spectrum given its positions in favor of pro-business policies and re-centralization in matters of state organization, seemed a plausible source of parliamentary support for the PP. However those two parties together held thirteen fewer seats than needed for an absolute majority. With the opposition of Catalan nationalists and forces to the left of the Socialists assured, the PP's only path to continuing in government involved either coalitional support or at a minimum abstention by the Socialists. The Socialists had two parliamentary pathways to winning the support needed to govern. If they could somehow secure simultaneous support from Ciudadanos and Podemos—the parties to their right and left—they would have enjoyed a support base more than twenty seats greater than needed for an absolute majority. However, both Podemos and Ciudadanos expressed skepticism about this pathway. If the Socialists made concessions to one of these parties, doing so would increase the political distance separating the PSOE from the other desired source of support. The Socialists had another highly plausible pathway to governing. The three electoral lists of the Left—the PSOE, Podemos, and Izquierda Unida (IU)—had secured 3.7% more votes than the two parties of the right, Ciudadanos and the PP. In terms of parliamentary seats, a clear plurality needed for the Left bloc to govern would have also required support from the Basque Nationalists (PNV) who have historically favored governments of the Left over governments of the Right when offered that choice.[14] Active support from Catalan nationalists, focused on winning independence from Madrid, was not necessary; if the Catalans abstained in a parliamentary vote of investiture, support from the parties to their left and the PNV would have provided the PSOE with the votes needed to form a government.

Despite the existence of differences between the two cases in the election results and in the makeup of the newly chosen parliament, the fundamental choice faced by the Socialists in the two countries was at least partially similar. Nonetheless, the Portuguese and Spanish parties handled that choice in very different ways. The Portuguese Socialist leader quickly reached agreement with the PCP and the BE to push for a Socialist government committed to reversing austerity-era policies. The arrangement they agreed on was for a single-party government by the PS with regular consultations between the three parties on matters of policy and legislation. The right-wing government of Prime Minister Passos Coelho attempted to remain in government but was quickly voted out of office by the now unified Left bloc of deputies, and the Socialists assumed governmental power. In Spain the PSOE suffered from serious internal divisions over the best course to follow. Party leader Pedro Sánchez indicated an interest in forming a governing majority, once it was clear that the PP could not do so, but he was subject to strong pressures to avoid collaboration with parties to his left or with peripheral nationalists. Podemos proposed forming a coalition government, dividing up governmental responsibilities—a proposal that most Socialists viewed as unacceptable. Although Sánchez expressed interest in negotiating with both Podemos and Ciudadanos, as a practical matter the PSOE prioritized negotiations with Ciudadanos and reached an agreement with that party on the program for a new government. The agreement included concessions by both parties. The Socialists attempted to persuade Podemos to support the accord, but their response was negative. Neither Podemos nor the peripheral nationalists were comfortable supporting the arrangement that had incorporated concessions to Ciudadanos, thereby moving the Socialists further away from the allies needed to win a parliamentary vote on the formation of a new government. No governing majority was possible.

The Spanish Socialists' operational exclusion of forces to their left and peripheral nationalists from the intensive negotiations with Ciudadanos over the program for a new government doomed the project to failure. New elections were required; they took place in late June 2016, yielding another complex outcome. The PP won increased support but still lacked a clear pathway to governing without acquiescence from the Socialists. The pathway to government by the PSOE was now somewhat more complicated than it had been after the elections of December 2015 and required active support from both the forces to its left and virtually all of Spain's peripheral nationalists—the Catalans included—or the unlikely combination of support from Podemos on the left and Ciudadanos on the right. Party leader Pedro Sanchez refused to offer support or abstention to the PP and seemed potentially open to the search for an understanding with those to his left and the peripheral nationalists. Unhappy with that prospect and with the possibility of a third set of elections if no government could be formed, the PSOE's establishment wing forced Sánchez to resign on October 1 and led the party toward its decision to abstain in the parliamentary vote permitting the PP to continue governing. Sánchez eventually returned to power in the PSOE, after winning a primary election for the post as party leader in June 2017, but for the time being the PSOE's reluctance to accept the inclusion of Podemos and peripheral nationalists in negotiations on the formation of a new government had led to an internal party crisis and continuing rule by the PP. The contrast between the inclusionary approach of the Portuguese Socialists and the de facto exclusionary approach of large sectors of the PSOE had led to sharply different governmental outcomes in the two countries. Spain's 2016 outcome ultimately proved unsustainable, and the Socialists returned to power in June 2018, having at least temporarily overcome their earlier unwillingness to reach understandings with peripheral nationalists and Podemos. That turn of events is taken up in the discussion of cultural change in chapter 7. Thus not only distributional outcomes but also strictly political ones provide evidence of how nationally predominant forms of democratic practice can shape the politics of crisis.

Another major set of political consequences of the crisis is to be found in the major mobilization of social protest against austerity in Spain, Portugal, and the rest of the Euro-zone's periphery. Despite the shared exogenous shock of the economic crisis and the accompanying austerity regime, major differences can be identified in the way social movements responded to austerity in the countries involved (Ancelovici, 2015; della Porta, 2017). Some of those contrasts involve the pattern of interconnection—or separation—between those active in protests in the streets and institutional office holders (della Porta, 2017). As this book's argument would predict, Portuguese movements of protest often developed close connections with institutional players in the existing system of representation (Baumgarten, 2013; Accornero and Ramos Pinto, 2015; Fernandes, 2017). At the same time, many of those active in Spanish protests sought to mark their distance from institutional power holders. Although the protest movements did innovate in various ways, a theme to be taken up in chapter 7 in the discussion of cultural change, memories of the past such as the continuing symbolic importance of the Carnation Revolution continued to strongly influence the practice of protest (Baumgarten, 2017; Fernandes, 2017; Romanos, 2017). Moreover, power holders responded to protest in quite different ways in the two cases, as the discussion in this chapter has emphasized.

The pattern of cross-national contrast in democratic practice that was evident both in the conduct of political actors and in survey data collected before the crisis has remained largely in place. The crisis changed a great deal, but it did not eliminate the Iberian divide in political inclusion. Instead it showed the extraordinary ability of that divide in democratic practice to shape a wide range of outcomes. New evidence of Portugal's inclusionary practice continues to emerge. The Minister of Education of Portugal's post-austerity Left government emphasized in May 2017 the importance of systematically listening to the voices and recommendations of students when contemplating curricular reform and other challenges—an approach that has earned praise from the OECD as an example for other countries.[15] The inclusionary political instincts of the Portuguese system remain in place—producing outcomes that clearly bear their mark. We now turn to another test of the book's central arguments, namely the way the Spanish political system has dealt with growing disagreement over the status of Catalonia.

 Does National Conflict within
Spain Undermine or Reinforce
the Argument?
The Catalan Crisis and Its Antecedents

I. Introduction

Intense political conflict over the status of Catalonia, still ongoing when
this book goes to press in July 2018, raises numerous important issues for
students of democracy and, inevitably, for readers of this book. The region[1]—
or, for many of its residents, the nation—located in the northeastern corner
of Spain along the Mediterranean and adjacent to France, had long been the
scene of political efforts designed to find some sort of legal expression for
the territory's distinctive identity and history. The aspiration of large sectors
of Catalan society to win full independence from Spain, and the handling of
the Catalan question by Spanish political forces, produced a series of historically significant confrontations in the fall of 2017, capturing the attention of
observers throughout the globe. Efforts by Spain's government, and the police
responding to its orders, to prevent voting in a referendum on independence
that had been called for October 1 by Catalan regional authorities produced
numerous scuffles and injuries inside polling stations, this constituting the
most dramatic episode in a long series of events that dominated the public
life of Spain for months on end. Waves of demonstrations and counter-
demonstrations in the Catalan capital of Barcelona and the jailing—in many
instances without bail—of numerous Catalan political leaders accused of
sedition and rebellion transposed much of the substance of the country's
political life from activities inside elective institutions to other venues, including courtrooms. An utter lack of consensus over a number of crucial

matters—including the nature of democracy and of national sovereignty—
had produced a major crisis that shook the foundations of the Spanish
system.

Conflict over national identity, the desired location of state sovereignty,
and the essence of democracy had at least temporarily undermined the
normal institutional contours of political life in ways that roused both fears
and hopes. At several points during the months of September and October
2017, elements of incipient "dual sovereignty" within Catalonia seemed to
open the possibility of a full breakdown in the existing legal order and of a
new revolution in both the streets of metropolitan Barcelona and the Catalan
hinterland—in the very locations where a social revolution during Spain's
civil war of 1936–1939 motivated George Orwell to write his memorable
Homage to Catalonia (Orwell, 1952[1938]). During 2017, Spanish and Catalan
elected governments made competing claims of ultimate authority within
Catalonia, and in the run-up to the October 1 referendum the autonomous
region's police force, the Mossos d'Esquadra, operated with enough operational independence from Spanish police—also actively involved in the use
of official force within the region—for the full development of dual sovereignty to seem a plausible scenario at least in the short run. The promise of
the elected Catalan authorities in the region's autonomous government, the
Catalan Generalitat, to override and supplant Spanish legality after the victory of a pro-independence list in elections held in September 2015 had set
the stage for what some political actors referred to as a likely "train collision."

The move toward the dual sovereignty scenario was somewhat slower and
more uncertain than had seemed possible on election night, September 27,
2015, when pro-independence forces won a majority of seats in Catalonia's
parliament with just under 48% of the votes cast in the regional elections held
that day. The over-representation of the Catalan hinterland in the regional
legislative body had predictably provided pro-independence forces with a
higher percentage of seats than of votes. The parliament's decision some
two years later, in September 2017,[2] to push forward with a binding referendum on independence that was ruled illegal by the Spanish Constitutional
Court, coupled with partial operational autonomy by the Mossos d'Esquadra,
appeared to fit at least some elements of what is arguably the most useful
scholarly definition of revolutionary situations—namely the emergence of
two or more effective and competing claims to state sovereignty within a
given territory (Tilly, 1978: 190–193). That extreme scenario never fully took
shape; the Catalan Generalitat's incipient claim to sovereignty in 2017,
prior to its actual declaration of independence on Friday, October 27 of that
year, was never matched by an ability to carry out most state functions with

genuine operational independence from Madrid, or by international recognition of the claim's validity. The one significant exception to this general shortfall in the *effectiveness* of Catalonia's assertion of sovereignty was the remarkable capacity of pro-independence forces to successfully organize voting in announced polling places on October 1, 2017—despite the efforts of the Spanish government and police to prevent that from happening (Vicens and Tedó, 2017). With this one highly visible exception, dual sovereignty—and the revolutionary situation it would have brought "onstage"—remained relevant merely as a hypothetical or counterfactual "road not taken" by the historical trajectory of events. Nonetheless, the great outpouring of emotions that *did* take place refocused the political energies of countless Catalans and Spaniards, placing large systemic questions at the center of politics. In Catalonia, political mobilization, as manifested by the breadth of participation in both elections and demonstrations, attained rarely seen heights that reflected the public's polarization over the issues at stake.

Conflict over the territorial definition of Spain, and the place—if any—of Catalonia in that larger unit, had essentially displaced normal political life throughout Spain. Within Catalonia itself, the salience of these large issues had occupied space normally taken up by much private life as well. During late 2017 and early 2018, frequent street and highway blockages by demonstrators served as a relatively small but directly physical reminder of the larger sense in which the conflict over Catalonia's status had come to occupy numerous arenas that Catalans had previously dedicated to concerns that stand largely beyond the political sphere. Outside Catalonia the reaction of Spaniards to these developments was generally quite hostile to the aspirations of the independence movement. Many citizens hung Spanish flags on their balconies or outside their apartment windows, and for the most part public sentiment in the rest of the country rallied to the side of the defenders of central government authority. One could scarcely ask for clearer evidence that major lines of internal division within Spain's borders limit the breadth of shared understandings and conceptions on at least some important political matters. The Catalan crisis brought into unmistakable view the existence of large-scale differences within Spain over national identity and certain other important elements of political life. Of course, that lack of consensus over national identity was not a new matter within Spain. The growth of a Spanish national identity, especially in the nineteenth century, was soon accompanied by the development of countervailing national claims in Spain's periphery—especially in the Basque Country and Catalonia (Alvarez-Junco, 2001; Linz, 1973; Díez Medrano, 1995). The assertion of a distinctive Catalan identity is as much a part of Spanish history as the growth of an overarching Spanish identity. However, the significance of the Catalan story clearly extends well beyond the borders of that territory and of Spain, holding implications for the European Union and for national independence movements and existing states in other contexts of disputed sovereignty.

The Catalan crisis raises numerous issues that will occupy scholarly researchers and theorists for decades to come; although many of these matters cannot be definitively resolved now, they cannot be fully deferred to the future. Several questions posed by the current conflict are of direct relevance for this book's argument, and thus despite the recent and—as of this writing—the *ongoing* nature of the events in question, it is appropriate to take up and examine the implications of the crisis for this book's claim that democratic practice in the neighboring countries of the Iberian Peninsula differs by country in ways that reflect long-term legacies of pathways to democracy during the 1970s. The central question that the Catalan events pose for readers of this book is a rather simple—if large—one: Does the bitter conflict over the status of Catalonia provide evidence of the *absence* of a predominant form of democratic practice—and instead the salience of widely *divergent* forms of political conduct, and systemic perspectives, within Spain—or does it instead confirm the existence of the type of democratic practice that this book identifies as emblematic of the Spanish case? In a related vein it is crucial to ask whether Spanish democratic practice has decisively conditioned the handling of the Catalan crisis and if so with what effects.

II. *The Approach of This Chapter: Summarizing the Argument*

I offer in what follows a discussion of antecedents to the crisis, a rudimentary chronicle of the pathway to crisis and of its unfolding in 2017 and early 2018, and an analysis of this case's significance for the book's larger argument. I have found it impossible to take up and address this important theme without attempting to provide a minimal accounting of the historical background to recent events. This is crucial for at least two reasons. It seems important to provide readers, including those who are unfamiliar with Catalonia and Spain, with some basis to assess the decisions and conduct of key actors in 2017 and 2018 through a lens that takes into account the nature of the challenges that they faced. Indeed, even readers who are generally acquainted with the Spanish case may lack some crucial elements of information about the history of the Catalan question. Additionally, the consideration of certain antecedents to crisis provides a useful occasion to address the nature of democratic practice within *Catalonia itself* before (and during) the onset of crisis. Taken as a whole, the material examined in this chapter provides valuable evidence on the central claims advanced in the book. Given the unavoidable density of the material covered here, I have included at the end of this section a very brief summary of the chapter's overall line of argumentation as an instrument intended to aid readers.

I draw on a wide range of sources including scholarly analyses of antecedents to crisis, written accounts of the Catalan "process," relevant data from surveys, and extensive discussions with relevant actors and observers. This last component of the overall set of sources on which I have relied is obviously the least systematic, yet I have not hesitated to include perspectives and knowledge developed in the course of a long personal history[3] of in-depth conversations with many Catalans—and other Spaniards—with political preferences covering the entire spectrum of viewpoints on the Catalan question. In some instances these conversations involved individuals who have played a role of considerable significance in the political trajectory of Catalonia. But in most cases they involved more ordinary, informed observers and rank-and-file participants on multiple sides of the Catalan question. Ethnographic accounts by scholars regularly rely on such evidence for their interpretations, and I find it highly useful to do so here as well. Given the recent, indeed ongoing, nature of the events discussed in this chapter and their inherently controversial nature, the claims advanced here should be treated as more "provisional" or exploratory than other claims advanced in the book. Nonetheless, the deep importance of the Catalan crisis and its evident relevance for the book's central arguments amply justified the inclusion of this chapter.

This chapter argues that the complex lines of development of Catalan society and culture have provided the basis for an essentially three-way division of preferences in the post-Franco period, as Vallès (2017) and other major analysts of Catalan politics have noted. The more or less distinct sectors of Catalan society can be thought of as three "thirds" even though the distributional breakdown of the region's population does not fully conform to that arithmetic characterization. In principle this structure of opinion—and of underlying identities—created a plausible basis for two different majoritarian coalitions within the region: a "Catalanist" alliance of forces interested, above all, in promoting and preserving the region's distinctive language and culture, and an autonomist but "unionist" alliance oriented in large measure toward forms of solidarity with other Spaniards. Either possible majoritarian coalition would require substantial support from the intermediate "third" of Catalan opinion favorable to *both* of these objectives, thus pulling the region's politics toward relative consensus in favor of developing a robust form of self-government—within Spain. Political forces located in one way or another within that "middle" third of Catalan society—favorable to these two objectives—led the region's autonomous government throughout virtually the entire post-Franco period. Granted, differences on other matters divided both the intermediate "third" and Catalan society writ large on the ideological dimension differentiating between left, right, and center, but on the major question of Catalonia's status, the three-way structure of division seems clear. This has created substantial support for a pathway of potential reform frequently referred to as "the third way," that is, the development of enhanced autonomy and recognition within the larger structure of Spain.

Political life is, of course, inherently "relational" (McAdam, Tarrow, and Tilly, 2001), and for that reason the ability of the intermediate third to govern Catalonia by pursuing one version or another of the middle "third way" is contingent on the conduct of political forces located outside the region.[4] I argue that the exclusionary tendencies that characterize much Spanish democratic practice have made it increasingly difficult for advocates of a Catalan "third way" to gain credible concessions from Spain's central government and institutions. As a result, sectors of the "intermediate third" of Catalan society have evolved politically, in some instances viewing the goal of full independence with increasing sympathy. Yet even with that shift, a somewhat diminished intermediate "third" has remained in existence. The Catalan question could have been relatively easily handled if Spanish political actors had been willing to treat the expression of sentiments in a nonbinding referendum as a normal element of democratic political life, as has been the case in many democracies. Had they done so, available evidence strongly suggests that the independence option would have been defeated at the ballot box. Central government concessions would have been extremely likely during the campaign preceding such a referendum, if not earlier, thus helping to avoid crisis. But in the eyes of crucial Spanish actors that scenario appeared both risky and unacceptable, just as readers of this book would expect given Spain's restrictive and segmented sense of democratic practice. At the same time, political actors within Catalonia have also practiced their own forms of exclusion. A type of democratic practice rooted in the 1970s democratic transition turned a complex but manageable set of challenges into a pathway leading toward the much feared train collision—with potentially grave consequences for democracy itself.

Thus I argue that Spain's institutionally segmented and frequently exclusionary democratic practice has powerfully conditioned the conduct of political actors both in Madrid and within Catalonia itself. Without this crucial conditioning factor, the conflict would have been quite manageable. The magnitude of the Catalan crisis underscores the political costs that this type of democratic practice can impose. At the same time, the prevalence—even within Catalonia—of the type of democratic practice outlined in chapter 3 serves as strong evidence of the ability of historical legacies to shape ongoing forms of political conflict.

III. Antecedents of the Catalan Crisis

The crisis that reached dramatic proportions in the fall of 2017 has had a long prehistory extending backward in time long before the Spanish transition from Francoist dictatorship to democracy in the 1970s. The origins of modern Spain lie in a large number of initially separate political units that emerged in the course of the protracted military confrontation between Islamic and Christian forces for control of the Iberian Peninsula. Following the eighth-century conquest of the Peninsula by Islamic rulers from North Africa, the centuries long Reconquista by Christian Spaniards provided the historical and sociopolitical parameters for the emergence of modern Spain. The Reconquista began in small mountainous territories in the northern extreme of the Iberian Peninsula and just across the Pyrenees Mountains, in the Carolingian Kingdom of France, which was itself engaged in the larger struggle. The origins of Catalonia lay in the extension of French Carolingian military activity southward across the Pyrenees, providing the foundations for the ultimately independent County of Barcelona. During the Middle Ages, the political institutions, language, and socio-cultural makeup of Catalonia developed independently from those of Castile—the region that played the predominant role in the eventual construction of modern Spain. The Catalan language retained significant marks of the region's socio-cultural origins in the southern extension of Carolingian France into what is today Spain.

Medieval Catalonia created a representative parliament with significant powers and other political institutions to which twentieth- and twenty-first-century Catalan nationalists have looked for inspiration and historical legitimacy. However, two dynastic unions through marriage connected Catalonia first to Aragon and later to Castile and the rest of Spain as well. With its language and many of its institutions at least initially intact, Catalonia developed as a part of Spain. That said, some elements of substance in Catalan history and its interpretation have been matters of cultural and political conflict. The long pre-history to the early twenty-first-century confrontation involves a great many matters of ambiguity (such as the specification of historical periods in which Catalonia could be considered a fully sovereign entity), elements of considerable complexity (such as the linguistic boundaries of Catalan predominance within the Crown of Aragon), and questions that motivate ambivalence.

The newly unified Kingdom of Spain was brought together through the marriage of its monarchs in 1469, but its constituent territories remained distinct from one another in their institutions, linguistic usage, and related matters. Catalonia was now part of a larger political unit in which the Castilian language—the historical basis for modern Spanish—strongly predominated. Complex tensions between efforts to homogenize the regional components of Spain and attempts to preserve regional distinctiveness and institutions marked the centuries that followed. Both Spanish national identity and Catalan identity are complex socio-cultural constructs that have taken multiple forms, most of them subject to contestation of various sorts (Alvarez-Junco, 2001). That contestation has taken multiple forms—some internal to the two identities, that of Spain and that of Catalonia, and others external to them (Muñoz, 2012). This pattern of contestation is quite typical of the broader cross-national experience of national identity formation.

What has taken Catalonia, and with it Spain, to a situation of extraordinary crisis has been the political *handling* of such complexity—not the fact of its existence. Indeed, numerous free and representative political systems are, like Spain, *multi-national states* in which diverse national identities and projects co-exist in democratic "space" within the borders of a sovereign state such as Spain, India, Canada, or the United Kingdom (Stepan, Linz, and Yadav, 2011). In all such cases, the multiple identities at play have emerged in complex historical processes of socio-cultural construction, but once the democratically expressed preferences of voters clearly manifest the existence of more than one national identity within a sovereign state, it falls on elected political leaders to collaboratively develop institutional and political arrangements allowing co-existence within that state. As the masterful analysis of Stepan, Linz, and Yadav (2011) has persuasively shown, although the challenges involved in building and sustaining democracy in multi-national states or "state-nations" may be greater than in the case of unitary nation-states in which only one national identity is present, those challenges have been successfully resolved in numerous cases.

Typically, some political actors in multi-national democracies would prefer their state to have a unitary national identity—eclipsing the minorities' national sentiments—but on this point as on others, democracy ultimately requires the coexistence in "mutual tolerance" of actors that disagree on matters of importance. Political actors who feel only the larger state-based national identity can become accustomed to referring to the institutions and identities of the periphery in terms that acknowledge the *national* self-definition of those most directly involved. In this sense, the legislative chamber of Quebec, Canada's large French-speaking province, is universally referred to as the Assemblée Nationale. Politicians in the two principal parties of the United Kingdom often refer to the collective interests or aspirations of Scotland as Scottish *national* matters. However, Spanish political forces outside the country's multi-national periphery tend to reject the legitimacy of using the term *nation* to refer to Catalonia, the Basque Country, or Galicia.[5]

In what follows I provide much evidence of certain types of Catalan distinctiveness, but argue that the predominant pattern of democratic practice in this territory—as in the case of Spain as a whole—is marked by historical influences that have diminished broadly inclusionary forms of conduct. Most of this book focuses on the implications of broad country-wide forms of democratic practice for the incorporation of low-income and socially marginal actors into institutionally recognized political life. This chapter focuses in partially related fashion on the treatment of socio-cultural outsiders who strongly feel a collective identity that is shared by only a minority of citizens in the larger polity. When exclusionary and segmented democratic practice limits the incorporation of low-income sectors, the principal negative effects involve a shortfall in democratic depth and unnecessarily painful distributional outcomes. In the Catalan case the "damage" exacted by relatively restrictive democratic practice appears to have touched on democratic *authenticity* and *consolidation*. The Catalan crisis may seem in some respects peripheral from the standpoint of this book's larger argument, but in this chapter I seek to provide recent and significant evidence of the widespread difficulties that can be generated by a politics of exclusion. The Catalan case helps to identify the full magnitude and significance of the Iberian divide in political inclusion.

IV. Catalan Nationalism and Its Oppositions

Modern Catalan nationalism emerged during the nineteenth century, developed and evolved politically during the twentieth century, and recently turned overwhelmingly toward the advocacy of full independence from Spain (notwithstanding continuing ambivalence on this point by some Catalan nationalists who prefer a "third way" out of the crisis through enhanced autonomy within Spain.) This nationalist movement initially developed in a context conditioned by the growth of modern Spanish national identity and by the industrial development of Catalonia (Diez Medrano, 1995). The economic factor, in turn, helped to motivate large-scale immigration to Catalonia from other Spanish regions.

The attraction that Barcelona exerted within Spain—drawing migrants from throughout the larger country—was not exclusively economic. Catalonia's capital city was a center of cultural and political innovation located close to France and seemingly far removed from the country's bastions of conservative resistance to transformation. Pablo Picasso chose to spend some of his early years in the city and the Catalan-born architect Antoni Gaudí, along with others in the Art Nouveau movement, worked primarily out of Barcelona, creating new aesthetic approaches to the built environment that have attracted worldwide fascination. Catalonia has been a magnet for many non-conformist Spaniards from other regions. Internally it has been divided between those forces focused on reshaping the larger political entity—Spain as a whole—and others who have preferred to exclusively defend Catalan distinctiveness. Of course, these two tendencies were not always fully incompatible with one another and they also stood in competition with more conservative currents, but the contrast in focus between progressives interested in building Spain-wide alliances and others interested in asserting specifically Catalan interests has been an enduring element of the region's modern politics.

Both Catalan aspirations to promote the region's distinctive identity and various other projects of social and political transformation reached their maximum twentieth-century apogee during Spain's Second Republic, declared on April 14, 1931. Despite the hopes and popular energies that characterized the Republican years, severe political and social polarization, the growth of anti-democratic forces, and a decline of mutual toleration among political adversaries undermined democracy's prospects. The Republic's final parliamentary elections were held in February 1936. The Popular Front of Left Republicans, peripheral nationalists, Socialists, and their allies won the elections, but right-wing military conspirators and their civilian allies planned strategies to overthrow the Republic. On July 18, 1936, a military uprising led by Franco marked the beginning of the civil war. The country's military was predominantly supportive of the right-wing coup, but many officers and units remained loyal to the Republic. Workers' militias and other civilian supporters of the Second Republic joined with those loyalist units to defend the Republic. Within days the country was divided between zones controlled by the two sides; the civil war was underway. In this long battle Catalonia was a firm component of the loyalist Republican coalition—despite the obvious existence of internal divisions within the region, some of them accentuated by the social revolution that soon took place. The civil war of course ended with the defeat of the Republic—and with deep consequences for Catalonia. Catalan society and politics were fundamentally changed by the long decades of Francoist repression and the struggle of large sectors of Catalan society in opposition to that regime. The early twenty-first-century conflict over the place of Catalonia in Spain is heavily conditioned by legacies of the Franco period—the theme to which we now turn.

V. Catalonia under and against the Franco Regime

When the military forces commanded by Franco took full control of Catalonia in 1939 during the closing days of Spain's civil war, they imposed a harsh new regime intended to do much more than simply deactivate the political forces that had supported the Republic. They also sought to fundamentally change Catalan society and culture, ending the predominant position of the Catalan language in both public and private life, replacing it with Spanish. This effort left an enduring mark on Catalonia, one that continues to shape underlying conditions that influence political conflict over the region's status. The harsh anti-Catalan repression was especially severe in the early years of the new regime, but despite the partial relaxation in later years, some restrictions on the Catalan language remained in place until after the death of Franco in November 1975. Crucially, the lasting impact of this element of Franco regime policies was amplified by the historical overlap between official restraints on the Catalan language and a period of intense in-migration to Catalonia brought about by the region's rapid economic growth and urban development during the second half of the Franco years, especially after 1960. New immigrants to Catalonia, along with everyone else, experienced public life, education, and interactions with state authorities in Spanish rather than Catalan. The effects of this historical overlap have proved lasting; language-use surveys show that Catalan has lost its majority use status within the region despite the implementation of policies intended to favor the language's recovery from the effects of repression. The most recently available monographic survey on language use dates from 2013. The results show that despite the strong growth of active knowledge of Catalan, promoted by the Generalitat's educational policies, in routine daily usage the language has not recovered the majority status that it enjoyed prior to the Franco regime.[6] Virtually all residents of the region know Catalan, but a narrow majority tends to use Spanish more often than Catalan in daily life.

The historian and lawyer Josep Benet, a leader of the anti-Franco opposition in Catalonia, carried out meticulous research on the regime's repression against the region's language, publishing the first results of his study in Paris in 1973 under an institutional pseudonym (L'Institut Catala d'Estudis Politics i Socials, 1973). After the return of democracy in 1977 Benet completed his study, publishing the full results in 1995 (Benet, 1995). In this work Benet exhaustively documents the comprehensive effort to reduce the use of Catalan to private and family settings, prohibiting its use in public in cultural, governmental, educational, and commercial endeavors. During the war itself, the use of the language in purely private conversations that could be overheard in public—such as telephone calls from a public place or discussions among friends in a restaurant—was also often prohibited and could be met with fines (Benet, 1995: 152, 157). Efforts to prevent the use of the language even in private conversations that could be overheard by authorities continued after the war in certain settings, for example for troops conscripted into obligatory military service. This devastating pattern of collective cultural repression did more than simply hamper the use and transmission of the Catalan language. It also produced a great deal in the way of personal indignities for residents of Catalonia. As Benet documents, in the first months of the new regime personal correspondence was routinely censored. Letters of all types had to be made available for inspection prior to posting them and it was required that they be written in either Spanish or foreign languages. Catalan was prohibited in personal correspondence until January 1940, nine months after the victory of the Franco forces (Benet, 1995: 367–368). Other forms of indignity were also experienced by many Catalans as a result of the prohibitions on their language. Residents of the region often reminisce about how they, or members of their families, were admonished by pro-regime troops or even by classroom instructors, for using their language. During the long years of the Franco regime, official limitations on the use of Catalan, along with other forms of repression, were partially relaxed over time, but many restrictions remained in force until after the death of the dictator in November 1975. To state the obvious, the use of Spanish was never subject to linguistic repression during the Franco period.

The Franco regime managed to reduce the use of the Catalan language, but in the process it generated widespread collective grievances and reinforced the strong sense of identity felt by most Catalans. At the same time, socio-economic grievances were building up among workers and urban residents located in areas that grew dramatically in population due to rapid economic growth following a change in regime policies in the late 1950s (Fishman, 1990b). Despite quite significant levels of repression, an increasingly powerful labor movement developed in opposition to the regime (Balfour, 1989; Fishman, 1990b). Strikes and other forms of collective protest grew in frequency as did the strength of leftist parties allied to the labor movement. Within the region, opposition to the regime developed both among labor activists on the left and Catalan nationalists. Others also became active in the opposition. By the end of the Franco period, opposition to dictatorship was extremely widespread within Catalonia, as the results of the first post-Franco elections, held on June 15, 1977 (Gunther, Sani, and Shabad, 1986; Linz et al., 1981, Linz and Montero, 1986), clearly suggest. Parties that owed their origins to elements of the Franco regime, including the Unión del Centro Democrático (UCD) of reformist Prime Minister Adolfo Suárez, won a total of just over 20% of the total vote in Catalonia. In the rest of Spain only the Basque Country generated a similarly low vote for the political forces born inside the Franco regime. For Spain as a whole, electoral support for "successor parties" (Loxton and Mainwaring, 2018), was more than twice as high as in Catalonia and the Basque Country.

In the context of growing opposition to the dictatorship, a crucial development took place. Parties of the Left that enjoyed widespread support in Catalonia adopted as their own the cause of Catalan autonomy, the linguistic recovery of the Catalan language's pre-dictatorship position and other Catalan goals. The demand for a new Statute of Autonomy was itself a constant theme in opposition rallies and congresses within the region during the transition period leading from Francoism to democracy. Union and party congresses of the Left and demonstrations led by the same forces routinely ended with the joint singing of two songs: the "Internationale" and "Els Segadors," the anthem of Catalan nationalism that refers to the seventeenth-century revolt of the Catalan "reapers." Parties of the Left, with their social base in a working class that included large numbers of immigrants from other regions of Spain, most of whom continued to speak primarily Spanish, joined in the widespread demand for the reassertion of Catalan collective rights and institutions. Their shared subjugation to Francoist repression had helped to build a sense of solidarity that built linkages between economic and cultural grievances. As the social movement scholar Hank Johnston has persuasively argued in his study of Catalan opposition to Francoism (Johnston, 1991), the nationalist defense of Catalan collective interests and objectives had become a central and unifying demand of the region's widely supported anti-Franco movement.

At the same time, de facto linkages between Catalonia and the rest of Spain grew in strength during the Franco period. The previously discussed rise of the Spanish language to dominant status in daily usage was one element of that change, but there were others. The growth of a large-scale Spanish language publishing industry in Barcelona and the increasing marriage and family connections between the region and the rest of Spain are two elements of this larger pattern. The Franco period and its antecedents left in place conditions favorable to the prevalence of dual identities in Catalonia. As data collected by a crucial survey instrument developed by Juan Linz have shown (Montero, 2019; Coller, 2006; Alvarez, Echavarren, and Coller, 2017), most Catalans think of themselves as being both Catalan and Spanish. According to the most recently available data at the time of this writing, a post-election Centro de Investigaciones Sociológicas (CIS) survey carried out in January 2018, nearly three fourths of Catalan society feels to one degree or another *both* Catalan and Spanish; just under 22% feels exclusively Catalan.[7]

Many of those who organized in opposition to Francoism in Catalan nationalist parties and movements, rather than within Left-oriented and labor-movement-linked parties, owed as much to the conservative Catalanist tradition of the Lliga of the pre–civil war years as to the more radical tradition of Esquerra Republicana de Catalunya. Moderate Catalan nationalists of Convergència Democràtica de Catalunya (Convergència), led by the energetic political entrepreneur Jordi Pujol were joined by the Catholic-oriented moderates of Unió Democràtica de Catalunya in a long-lived electoral and governing coalition. At least discursively, Convergència i Unió (CiU) adopted the defense of the welfare state as an element of its program along with distinctively Catalan aspirations. The main forces of opposition to Francoism in Catalonia had coalesced around the defense of socially progressive and nationally distinctive objectives. Granted, the three main political forces involved—the Partit Socialista Unificat de Catalunya (PSUC) linked to the Communist international, the Partit dels Socialistes de Catalunya (PSC)[8] affiliated to the Socialist international and the moderate Catalan nationalists of CiU—were significantly different from one another in various ways. Nonetheless, in very general terms, the long period of Francoist repression had put in place conditions favorable to political consensus in Catalonia on a number of points. Underlying political sentiments within the region were further to the left than in most of Spain[9] and strongly favorable to the reassertion of Catalan distinctiveness.

However, at the same time the growth of the Spanish-speaking population in Catalonia had created the social potential for future political divisions over language use and educational policies (Miley, 2006). Catalan society in the post-Franco period is the product not only of the region's pre-Franco history but also of multiple forms of transformation experienced by the region during the long years of dictatorship. The constellation of factors linked to the legacies of the Franco years was favorable to the three-way division of preferences on the national question that has been persuasively noted by political scientist Josep Maria Vallès in the context of the alleged reduction of sentiment into a binary opposition between two opposing blocs (Vallès, 2017). Despite the polarizing events of 2017 and early 2018, the middle or intermediate "third" of Catalan society retains the balance of power in public opinion. This configuration in public opinion made likely relatively moderate forms of Catalan national self-assertion *within* the institutional framework of Spain. The extremes—on the one hand in favor of independence from Spain or on the other hand in support of de facto recentralization on matters of linguistic and educational policies—seemed unlikely to triumph. However, the viability of the moderate Catalanist pathway between the extremes was to be contingent on the willingness of Spanish political forces to negotiate and reach agreement with the Catalans. That willingness would, in turn, be sharply constrained by legacies of the transition and its "coda," with their tendency toward segmented and often exclusionary democratic practice. We now turn to Catalonia during the transition and in its aftermath.

VI. *Catalonia during the Transition and under Democracy*

During the transition itself, the compromise-oriented leadership of the regime reformer Adolfo Suárez contributed to making the hypothetical scenario of agreement between Spanish political forces and moderate Catalan nationalism into an empirical reality. In an extremely important symbolic move in October 1977, only months after the first free elections of the post-Franco period had taken place, Suárez invited Josep Tarradellas, the President-in-exile of the Catalan Generalitat, to return to Barcelona as provisional President of the region's autonomous government in formation. This would allow Tarradellas to participate in transition-era negotiations with Suárez and others. This move was widely seen as a symbolic recognition of the continuing legitimacy of the pre-Franco institutions of the region, a form of legitimacy that could be seen as prior to the soon-to-be-drawn-up Constitution of the new democratic regime. Suárez and many other key actors of the transition understood the importance for Spanish democracy of securing Catalan participation in the overall design of the new system and in forging a new regional Statute of Autonomy. The new Constitution drafted over the following year and approved in 1978 established a special accelerated pathway to autonomy statutes for the regions historically defined as "nationalities," namely Catalonia, the Basque Country, and in the country's northwest, Galicia.

The transition-era efforts of political actors to begin constructing an institutional architecture reflective of Spain's multi-national makeup offered considerable promise; steps were taken toward a form of "asymmetric federalism" facilitating autonomy arrangements for the multi-national periphery of the Basque Country, Catalonia, and Galicia. Many crucial details were left to be worked out later: The full elaboration of the potential embedded in the new Constitution of 1978 was to depend on numerous decisions made by political actors at multiple levels of the system over a prolonged period of time. Elected politicians, and judges charged with interpreting the Constitution, would play a large role in fully elaborating the country's incipient "State of Autonomies" which ultimately provided all regions with forms of autonomy. Those decisions would ultimately be shaped not only by the transition's openness to dialogue among *institutionally recognized* actors but also by the more restrictive form of democratic practice that came into full view after the 1982 transformation of the party system that is conceptualized in chapter two as the transition's "coda." In the handling of the country's multi-national periphery, the most exclusionary features of Spanish democratic practice only came to the fore after the Partido Popular (PP) had replaced the UCD as the principal party of the center-right following the 1982 party system "earthquake." The transition's "coda" powerfully shaped its enduring legacies.

During the transition years, and in their near-term aftermath, the political dynamics of the Basque Country appeared far more challenging for the Spanish system than Catalonia. Nationalist parties won a higher proportion of the vote in the Basque Country in the first post-Franco elections, and, more significantly, the region was home to ETA, a violent organization that used arms to pursue its goal of Basque independence. ETA's terrorism grew in intensity during the transition, becoming one of the most significant terrorist threats in a democracy at the time. In 1980 the number of deaths attributable to the organization surpassed ninety (Sánchez-Cuenca, 2001). In contrast, Catalonia appeared to be a success story. The pursuit of robust forms of autonomy enjoyed widespread support there, but pro-independence sentiment was substantially lower than in the Basque Country (Linz et al., 1981) and no major organization turned toward violence. However, the segmented form of democratic practice that came to predominate in the Spanish polity powerfully shaped underlying conditions for the treatment of Catalonia within the larger system, restricting the capacity to handle Catalan distinctiveness as successfully as Suárez had done during the transition itself. The predominant cultural rendering of the essence of democracy contributed to a climate in which major political forces cast doubt on the legitimacy of Catalan actors, objectives, and forms of action. That exclusionary tendency has greatly amplified the magnitude of the problem.

A new Catalan Statute of Autonomy was approved in 1979, and the first elections to its parliament produced a highly divided outcome that permitted the moderate nationalists of CiU, to form a government as the largest single formation in a divided regional parliament. That coalition was to remain in power in the region until more than twenty years later, when a left-oriented coalition of three parties, led by the Socialists (PSC) and including the left-nationalists of Esquerra Republicana de Catalunya (ERC) ousted CiU in elections held in 2003. The parameters of electoral and political competition among parties (Rodon and Orriols, 2014; Pallarès, 1991) hold inescapable relevance for the 2017 crisis. Before we turn to an examination of democratic practice within Catalonia, and an analysis of the crisis during late 2017 and early 2018, we first take up the important question of how and why pro-independence sentiment increased substantially, especially in three crucial years between 2010 and 2013.

VII. The Rise of Pro-Independence Sentiment and the Non-Binding Referendum of 2014

The emergence of severe conflict over Catalonia's status—within or outside Spain—is in part premised on the prior growth in pro-independence sentiment. That dynamic, and explanations that have been advanced to account for it, require brief treatment here. In what follows I up take several quite plausible explanations that have been offered and suggest that they have contributed in part through their interaction with another fundamental factor. I argue that Spain's often exclusionary democratic practice strongly conditioned both the growth of pro-independence sentiment and the central political system's handling of this new challenge once it emerged. I understand the dominant conception of democratic practice to have operated in combination with other causal dynamics such as the impact of the Great Recession on all of Spain—Catalonia included—but I argue that the magnitude of the crisis cannot be fully explained without introducing the factor emphasized here. Without the limitations imposed by the predominant way that democracy is understood and practiced in Spain it would have been far easier than has been the case for political actors to resolve the challenges posed by Catalan distinctiveness, and it is highly likely that support for independence would have remained substantially lower than the level that exists in 2018.

A reasonably long series of survey results on the status question is available from the Generalitat's opinion research institute, the Centre d'Estudis d'Opinió (CEO), however the interpretation of this data is at times challenging. In addition to the normal fluctuations produced by random sampling error and real-world changes in circumstances, in this instance answers are also conditioned by question wording. Support for independence is measured through a binary option and through a multi-option question that offers respondents the opportunity to express preference for the so-called third way of enhanced autonomy within a federal Spain. The inclusion of multiple options consistently reduces the level of support for independence manifested through the simple binary formulation. Thus, for example, in one of the highest readings of support for independence, a CEO survey carried out in October 2017, after the referendum, showed pro-independence sentiment at 48.7% in response to the simple binary question. However, when intermediate options were introduced in the same survey, support for independence dropped to 40.2%. Given that enhanced autonomy is an option that forms part of the political debate and on which voters may be asked to take a position, I consider the multi-option question the most valid rendering of the state of public opinion. The data reported in Figure 6.1 show the evolution of support for independence in the CEO's multi-option question.

The data show a slow increase in independence support even prior to the crucial 2010 Spanish Constitutional Court decision that invalidated

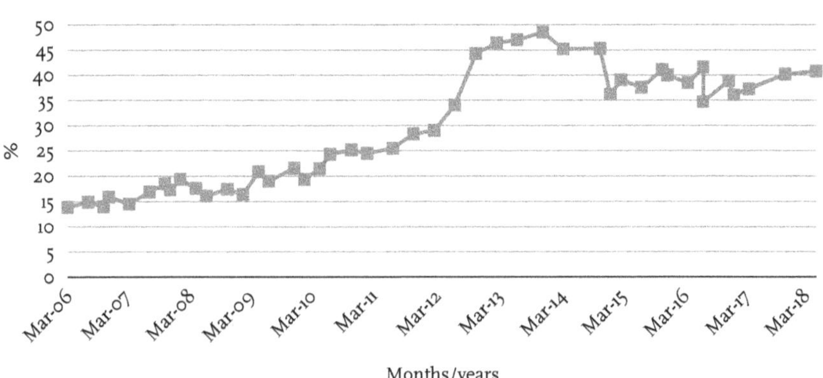

FIGURE 6.1 Evolution of the support of Catalonia being an independent state

SOURCE: Own elaboration based on graph on page 12 in: Generalitat de Catalunya (2018), "Political Opinion Barometer: 1st wave 2018." *Baròmetre d'Opinió Política Press Report.*

large components of Catalonia's new "third way" Statute of Autonomy that had been approved in 2006. That watershed Court decision, and the 2006 Statute that was partially invalidated by it, are taken up later. After 2010, support for independence grew rapidly until 2013, when those favoring this option reached 48.5%, close to the 50% threshold. However, after that 2013 peak, the data show constant fluctuations within a range that remained consistently below the crucial 50% mark. Three large-scale factors emphasized by scholars writing on this matter seem at least plausibly related to the large growth in independence support from 2010 through 2013 and the stagnation or drop-off after mid-2013. These factors include economic crisis, the electoral interests of political party leaderships in a competitive setting, and the impact of the 2010 Constitutional Court decision on widespread hopes for a "third way" leading to enhanced autonomy within Spain.

The major exogenous shocks—economic crisis and the Constitutional Court decision—appear in most scholarly analyses of the growth of independence sentiment, but other factors are also often mentioned. Some analysts have emphasized the perceived need of party leaders to compete with opposing electoral options under increasingly difficult conditions. The comparative political scientist Sonia Alonso (2012) argues that political decentralization or "devolution" may paradoxically increase the incentives for previously moderate peripheral nationalists to turn toward the demand for independence as a way of differentiating themselves from non-nationalist parties that fully accept regional autonomy and distinctiveness. This argument deserves serious consideration, but it is not entirely clear that it can adequately account for the timing of the rapid rise in independentism after the Constitutional Court decision and in the context of the Great Recession. A partially related claim often discussed by observers was made explicit by the astute political journalist Guillem Martínez in his book length analysis. Martínez suggests that for Convergència the turn toward support for independence offered the party a way to "rebrand" itself[10] after being tainted by a succession of corruption scandals and the implementation of austerity measures (Martínez, 2016: 161), and served as a strategy to compete with the more left-wing Catalan nationalist party, ERC (174). In a wide-ranging qualitative and theoretical analysis, Thomas Jeffrey Miley places emphasis on the economic crisis and the politics of austerity, arguing that these exogenous factors interacted with pre-existing political and institutional factors to produce the strong growth of support for independence (Miley, 2017). In a rigorous examination of competing explanatory hypotheses, Muñoz and Tormos (2015) argue that economic factors are not the primary driver of increasing support for independence among most Catalans who have embraced that objective. However, these scholars find a tangible economic effect for those not decisively moved toward independence by two other motivations: partisan loyalties or an especially strong Catalan identity.

Thus the growing scholarly literature on the rise of pro-independence sentiment offers at least some support for multiple explanations. There is substantial reason to believe that several quite distinct factors have interacted with one another in generating the large shift in popular sentiment and elite behavior on the status question. I emphasize the explanatory significance of Spain's restrictive democratic practice, conceptualizing it as a factor that operated in combination and often in interaction with other variables. The tendency to exclude from the sphere of normal politics forms of expression (such as referenda), perspectives, and collective actors that are valued by many Catalans has made the Spanish political system increasingly unattractive for large sectors of Catalan society. Moreover the restrictive conception of acceptable forms of political conduct has led Spanish political forces away from potentially fruitful avenues of negotiation with Catalan elites and has tended to push actors on both sides toward confrontation. As arguments advanced by a leading political theorist in favor of independence clearly show, the reluctance of centrally important Spanish actors to accept aspirations for enhanced autonomy as legitimate—and as plausible within the framework of Spain—has essentially made the "third way" lose credibility for many Catalans, leading them toward support for independence (Requejo, 2017: 24–25, 40, 169).

A new Statute of Autonomy approved in 2006 by the Catalan and Spanish parliaments and ratified by Catalan voters had provided renewed hope to many Catalans that their distinctive identity and aspirations could be institutionally incorporated within Spain's legal structures. The new Autonomy Statute had been elaborated by Socialists, Catalan nationalists, and post-communists eager to make the abstract idea of a "third way" into actual reality. The new text provided Catalan institutions with new powers and symbolic recognition. Spanish centralists in the PP and Ciudadanos responded quickly with a large-scale campaign calling for the text to be declared unconstitutional. The controversial Constitutional Court decision of 2010, declaring crucial sections of the new Statute unconstitutional, reduced the credibility of an approach to Catalan distinctiveness that had promoted the incorporation of peripheral nationalists into the broader Spanish project. As Sánchez-Cuenca (2018) and others have pointed out, this Court decision declared elements of the new Statute to be unconstitutional even though they had been patterned on existing components of other Autonomy Statutes in Spain that have not suffered the same fate.

The decision is often mentioned by relatively recent adherents to the independence cause as a determining factor in the evolution of their thinking. In their view, the Court's rejection of major elements of the *Estatut* had essentially closed off the "third way" scenario of increased recognition of Catalan distinctiveness within Spain. Admittedly, the terrain for such an interpretation of the Court decision had, in some ways, been actively prepared in advance by independence supporters who had expected such an outcome (Basta, 2018), but the linkage between the judicial decision and the evolution of Catalan politics (Rodón and Orriols, 2014) seems clear. The decision probably contributed significantly to a shift in perspective by highly placed elites in more than one political party, but the shift was not limited to elites. The trend line in public support for independence supports this view. Perhaps even more importantly, the public claims of pro-independence leaders and activists often draw on this Court decision as a way of supporting their stance in favor of leaving Spain. In both large-scale public debates among political leaders and small-scale discussions among friends or family, the Constitutional Court decision provided material that was actively used by those arguing in favor of independence.

The crucial Court decision soon produced a variety of direct and indirect effects. The Socialist-led coalition government that had ruled Catalonia since 2003 lost power, and the center-right Catalan nationalists of CiU returned to power in the Generalitat late in 2010. At the same time, the largest party in that center-right nationalist bloc, Convergència, shifted its position on the status question, moving toward support for independence or, at a minimum, an assertion of the "sovereigntist" insistence on Catalonia's right to decide its political future through a referendum. In a larger sense the Court's decision—important as it was—was emblematic of a significantly broader tendency in the treatment of Catalan aspirations by many Spanish political actors and institutions. The reticence of many within the PP, Ciudadanos, and even some sectors within the PSOE to see Catalan aspirations for increased recognition of the region's distinctiveness as fully legitimate made the path toward a broad-based agreement within Spain's institutional structures considerably more difficult than hoped for by advocates of the Catalan "third way."

Initiatives launched by Artur Mas, President of the Generalitat from late 2010 through early 2016, provide two crucial additional examples of how Catalan aspirations have been handled. Spanish parliamentary elections held in November 2011 had provided the PP with an absolute majority in the Spanish parliament, allowing party leader Mariano Rajoy to rule without the need to reach accommodation with other political parties. Both the Spanish government of Rajoy and the Catalan government led by Artur Mas faced strong external pressures to adopt crisis-era austerity measures that seemed guaranteed to elicit significant popular opposition. Indeed, austerity policies had been introduced earlier following the U-turn of the Zapatero government of the PSOE in May 2010. Hoping to diminish the pain imposed by this approach, Mas attempted to negotiate an improved fiscal arrangement for Catalonia, perhaps to be patterned on the system that the Basque Country enjoyed. The Catalan president also presented the Rajoy government with other aspirations, hoping they would serve as the basis for negotiations. For whatever reason or set of reasons, the Rajoy government was unwilling to offer substantial concessions to the Catalans. No fruitful negotiations took place. For many Catalans, disappointment over the Court decision was magnified by the inability of the Generalitat to secure meaningful concessions from the Madrid government. In this context, the Catalan government formed after new elections held in November 2012 (Rodon and Orriols, 2014) prioritized holding a plebiscite on the status question, allowing the region's electorate to express its preferences regarding the possibility of gaining independence from Spain.

Exactly why the Catalan government favored holding a referendum—in this first instance, a non-binding one—is still open to debate and uncertainty (Amat, 2017; Martinez, 2016), leaving a number of questions without definitive answers: Did the government genuinely hope to attain independence through a favorable voting outcome or did it hope to achieve goals other than independence? Was the planned referendum at least in part an effort to promote negotiation with Spain's central government, providing Madrid with a new strong incentive for offering greater autonomy within Spain? Was the referendum simply intended as a vehicle to "rebrand" its organizers for competitive electoral purposes? Or was it a genuine effort to make independence possible? Regardless of how one answers these questions, the initiative met with a rather harsh, and likely counter-productive, response from Spanish authorities. Indeed, had the Spanish government and judicial authorities accepted the holding of the non-binding referendum planned by the Catalan government, the electoral consultation would almost certainly have ended the matter with a clear defeat for the pro-independence forces, but instead, Spanish governmental efforts to prevent the electoral consultation from taking place reduced participation by opponents of independence and antagonized many Catalans who were in principle favorable to remaining within Spain.

My assertion that the Generalitat's plan for a non-binding referendum in 2014 would have produced a clear victory for those wishing to remain in Spain had voting participation been widespread is based on two specific features of the 2014 referendum as well as considerations equally applicable to any hypothetical referendum. The specific features involve the wording of the 2014 question and the definition of the electorate qualified to vote. Opinion polling on the Catalan status question consistently shows that support for full independence is substantially reduced when "third way" options such as enhanced autonomy in a federal Spain are included in the set of choices made available to respondents. The 2014 referendum in effect did so, increasing the likelihood that independence would receive well under 50% of the total vote. Secondly, the electorate entitled to vote[11] included virtually all residents of Catalonia, including most non-citizens. In 2014 non-citizen immigrants made up as much as 14% of the total Catalan population and all indications were that most of the immigrant population was strongly opposed to independence. Both linguistic usage and the understandable interest of immigrants in facilitating their own freedom of movement predisposed non-citizen residents of Catalonia against independence. However, even without these two specific features of the 2014 referendum, a victory for the pro-independence forces seemed extremely unlikely if voting participation had been widespread. The underlying structure of national identity in Catalonia, although favorable to the pursuit of enhanced autonomy, is unfavorable to full independence. Those who hold an exclusively Catalan identity, and who do not consider themselves to be Spanish at all, are slightly fewer than one quarter of the population, according to the most recent data.[12] This helps to explain the consistent difficulty that the pro-independence option has had surpassing the 50% threshold in opinion polling.

The Rajoy government in Madrid responded to Catalan plans to hold a non-binding referendum in November 2014 by asking Spanish Courts to block the initiative. The Constitutional Court ruled in favor of the requested prohibition—arguing that the planned vote was unconstitutional. When the Catalan government responded by reframing the vote as an unofficial exercise in civic participation without legal ramifications of any sort, the government in Madrid and the Constitutional Court reasserted the ban on voting—thereby losing an opportunity for a voting outcome favorable to their perspective, while also antagonizing many Catalans who saw in the prohibition on voting a disturbing limitation on their democratic rights, one that seemed to differentiate Spain from countries such as the United Kingdom and Canada that had permitted such referenda. The vote was held, but participation fell substantially below 50% of those eligible, most opponents of independence having chosen not to participate. Among those voting, approximately 80% expressed their support for independence. The Catalan President, Artur Mas, and others involved in holding the electoral consultation were subsequently subject to significant legal penalties. Mas, who was one of the most right-of-center leaders in the larger Catalan nationalist movement, would have been a plausible negotiating partner for the Spanish Prime Minister, Mariano Rajoy. After all, they had both implemented neo-liberal austerity policies, they both had both been the targets of large-scale street protest critical of budgetary cutbacks and both of them led parties that found themselves confronting a series of corruption scandals. Nonetheless, they became enmeshed in an increasingly bitter confrontation that held especially large legal ramifications for the then Catalan president. It was in this setting that the Catalan leadership would turn toward the holding of "plebiscitary elections" in September 2015, a precursor to the crisis that deepened in 2017.

What motivations led Spanish and Catalan politicians down the road toward increasingly bitter confrontation? An insightful account by the journalistic author Jordi Amat stresses the role of irresponsibility and narrow electoral calculations on both sides (Amat, 2017). The important recent analysis of political scientist Sánchez-Cuenca argues that the crisis reveals certain shortfalls in the functioning of Spanish democracy. His argument emphasizes the tendency of the system to treat political matters in a hyper-legalistic way that often loses sight of the essence of democracy (Sánchez-Cuenca, 2018). This argument captures major elements of the dynamics at work. In his analysis, Sánchez-Cuenca introduces two highly telling comparisons. Whereas the Canadian Supreme Court's favorable decision on Quebec's independence referendum drew simultaneously on the written law *and* the essential principles of democracy, Spain's highest Court, and the government that appealed to it, seemingly looked only to written law in designing a response to Catalan aspirations for a referendum. And whereas the Italian government, when faced with a formally illegal independence referendum in the northern part of the country, chose to essentially ignore it given the lack of practical implications, the Spanish government implemented a harsh legal response to the non-binding and unofficial vote held in November 2014. Sánchez-Cuenca's analysis provides important substantive contributions along with its insights about the tendency of the Spanish government to rely on the judicial system to handle the political issues posed by Catalan aspirations. However, that said, there is room to question whether the driving factor motivating the official handling of the Catalan challenge was an obsession with the literal application of the law or something rather different.

In Spain as elsewhere, the use of the law to restrain or prevent actions that are illegal is almost inevitably somewhat selective. When the law is put to work, its application can be exercised with leniency, with an insistence on the literal and full adherence to the strictest possible requirements, or with an effort to discern the underlying spirit and purpose of legislation. These three approaches can yield quite different judicial findings. However, on occasions, and whether for political or practical reasons, the law is *not* put to work. In the Spanish case the interpretation of the law on matters related to Catalonia has become increasingly strict. Important legal scholarship has argued that Spain's Constitutional order does, in principle, permit the calling of a non-binding status referendum by autonomous communities such as Catalonia (Vilajosana, 2014), but that view has not been reflected in judicial decisions. The tendency of some political actors to adopt the most restrictive and harsh possible interpretation of the law reaffirms the political system's more general tendency toward an often exclusionary form of democratic practice. I argue that the underlying dynamic at work involves a cognitively embedded inclination to make decisions that entail a de facto exclusion of certain actors, themes, and forms of practice from the sphere of legitimate political life. In other words, I argue that the Spanish approach to democratic practice, introduced in chapter 3, has strongly conditioned the handling of Catalan aspirations. In this case the definition of the excluded "other" is a cultural one, rooted in matters of national identity, rather than a socio-economic one. Spain's predominant form of democratic practice, acting in interaction with other factors, has limited the country's ability to successfully handle the challenge offered by the multiplicity of national identities within the country.

The tendency of some actors to view Catalan nationalists as an unwelcome "other," lacking full legitimacy to participate in Spain's politics, has long been evident. The critique of Catalan nationalism has been especially pronounced among Spanish rightists, but can also be found among some supporters of left-of-center parties or movements. One of the most memorable and telling instances of this pattern took place in March 1996, when crowds outside the headquarters of the conservative PP celebrated the center-right's first electoral victory since 1979. The crowds that gathered on Génova Street in central Madrid on election night apparently viewed not only the Socialists who lost power in the 1996 elections but also the Catalans of CiU as their political adversaries. One of the most common chants of the crowd of PP supporters that evening was "Pujol, enano, habla castellano," in English, "Pujol, shortie, speak Spanish!" Ironically even though the crowd seemed eager to admonish Catalan President Pujol for his past support of the Socialists and his unsurprising tendency to address the Catalan public in their language, by the time all the votes had been counted it became clear that the PP would need to rely on an agreement with CiU to attain a governing majority in the Spanish parliament. Nonetheless, the words of those gathered had made abundantly clear the underlying sentiments of many PP supporters.

Years later when a new center-right party was launched, initially in 2005[13] in Catalonia and later throughout Spain, it defined its political identity in part through its opposition to Spain's peripheral nationalisms, especially in Catalonia and the Basque Country. That party, Ciudadanos, prioritized its critical perspective on the Catalan drive for linguistic "normalization," that is the set of policies intended to erase enduring effects of the Franco regime's linguistic repression. The Generalitat's language policy sought to promote the use of Catalan in schools, the public administration, and in other public ways. Ciudadanos viewed this language and educational policy as discriminatory toward Spanish speakers, much as critics of affirmative action policies intended to correct the long legacy of past injustices in the United States claim that such policies produce new forms of discrimination. In a broader sense this party opposed special forms of recognition for Catalonia or the Basque Country, arguing that such an approach broke with the principle of equality for all Spaniards. Ciudadanos has been quite explicit about seeking to exclude Basque and Catalan nationalists from participation in the construction of parliamentary majorities needed to form governments.[14] This relatively new party does not ask Catalans or Basques to renounce the usage of their language but does in effect ask them to abandon their search for a distinctive status linked to their history. Ciudadanos, like the crowds on Génova Street in 1996, has seen the collective assertion of a strongly distinctive Catalan identity as unwelcome. Thus multiple actors in Spanish politics have sought to marginalize Catalan aspirations and initiatives, hardly a strong basis for incorporating the region's distinctive identity within Spain. The rise of support for independence was conditioned by this factor in combination with economic crisis and political party agendas.

Yet if Spanish democratic practice conditioned the handling of Catalan aspirations and reduced opportunities for agreement between political authorities in Madrid and Barcelona, this leaves open an important related question: Was democratic practice within Catalonia substantially more inclusionary—as in Portugal—or did it follow patterns that were decidedly Spanish? As I explain in what follows, much evidence points to the congruence of democratic practice in Catalonia with the pattern that predominates in the rest of Spain.

VIII. *Democratic Practice in Post-Franco Catalonia*

Although the makeup of the Catalan party system and the center of gravity in public opinion within the region are substantially different from the pattern to be found in the rest of Spain that offers no guarantee about the pattern of democratic practice to be found in the region. In examining this question I have cast a historically expansive net, carrying the discussion forward to the 2017 crisis itself. I seek to show that despite the differences in identity and political preferences that distinguish between Catalonia and Spain as a whole, the prevailing conception of democracy and predominant forms of conduct within the region have shown strong parallels with the rest of Spain. I argue that this, in turn, is a result of Spain's shared history. The key recent elements of that shared history involve Francoism and political transition, as examined in chapter 2. There is however an important caveat: Democratic practice, like most cultural phenomena, is best conceptualized as constituting a *repertoire* of possibilities with some internal variation in specific manifestations of the phenomena involved—a point emphasized by much theoretical work within the field of cultural sociology that is discussed in chapter 1. At times, Catalan democratic practice has indeed strayed somewhat from the overall Spanish pattern. But as late as the declaration of independence approved by the Catalan parliament on October 27, 2017, elements of *convergence* with Spanish democratic practice stand out strongly. The remarkable story is one of overlapping forms of democratic practice deployed by actors pursuing diametrically opposed ends.

Democratic practice in Catalonia—as in the rest of Spain—frequently manifests a hierarchical segmentation of political conduct in which action centered *within* official representative institutions is strictly set off from political expression located *outside* their bounds—frequently in streets and plazas. The use of force by police who have been ordered to maintain that strict separation has been a "normal" occurrence both in the rest of Spain and in Catalonia. The related tendency of dominant actors to exclude others they see as social or political outsiders, and to restrict the range of themes subject to full discussion in the institutional core of the political arena is to be found frequently both in the rest of Spain and in Catalonia. Despite major differences between Catalonia and the rest of Spain in identity, language use, and the structure of political preferences, Catalan democratic practice has been remarkably Spanish.

Some of the most dramatically clear evidence dates from the period between late 2010 and late 2012 when the moderately nationalist and center-right formation, CiU, held power under the leadership of Artur Mas. Admittedly, this was an extraordinarily challenging time to rule given that all of Spain was enmeshed in a deep economic crisis that led to a severe rise in unemployment, drastic budgetary cutbacks and frequent protest in the streets. However, the pattern is not limited to this period. A great deal of evidence from other periods of time shows much the same as this two-year time span. Moreover, as the discussion in chapter 5 showed, Portuguese and Spanish political actors handled the exogenous shock of the "great recession" and the Euro crisis in remarkably different fashion with consequences that have endured. During this crucial period of time democratic practice and distributional decisions followed quite different patterns in Portugal and Spain. Catalonia largely followed the pattern observed in the rest of Spain.

In May 2011 Spanish political authorities—including the government of the Catalan Generalitat under then-president Artur Mas of CiU—were the object of rising public discontent over major budgetary cutbacks induced by the sharp turn toward neo-liberal austerity one year earlier. On May 15, 2011, protestors, widely known as the *indignados*, filled the central squares of Madrid, Barcelona, and other Spanish cities, initiating a movement that sought to shift the country's political atmosphere. The 15-M movement, analyzed at greater length in the next chapter, brought to the fore a wide range of demands and concerns that had largely fallen off the agenda of institutionalized politics. The spaces that the protesters sought to occupy were simultaneously *physical venues* of urban life and, politically relevant *discursive "arenas"* that shape the formation of public opinion and agendas. The governmental response was also motivated by an effort to assert control over both the physical center of large cities and the more symbolic "center" of political debate and discussion. The *indignados* established around-the-clock occupations of the central squares, hoping to reorient the direction of political life. Meanwhile, governmental office holders contemplated ways to clear the plazas of the 15-M movement.

Less than two weeks after the occupation of plazas had begun, on the morning of May 27, 2011, police forces in Barcelona, responding to the orders of the Catalan autonomous government, tried to clear Plaza Catalunya, but the *indignados* decided to stay in place. The police then acted with considerable force, using a range of methods to clear the plaza. Over one hundred people were injured.[15] The police operation in Barcelona is generally seen as the most forceful and controversial episode of police coercion in governmental efforts to dislodge the *indignados* from Spain's plazas. The confrontation between the Generalitat and the *indignados* involved not only the space available for political expression but also matters of policy substance. The Catalan government planned to secure approval for large budgetary cutbacks in a parliamentary session scheduled for June 15, exactly one month after the arrival of protesters in the plazas. The *indignados* responded with a new strategy: They decided to protest directly in front of the Catalan parliament, hoping to prevent passage of the austerity cutbacks. This strategy, combined with the approach to crowd control manifested by the May 27 clearing of Plaza Catalunya, produced a major confrontation and ongoing controversy.

The protesters concentrated outside the Catalan parliament in mid-June 2011, jeered the entering parliamentarians, in extreme instances using physical force or intimidation. Some observers have alleged that the genuinely violent incidents that marred the protest were actually the work of *provocateurs* unrelated to the *indignados* and perhaps linked to official security services.[16] The accomplished journalist Guillem Martínez asserts, "many police were identified among the most active demonstrators" (Martínez, 2016: 147). Whatever one concludes regarding the role of *provocateurs* external to the movement, the protest was met by police force and arrests leading to criminal prosecution. Artur Mas and members of his Catalan government entered the parliamentary chamber by helicopter. The protest of the *indignados* outside the parliament, hoping to halt adoption of major budgetary cutbacks, had served to underscore the sharp separation between politics inside representative institutions and the expression of citizen sentiments outside their bounds.[17] Following these events, criminal prosecutions against arrested demonstrators led to eight convictions with three-year jail sentences. Although some of those convicted were found to have engaged in physically abusive acts such as spray-painting a parliamentary deputy attempting to enter the chamber, at least three of the eight convicts were only found to have verbally critiqued the budget cutbacks while also admonishing a parliamentarian to the effect that he did not represent them.[18] During a period of time in which Artur Mas and the party that he led were moving toward an embrace of the pro-independence cause, Catalan political life was marked by a conception of democratic practice that fits this book's characterization of the broader Spanish pattern. Actors on both sides of the cognitive divide between protest in the streets and life inside the parliament had failed to prioritize dialogue and mutual recognition between these two worlds of political life.

In a perhaps surprising confirmation of the broader pattern, a tweet sent in 2010 by Carles Puigdemont conveyed a perspective on protest that fits the predominant Spanish approach. Even though he would later lead the drive for Catalan independence while serving as president of the Generalitat, in 2010 Puigdemont appeared irked by the tactics of picketing strikers. In response to an anti-austerity general strike in September 2010, Puigdemont admonished the strikers for their use of conventional labor movement picketing, complaining that "this [business of] picketers who block access, services, etc. seems to me lamentable."[19] More recently, on crucial moments in October 2017, Puigdemont sought to contain protest, limiting its expressive impact on official institutions.

Perhaps the most decisive evidence comes from the two occasions when the government of the Generalitat contemplated issuing a unilateral declaration of independence. On October 10—less than two weeks after the controversial October 1 referendum—President Carles Puigdemont suspended plans to ask the Parliament to approve a declaration of independence and instead issued a call for negotiations with the Madrid government. Pro-independence demonstrators had planned to gather outside the parliament, presumably to celebrate the declaration that they anticipated, but Catalan authorities decided to limit access to the park in which the parliament is located. Demonstrators were restricted to a street adjacent to the park, the Passeig de Lluis Companys, located roughly half a kilometer away from the parliament building.[20] Nearly two weeks later, on October 27, 2017, when the Catalan parliament did vote to declare independence, demonstrators were again kept rather far away from the representative institution as it contemplated and voted on the declaration.[21] Much like their counterparts in Madrid, and even when they were contemplating a historically monumental decision, elected Catalan authorities attempted to erect a sharp demarcation between the workings of their representative institution and the articulation of citizen preferences outside its bounds.

The applicability of this claim to governments led by parties of the Left is clearly relevant. Barcelona has been governed by mayors of the Left during all but one four-year period following the return to elected municipal governments in 1979. The industrial belt of cities surrounding Barcelona has also, for the most part, been governed by parties of the Left and at the level of the Catalan regional government a three-party coalition of Socialists, post-communists, and the left-nationalists of ERC governed the Generalitat from late 2003 through late 2010. The argument advanced in this book is not intended to challenge the widely held assumption that the ideological placement of governing parties actually matters—helping to shape major outcomes. Instead the argument is that nationally predominant forms of democratic practice interact with widely recognized explanatory variables—such as the ideology of governing parties—thereby helping to shape outcomes. Undoubtedly some Catalan policy decisions have, in fact, reflected the electoral strength of parties of the Left. Thus for example the geographer Oriol Nello (2015) argues that the urban form of greater Barcelona is reflective of political dynamics rooted in the strength of Left parties. Nonetheless, the broader constellation of outcome variables fails to show a comprehensive pattern of major contrast with the rest of Spain parallel to the large divergence between Portugal and Spain.

A number of incidents suggest that the predominant Spanish pattern of democratic practice has also frequently emerged under Left rule in Catalonia. In the fall of 2010 while the post-communist leader Joan Saura served as the Generalitat's cabinet member in charge of police and security issues, major confrontations took place between police responding to his decisions and urban Okupas. In connection with one incident the police made sixty arrests.[22] Several years earlier, in 2007, Saura had justified the police use of batons to deliver blows to demonstrating militants of the Okupas movement.[23] Regardless of how one assigns responsibility for confrontational police/protester interactions, the pattern seems quite in line with broader Spanish practice and decidedly unlike the dynamic to be found in neighboring Portugal. During the same period of time, Sabadell, an old industrial city within the Barcelona metropolitan area, was the scene of numerous harsh encounters between members of a housing-oriented movement and authorities. The Assemblea per un Habitage Digne de Sabadell (AHDS) organized protests at city hall and in other public places; their relations with the Socialist-led municipal government were quite antagonistic. In one instance, militants complained that a demonstration they held on October 6, 2007, was subject to police harassment and intimidation.[24]. In the broader Catalan context, at roughly the same time, the housing-oriented movement V de Vivienda initially focused its mobilizations primarily on civil society targets rather than the chambers of elected office holders, presumably on the assumption that direct appeals to office holders were unlikely to be effective. In Catalonia, as in the rest of Spain, the hope for genuine "conversation" between protesters and office holders failed to achieve the status that idea enjoyed in Portugal: as a normal form of democratic public life (Fishman and Everson, 2016).

An enthusiastic proponent of the independence movement, eager to build the case for the distinctiveness of Catalan democratic practice might, conceivably, argue that the effort to organize a referendum on the region's status somehow showed a broader and more inclusionary conception of democracy than that found in the rest of Spain. There is, of course, an argument to be made that referenda represent "direct democracy," placing in the hands of ordinary citizens the right to make major decisions (Altman, 2011; Morel, 2007; Jaume López, 2017). The scholarly literature on the use of the referendum raises reasonable doubts on that optimistic conception of plebiscitary democracy, but quite apart from the general debate, in the Catalan case several matters raise questions about whether the political conduct of the Generalitat has been genuinely inclusionary. Indeed, pro-independence Catalan elites have often shown an inclination to view democracy as a system that empowers elected representatives to exercise institutional power in often rather exclusionary ways, without paying great attention to the expression of citizen preferences outside the bounds of representative institutions.

The decision of the government of the Generalitat in early September 2017 to call a referendum for October 1 of that year led to a successful collaboration between the Catalan government and the allied pro-independence social movement (della Porta O'Connor, et. al. 2017). Together they managed to hold the referendum despite determined opposition from the Spanish government, legal system, and police. In the process they secured for the independence movement its most dramatic public relations victory. However, the pro-independence parties that were governing Catalonia had not always been committed to holding a referendum on the status question and even when they did adopt this commitment, key elements of their conduct raised important questions about their full allegiance to democratic inclusion and responsiveness. The astutely critical Catalan journalist Guillem Martínez has noted that CiU and ERC actually voted in 2010 *against* the possibility of holding a referendum at a time when it might well have been possible to do so legally had they supported the initiative (Martínez, 2016: 122–123). Pro-independence forces subsequently embraced the effort to hold a popular vote on the matter. The Catalan government elected in 2012, and led once again by Artur Mas, organized a non-binding referendum for November 2014, as discussed above, but after the central government of Spain managed to restrict the effectiveness of that initiative through a variety of means, the independence forces turned instead toward the idea of "plebiscitary elections" in which votes for representatives to the Catalan parliament would be taken as a de facto statement of voter preferences on the national status question. Faced with the difficulty of holding a referendum, and unable to negotiate successfully with the Madrid government on other matters, Artur Mas called new elections for September 27, 2015, declaring them to be plebiscitary in nature.

The turn toward parliamentary elections as a way of resolving Catalonia's ongoing deadlock over its status crucially shifted the institutional basis for a key political decision to one in which a central premise of referenda—that all votes count equally—would not hold. In principle, calling the elections "plebiscitary" invited all involved to add up the votes for electoral lists that shared a joint perspective on independence as if the election had been a referendum. However in institutional terms the elections chose members of parliament and clearly many voters—and parties—did not see the elections as fully equivalent to a referendum. Catalonia's electoral system for selecting its parliament affords greater weight to the region's hinterland than is justified by strict adherence to the principle of political equality among all voters. Parliamentary deputies are allocated to the region's four provinces through a procedure that benefits the three provinces that lie beyond the edge of the Barcelona metropolitan area. Barcelona province has nearly 74% of Catalonia's total population but is entitled to roughly 63% of the elected deputies. The representational bias in favor of the heavily pro-independence less populated provinces is not an overwhelming one, but it has been large enough in magnitude to provide pro-independence parties with a narrow majority of parliamentary seats despite enjoying support from under 50% of the Catalan electorate. By denying Catalans the right to a non-binding referendum on their region's future—a right that had been exercised by residents of Quebec and Scotland—the Spanish government and supporters of its restrictive sense of democracy had shifted the terrain of political conflict to parliamentary elections, providing supporters of independence with a strong institutional advantage. How pro-independence political elites handled this situation was reflective of their own democratic practice.

The elections held in September 2015 provided Junts pel Si, a large pro-independence coalition between the two main nationalist parties, ERC and Convergència[25] (along with non-party members of the pro-independence movement), with a large block of sixty-two parliamentarians, six short of the sixty-eight deputies needed for an absolute majority. A far-left pro-independence coalition, the Candidatura d'Unitat Popular (CUP) won 10 seats, jointly providing the two pro-independence coalitions with four more seats than needed for an absolute majority. However, these two coalitions had together won just under 48% of the votes cast. In a sense, the supporters of independence had won the parliamentary election but they had narrowly lost the plebiscite on the region's status. Of the four remaining political forces that won representation, three opposed both independence and the holding of a referendum whereas the remaining one supported the holding of an electoral consultation on the region's status but not the call for independence. The leadership of Junts pel Si took the parliamentary majority as an electoral mandate to push ahead toward independence, in principle without the need to consult the population again before taking decisive steps in that direction. Paradoxically, the political forces that had conceptualized the elections as plebiscitary won the parliamentary contest but lost the plebiscite—and then proceeded to take the results as a victory. The political forces that had opposed the holding of a referendum focused on the de facto plebiscite outcome rather than the parliamentary elections result. Crucially placed actors on both sides of the status question seemed more concerned with promoting their preferred option than with achieving—and respecting—a full reading of the electorate's preferences.

If the disagreement over how to interpret the message of the September 27, 2015, elections—and, prior to that date, the rejection by many anti-independence forces of all efforts to hold a referendum—represented only temporary and passing instances of excessive zeal in the pursuit of large objectives, the conflict would be more amenable to a broadly acceptable negotiated resolution than has been the case. However, additional evidence suggests that such specific positions are reflective of an underlying conception of democratic practice on both sides that prioritizes the exercise of power by representatives in institutionally designated positions of authority. This perspective in effect minimizes the need to take account of viewpoints articulated outside those centers of institutional power. The result is an exclusionary understanding of democracy that differentiates hierarchically between what takes place in the center of institutional power and other expressions of political preference. Those placed on opposing sides of the conflict have disagreed over the official institutions that they prioritize—the Spanish parliament and courts or the Catalan parliament—but they have shared a tendency to strongly prioritize a center of formal institutional power. The practice of important actors in the major institutional power centers of both Madrid and Barcelona has often tended to exclude certain political forces, perspectives, and forms of action, treating them as peripheral or even dangerous. The tendency toward marginalization of many key actors has been practiced on both sides.

In early September 2017 the Catalan government definitively decided to hold a binding referendum on independence despite adamant opposition from Spanish authorities in government and in the judicial system. The goal of placing the status question in the hands of voters resonated deeply with inclusionary or participatory conceptions of democracy, but in practical terms the matter was far more complex than that. Even though a large majority of the Catalan electorate, including many opponents of independence, was in favor of holding a referendum (Requejo, 2017: 287; Rodon and Orriols, 2014: 27) three major parties were opposed and a fourth political grouping was ambivalent—supporting the principle of holding a vote on the region's status while articulating major reservations about the specific formula adopted in 2017 by the Catalan government. The proposed referendum was legislatively defined as legally *binding* despite the large logistical difficulties posed by the adamant opposition of the Spanish government and, the related likelihood that a large portion of the electorate would refuse to participate. Moreover, the legislation calling the referendum was to be immediately voided by the Constitutional Court rendering it formally illegal. In pushing forward, the pro-independence majority in the Catalan parliament suspended normal legislative procedures, blocking opposition parties from many standard parliamentary actions and drastically limiting the time available for debate. In the limited time available, the opposition complained that the framework for holding the referendum lacked adequate guarantees. The standard legal review of the proposed legislation by the chamber's juridical experts was also circumvented. In a highly anomalous procedure, the law calling a binding referendum was approved in expedited sessions held on September 6 and 7 under strong protests from the opposition.[26] A key initiative that appeared to place ultimate decision-making authority in the hands of the Catalan electorate was pushed forward through parliamentary procedures that many saw as exclusionary.

This scenario made it terribly difficult to establish consensus about the people's will. The legislative designation of the referendum as legally binding, even though challenges to its legitimacy raised the possibility that a majority of voters might choose not to participate, could be critiqued as a de facto exclusion of a large proportion of the electorate, perhaps a majority, from a historically important collective decision. On the other hand, from the standpoint of pro-independence forces it could be claimed that the very real limitations on the ability of the referendum to accurately reflect popular sentiments were largely induced by the central government's efforts to prevent voting from taking place. Yet the reality is that both actual election outcomes and the long series of public opinion data suggested that support for full independence remained below a full 50% of the Catalan electorate, especially when "third way" or intermediate options were offered to voters. A large majority of Catalans, according to available opinion data, wished to vote in a legally recognized consultation on the status question, but many of those wishing to vote did not support independence.

Regardless of how one attributes responsibility for impasse, much of the political leadership in both the pro- and anti-independence camps had shown more interest in advancing its ultimate objectives than in guaranteeing an accurate reading of the citizenry's preferences.[27] In the process of doing so, many actors had shown strong evidence of the segmented and often exclusionary form of democratic practice discussed at length in chapter 3. The pro- and anti-independence forces differed in the designation of the institutions they chose to see as central to decision-making. But in both cases many actors saw sentiments that were at odds with the majority inside those institutions as inconvenient, politically marginal, and essentially irrelevant to resolving the status question. Those who believed that the only way to consensually resolve the conflict was to fully and accurately consult the Catalan electorate in a legal referendum with widespread participation were caught in the middle—unable to push the handling of the controversy in that direction. The available survey data strongly suggest that the independence option would have been defeated in such a popular vote and that the decisive intermediate sector of opinion continued to favor the third way of enhanced autonomy. However, many key actors on both sides actively sought to marginalize defenders of the "third way."[28] Paradoxically, much political conduct showed evidence of the predominance, even in Catalonia, of the form of democratic practice that has characterized post-Franco Spain. Some political forces have attempted to promote a shift in that practice but to date their efforts have not been successful.

IX. *Paradoxes of Conflict over the Referendum and Its Aftermath*

The decision to hold a binding referendum on October 1, when juxtaposed with the adamant opposition to this step by the Spanish government and others in the Spanish political and legal systems, put in place dynamics that would lead to a series of dramatic and often paradoxical events. Beginning in September 2017 the test of wills between pro-independence actors and Spanish authorities led to an escalating series of confrontations that held many surprises and uncertainties for all involved. The matter so absorbed public attention that it was often referred to in conversation as the "monotheme." Given the uncertainties and the drama of the autumn of 2017, stories circulated in Barcelona that the city's pharmacies had exhausted their supply of sleep medication. A chronicle of all of the most important and memorable episodes of the larger conflict would fill the pages of a rather substantial book. Surely there will be many important volumes on this theme; I leave to others the narrative task of relating the major steps of the crucial actors from September 2017 onward. I limit myself here to a brief discussion of several of the most important elements of the larger story that hold analytic significance for this book's major concerns.

The Spanish government responded to the referendum plans with a large battery of legal and police measures, and with firm public assurances that the referendum would not take place. The Madrid government's position quickly won support from the Constitutional Court, legally banning the electoral consultation. The Catalan government, the large social movement committed to the sovereigntist project, and large elements of the Catalan public countered with increased adamancy and with ingenious strategies to move ahead with existing plans. A series of police raids sought to confiscate the ballots, voting bins, and electoral registration lists that would be needed for the referendum to take place. The most important police action took place on September 20 at the Catalan Department of Economics presided over by the Catalan Vice President, Oriol Junqueras. Before the police action was completed with several arrests and the confiscation of material related to the referendum, a crowd of many thousands had formed outside to express support for those inside the building. A key ERC leader, Joan Tardà, and others made vociferous calls for the crowd to act peacefully, insisting on the rigorous commitment to non-violence, and for the most part the crowd strictly adhered to that guideline. However, two Spanish Civil Guard vehicles present at the site were vandalized while the Civil Guards were in the building. Stories circulated widely in Catalonia about potential voters who felt ambivalence or even hostility toward independence but who decided during late September to participate in the referendum as a way of protesting Spanish government attempts to prevent the voting from taking place.[29]

The Catalan government's determination to push ahead with the referendum would not have succeeded absent two crucial forms of "bottom-up" participation. A new movement organization, the Committees in Defense of the Referendum (CDRs), formed, providing a large network of volunteers willing to hide the voting urns and ballots from the police and to take them to polling stations in time for voting on October 1. The CDRs also provided the necessary volunteers for the organization of voting and vote counting on the day of the referendum. The police entered numerous polling stations and shut down voting in some of them, but the referendum organizers countered by permitting voters to shift to new polling stations. A unified voter list was maintained throughout the day to prevent voters from voting twice and for the most part it seems to have worked, despite the difficulties posed by the widespread police efforts to bring voting to a close.[30] The police efforts to prevent voting from taking place, extensively covered on television, seem to have been counter-productive, motivating many undecided or skeptical Catalans to go to the polls to protest the treatment befalling their fellow citizens who had chosen to vote. Journalists and others reported stories of individuals who decided to vote on the very day of the referendum in response to the police actions that injured many voters inside and adjacent to polling stations. Typically, it is difficult to assess such reports with scholarly rigor, but in this case one source helps to make that possible. A reputable survey by the CEO found that virtually one fifth of the Catalan electorate,

19.9%, reached a decision regarding voting on October 1 during the final three weeks before the referendum, that is, while police efforts to prevent the referendum from happening were underway. A full 7.7% reached a decision regarding voting on the very day of the referendum.[31] The official Spanish governmental efforts to prevent the referendum from taking place backfired badly, increasing both participation in the consultation and, at least temporarily, support for independence.

The pro-independence movement won a large public relations victory on October 1 but little more than that. Although Catalan President Puigdemont and others in the pro-independence movement tried to frame the outcome as a clear statement of the Catalan people in favor of independence, the reality was that a majority of those eligible to vote had chosen not to do so, acting in congruence with the opposition's call to boycott the voting. Roughly 10% of those who did vote had opposed independence. In the emotional climate of a referendum that was successfully held despite the fact that it had been legally prohibited, the pro-independence forces once again fell well short of the crucial threshold of 50% of the Catalan electorate. Equally importantly, it soon became apparent that the proponents of the referendum lacked the infrastructural ability to press forward toward effective independence. Absent the genuine support of a majority of Catalans, the infrastructural capacity to form a new state, and any international recognition, the pathway to independence looked far more questionable than the movement's ability to successfully hold the vote on October 1. It seems likely that some leaders within the independence movement had hoped to make use of the large-scale confrontation to relaunch negotiations with the Madrid government, searching for enhancements in Catalan autonomy instead of full independence. However, it is far from clear how widespread that more or less pragmatic stance was within the leadership circles of the pro-independence forces.

In the turbulent days after October 1, much uncertainty surrounded the path forward for all actors, regardless of their perspective. Numerous firms announced plans to move away from Catalonia in response to this uncertainty and to the danger that Catalonia would be left outside the European Union if it achieved independence. The uncertainties were felt not only in the mass public but also by decision-making elites. On at least two crucial occasions in October, Catalan President Puigdemont announced plans to address the public only to cancel those plans—having changed views on the best course of action to follow. On October 10 the Catalan leadership prepared to issue a unilateral declaration of independence, but instead stepped away from that historic move, issuing a call for negotiations. On the same day, pro-independence parliamentarians personally signed a pledge to build an independent Catalan Republic while opting out of a formal parliamentary vote on the matter. The public handling of the declaration by the Catalan government was so opaque that many observers were left wondering whether independence had or had not been declared. An especially witty Catalan analyst, Pere Rusiñol, remarked on the occasion that the day was truly historic, due to its surrealism.

Spain's Prime Minister, Mariano Rajoy, indicated a willingness to negotiate with Puigdemont if the Catalan President would affirm that independence had not been declared on October 10. Puigdemont's initial reply was somewhat ambiguous, but his second reply on October 19 clearly stated that independence had not been declared. Rajoy was still not satisfied, at least publicly, but rumors circulated of indirect negotiations involving intermediaries. The following week Puigdemont reached a decision to call routine elections to the Catalan parliament within the existing legal structures as a way out of the crisis and in order to avoid the imposition of direct rule by the Madrid government. However moments before issuing the promised announcement, Puigdemont changed plans, citing a lack of guarantees from the Spanish government that the calling of new elections would in fact halt plans of the Rajoy government to make use of the Constitutional provision allowing for direct rule. On Friday, October 27, The Spanish government instituted direct rule through the use of Article 155 of the Spanish Constitution, essentially suspending Catalan self-government. The Catalan parliament then declared independence, as a Republic—with most opposition deputies walking out in protest. Making use of direct rule powers, the Spanish government called new Catalan elections for December 21.

In the interval between October 27 and December 21, the Catalan leadership, now legally removed from its position of institutional power in the Generalitat, was unable to make any progress in its pursuit of independent status. Much of the pro-independence leadership was arrested, charged with sedition and rebellion, two crimes that involve the use of violence to subvert the state and that carry long jail sentences. Those accused were jailed, in many cases without bail. Puigdemont left Spain secretly during the weekend after the independence declaration and reappeared in Belgium, announcing plans to remain there to avoid arrest. The Spanish government encouraged all political forces to participate fully in the December 21 elections and despite some doubts, all did so. But the top leadership of the pro-independence forces was either in jail or outside Spain hoping to avoid arrest. The election campaign took place under highly unconventional circumstances. Much of what happened during the fall of 2017 seems to fit the lament of Jordi Amat (2017) that multiple political forces, including prominent leaders on both sides of the independence question, had behaved quite irresponsibly. But the problems that had come unmistakably into public view involved more than irresponsibility. They involved matters that strike to the core of democratic practice.

In response to the imposition of direct rule over Catalonia by the Spanish government and the jailing of many pro-independence leaders, many Catalans turned to militant forms of protest. The CDRs re-emerged as committees for the defense of the Republic—instead of the referendum—leading militant supporters of independence in frequent street and highway blockages. On one occasion train lines connecting Catalonia to the rest of Spain and to France were blocked by demonstrators. However, attention soon turned to the campaign for the December 21 elections. On this occasion the supporters of independence ran three separate lists instead of two; the principal parties inside Junts pel Sí ran separately. The results gave pro-independence forces a slightly reduced absolute majority of parliamentary seats. However, with Puigdemont in Belgium and many other pro-independence leaders in jail, forming a government proved more difficult than under conventional circumstances. The strongly anti-independence party Ciudadanos had actually received more votes than any other single party, but it had no plausible path to governing, lacking the ability to win a vote of governmental investiture in a parliament where pro-independence forces held a majority of seats. On May 14, nearly five months after the elections had taken place, a rather secondary leader of the independence movement, Quim Torra, was narrowly chosen by parliamentary deputies as the new President of the Generalitat. Opposition deputies criticized him for statements he had made that used derogatory terms to refer to Spaniards and Spanish speakers. The independence movement had managed to formally elect a new governmental leader, but his past statements raised concerns of continuing polarization. The change of government in Madrid in June 2018 reopened hopes that some sort of accommodation might be possible.

An ultimate but revealing irony of the crisis deserves mention. Many actors on both sides of the divide over independence have accused their adversaries—on the other side—of carrying out a "coup" against democracy.[32] Both sides profess strong loyalty to democracy and complain that their adversaries have violated fundamental principles of free and representative polities. These mutual charges can be seen in part as a reflection of the segmented and often exclusionary view of democracy that has predominated in Spain—leaving many expressions of sentiment and forms of action outside prevailing understandings of democracy. A broad and inclusionary understanding of democracy allows political actors to sharply criticize their adversaries without questioning their democratic rights or alleging that they seek to eliminate government by and for the people. In this case both sides have multiple grounds for complaint, but neither side has eliminated the central and defining institutions of democracy—carrying out a "coup." The magnitude of the crisis and the mutual charges that the other side is guilty of a "coup d'état" suggest just how serious the consequences of restrictive and segmented democratic practice can become. Most of this book analyzes the impact on democratic depth and societal outcomes of variation among democracies in their inclusion of socio-economically marginal actors. This chapter examines the consequences of a deep-seated tendency to exclude cultural "others," and their aspirations, from fully legitimate status in institutionalized political life. This tendency has led to an unnecessarily deep crisis and to new shortfalls in democratic authenticity and consolidation. Spain remains a democracy, but the jailing without bail of numerous political leaders has clearly impinged upon the normal functioning of democratic life. Just as troubling is the de facto loss of mutual tolerance among political adversaries—a possible sign of the deconsolidation of democracy. It remains uncertain where the crisis will lead, but its consequences for democracy have been deep and potentially dangerous.

 | # Change or Continuity in Cultures?
Theorizing the Iberian Peninsula Experience

I. Introduction

The central claim of this book concerns cultural legacies of historical change and their ability to shape political and social outcomes long after the triggering historical processes have faded away into distant memories. In that sense, the book is premised on the assumption that culture has staying power. Yet at the same time the story of democracy in the contemporary Iberian Peninsula is replete with episodes of cultural change and innovation. In the scholarly community that studies such questions, contemporary students of culture are virtually unanimous in rejecting the old essentialist conception, which assumed that somehow cultures automatically and unfailingly reproduce themselves, thereby generating unchanging differences between countries. That view has nonetheless more or less survived among some social scientists who focus primarily on other substantive areas— helping to explain why some scholars implicitly or explicitly assume the existence of a centuries-old Iberian cultural "essence" that somehow unites Spain and Portugal (Wiarda, 1989). Clearly, the argument about democratic practice presented here is thoroughly at odds with such claims. This book's argument is as much about cultural change—in the first instance in the context of the 1970s transitions to democracy—as about continuity, thus it is thoroughly incompatible with the essentialist view, but underscoring that point does not resolve the difficult question of how we conceptualize and explain instances of change and of continuity in cultures; it simply opens the door to seriously taking up a very large and complex question. In this chapter I focus on identifying causal mechanisms that can account for instances of cultural change and continuity, and search for their manifestations in the two cases studied here.

Before we turn to instances of cultural change and continuity in the Portuguese and Spanish cases, as well as mechanisms that can help account for them, I offer a few general considerations on the theoretical effort to grapple with the dynamics that lead to cultural change or continuity. This brief discussion is not intended to review or address the overall corpus of theoretical work on this question; the goal is simply to pose a few considerations that are intended to be helpful in our examination of the tension between dynamics of change and continuity in the democratic practice of the Iberian Peninsula neighbors. One fundamental theoretical point should be underscored at the outset: Many cultural phenomena may thrive as predominant understandings, expressive "scripts," or forms of practice within social contexts of widely varying scale: within a society as a whole or only within more restricted circles—often seen as "subcultures."[1] This is certainly the case for religious practice, gender norms, and household practices—recently theorized by Esping-Andersen and Billari (2015) as subject to coalescence in "multiple equilibria"—and many other objects of social research. Democratic practice is somewhat different from such cultural phenomena because it concerns the interactions or hoped-for interactions among all of the actors of relevance in a free and representative political system. Forms of democratic practice, and the understandings that underpin them, are inherently *relational* in their implications, and they typically aim to define actors' conduct at the systemic level of national democracies writ large—that is to say not only within subcultural venues. A country's predominant understanding of democratic practice may presume that most political conduct takes place in venues that are segmented by institutional, hierarchical, or ideological position; such divisions do not necessarily imply active contestation over the definition of the whole, the shared conception of the polity. Where such contestation does take place it signifies the existence of cultural conflicts over predominance within shared national political space.

Whereas various forms of socio-cultural segmentation—for example in the religious sphere—are compatible with the de facto retreat of societal segments into their own subcultural spaces for the exercise of their autonomy, in the instance of segmented democratic practice it seems more likely that the segments will ultimately meet in cultural and political "battle" of some type in the shared space of nationwide democratic governance and interchange. Those cultural and political battles may take numerous forms—in the streets, in other public venues, or within mainline political institutions. The massive anti-war demonstrations in the streets outside the

1968 Democratic Convention in Chicago, the recurring conflicts in Spain between demonstrators and governmental authorities over the availability of symbolically central spaces for protest activities, sharp disagreements within the Spanish parliament over the legitimacy of the forces present in the chamber, and as a result over the acceptability of various mathematically feasible coalitional majorities, and difficult conflicts within the Socialist Party (PSOE) over how to handle and resolve strategic disagreements about potential alliances with political "outsiders"—all of these episodes of conflict are examples of the types of cultural and political battles that are likely to ultimately emerge in free and representative political systems characterized by segmented democratic practice. A relatively less conflictual arena is found where the cultural assumptions and forms of practice constituting democratic practice are quite widely shared—either because all major actors accept the validity of segmentation by hierarchical or institutional position or—alternatively—because the political arena is generally understood to be *inclusionary*. This is not to say that nationally shared forms of democratic practice are likely to be conflict-free, but where the predominant form of democratic practice is highly inclusionary, as in Portugal, political conflicts—even those that pit relatively powerless outsiders against powerful veteran political insiders—typically take the form of "conversation" (Fishman and Everson, 2016) instead of confrontation.

Thus whereas some matters within society may be collectively handled through the reproduction of subcultural patterns that are dominant within rather separate worlds, the segments of a country divided over democratic practice are not so easily kept separate; their actions may lead to rather visible conflicts over the place that voices of discontent—and their political representatives—can legitimately occupy in national political life. In Spain, for much of the post-Franco democratic period demonstrators in the streets and representatives inside official institutions thought of their conduct as constituting two quite separate worlds. The system's segmentation was generally accepted, with relatively little thought given to the possibility of reconfiguring the unwritten cultural rules conditioning political life. However, several major episodes of change in forms of political participation have reopened the question of how the boundaries of inclusion and conduct should be drawn. The country's democratic practice is still segmented—given the tendency of some crucial political forces to define historically marginal actors and forms of conduct as unworthy of inclusion in the polity's central conversation. But the new form of segmentation is contestatory. The definition of rules of inclusion is now subject to ongoing political and cultural conflict. Internal divisions within the PSOE over the selection of negotiating partners in the search for a governing majority after the elections of 2015 and 2016 served to underscore the practical significance of such conflict. Even in the context of cultural change, the system continues to be segmented. At the same time in Portugal many types of cultural innovation or evolution in the political sphere end up simply fine-tuning, but not challenging, the deeply inclusionary character of the country's post-revolutionary democratic practice. Some changes fail to alter the logic of the systems where they take place.

The analysis of Mahoney and Thelen (2009), two historically minded and theoretically oriented social scientists who have done important work on institutional change, proves quite helpful. In their argument, the evolution and transformation of institutions is driven not only by the major exogenous shocks that scholars have long seen as crucial to the modification of sociopolitical or economic structures but also by endogenous dynamics linked to the normal functioning of institutions themselves. Those endogenous dynamics are multiple in their analysis; they include the agency of institutional leaders and activists and their struggles over power, ideas, and interests (1–37). Despite the differences between institutional and cultural analysis, the overlaps are significant and this approach proves to be helpful.

The Tocquevillean approach to the culture of politics provides highly complementary insights. Although many culturally oriented readers of Tocqueville focus heavily on his emphasis on "mores" or "habits of the heart" in his analysis of American democracy, I see an even deeper and more pervasive relevance in his discussion of the role of French philosophers and abstract thinkers in the radicalization of French political thought and action in the Revolution. Tocqueville's claim in his overarching comparison of France and the United States is that underlying human grievances and concerns may be either activated and channeled by political actors, or left more or less dormant. When human dissatisfaction *is* politically activated, it is system-wide political structures that play a decisive role in determining what type of actor is available for that decisive role. Thus in Tocqueville's analysis the contrast between pragmatically oriented and often locally focused politics in the United States and nationally oriented ideological politics in France was driven by the fact that the only space available for free political action and critique in ancien regime France was the intellectual arena in which the abstract thought of philosophers and "men of letters" predominated. In Tocqueville's conception of the United States, the American system provided considerable opportunities for pragmatically oriented local leaderships to develop with quite un-ideological framings of the issues on which they sought to mobilize people. From Tocqueville's perspective, the cultural framing of dissatisfaction in the two democracies was configured by the structural factors that determined what type of political actor would activate and channel dissatisfaction.

This side of Tocqueville—his theorization of ways in which the structure of political power helps to drive the socio-political "selection" of actors who operate within or even *against* (Goodwin, 2001) the system—points to the importance of understanding how political leaderships are socio-historically "selected" to play that function, and how the outcome of that process in turn helps to shape the cultural framing of much political life. More recent work (Valenzuela, 1991) has advanced considerably beyond Tocqueville in specifying determinants of the socio-historical "selection" of political leaderships, but Tocqueville's underlying insight remains of central importance. The historical selection or re-selection of competing national political leaderships—for example, in what I have called the "coda" of the Spanish transition—helps to shape the cultural course of political life in Spain, Portugal, and elsewhere. But whether cultural patterns persist or are transformed is not only a function of the selection of new leaderships. The balance between cultural continuity and change may be influenced by many other factors including the changing nature of the problems confronted by those leaderships. If we are interested above all in understanding outcomes—in this case the staying power or transformation of the nationally predominant forms of democratic practice theorized in this book—we have no choice but to cast a wide explanatory net that seeks to incorporate both exogenous and endogenous drivers of outcomes, that is to say sources of influence that can be seen as both external and internal to the cultural repertoires that we want to understand.

In a broader sense, the forging of connections between historical experience and cultural legacies clearly requires a great deal of work by cultural actors who select, interpret, narrate, and employ elements of the past. The important scholarship of della Porta and her collaborators in a cross-national study of how legacies of the past shape protest movements (della Porta et al., 2018) contributes significantly to this goal. Many of the effects identified in this book would not have taken shape without cultural work by actors who sought to build and sustain a living basis for tying the past to the present. The experiences of the Iberian Peninsula neighbors—embracing episodes of both cultural continuity and change—provide a great deal of material for examining how such work, and the broader substance of political life, contribute to cultural continuities or change. We turn next to an especially important example of cultural work that has helped sustain the living importance of the past in Portugal—the annual commemorations of the Carnation Revolution.

II. *Commemorating April and Continuities in Practicing Its Lessons*

The commemoration of Portugal's April 25 Revolution of 1974 provides an immense example of how large public rituals can contribute to both the reproduction of existing cultural practices and the breadth of their acceptance. This large enterprise forms part of the broader set of efforts of many Portuguese actors to mobilize memories of the Estado Novo dictatorship and the revolution as a foundation for confronting contemporary political challenges (Loff, 2014). The amount of cultural energy that goes into annually retelling the story of April, identifying its lessons, and underscoring its implications—for democracy and for Portugal—is difficult to fully transmit. The social and political breadth of involvement in the robust annual program of commemorations is quite staggering. A simple documentary reflection of the magnitude of the undertakings is provided by the 754-page volume published by the April 25 Association in 1996, listing all of the commemorative activities that had taken place in 1994 on the Revolution's twentieth anniversary (Associaçao 25 Abril, 1996). The organizers of those activities—and of the annual commemorations in subsequent years—include political office holders, civil society organizations, and activists of all sorts. Indeed the commemorations thoroughly blend together actions and actors located in official representative institutions and others firmly rooted in civil society. Just as the Portuguese pathway to democracy frayed the boundary between actions inside and outside the bounds of official institutions, so too do the commemorative activities.

A core feature of the annual program is a commemorative session of parliament,[2] which provides the occasion for representatives of the political parties present in the chamber and other institutional leaders—such as the country's popularly elected president—to make well-crafted speeches identifying the achievements of the revolution and their significance for contemporary Portugal. In this special parliamentary session, which is broadcast live on television, red carnations, revolutionary-era songs, and other symbols of the revolution are featured along with the carefully chosen words of political leaders. Unsurprisingly, the central features of the social revolution are more strongly underscored by representatives of parties on the Left than by those on the Right of the country's political spectrum. Thus, in 2008 it was José Soeiro, the speaker chosen to represent the Bloco de Esquerda, a political formation located to the left of the Socialists, who remarked, "Democracy is the strongest answer against all forms of domination—in the space of enterprises, schools, families, sexuality . . . [I]f there is one thing that April 25 teaches us it is that it is always possible to change everything."[3]

Many remarks by other political leaders and offered in other years have articulated socio-political commitments similar to those of this evocative call to remember the essence of the Revolution's overturning of multiple hierarchies. At the close of a long substantive address during the 2004 commemorative session, the country's Socialist President, Jorge Sampaio, offered the following summary of lessons of the Revolution: "The fragilities, the blockages, the errors of democracy are, therefore, corrected with more democracy, more participation, more initiative, more mobilization, more citizenship" (Sampaio, 2006: 46). Yet from a certain point of view it is the statements made by representatives of the center-right Partido Social Democrata (PSD) that hold the greatest interest, for it is their cultural expressions that ensure the wide political breadth evident in the annual celebration of the Revolution. The PSD speakers often articulate support for social commitments and a participatory understanding of democracy—linking those views to the legacy of April. Much of the discussion in earlier chapters suggests that these claims actually have a resonance with ongoing practice; the PSD has often been supportive of participatory budgeting (PB) initiatives and other efforts to encourage enhanced citizen participation. Through the memory of the April Revolution, even the country's principal center-right party puts such commitments in a historically grounded light, celebrating them as constitutive of the country's understanding of democracy. In 2004 Victor Cruz, the PSD representative who spoke at the commemorative session, declared, "Never was politics so close to poetry as in April."[4] Other remarks by PSD leaders that year, and in other years, have underscored that party's commitment to remembering and honoring the memory of April. In April 2004, José Manuel Durao Barroso, at the time Prime Minister—a position he left later that year to become President of the European Commission—remarked to television reporters after the ceremony that he identified with the message delivered by the country's Socialist President, Jorge Sampaio, and that in any event April 25 was not an occasion for emphasizing partisan differences.[5] The country's Left has consistently dedicated more energy than the Right to cultivating the memory of revolution, but the commitment to a minimum set of revolutionary symbols and principles extends well to the right of the Portuguese center.

Much in the conduct of the commemorative parliamentary sessions continues on with little change from year to year, but small modifications of one sort or another are regularly introduced. In the first austerity-era commemoration under a PSD government, the 2012 anniversary of April

25, center-right deputies made more extensive use of red carnations than their party's representatives had in the past, and many other symbols of the Revolution were given prominence. In that year's commemorative session of parliament, large screens projecting the image of speakers at the podium were placed on both sides of the speaker's dais. These screens enhanced the visibility of the "performance." Crucially, before the speeches began, the screens were used to display a constantly changing succession of photographs of key scenes from the 1974 Revolution. These photos conveyed the essence of popular involvement, of mass-level enthusiasm, and of the challenge to existing hierarchies, at least as forcefully as the words later spoken from the dais. The prominent public use of photographs of the original April 25 has been a constant in the annual commemorations, and in 2012 the leaders of the parliamentary chamber, controlled at that time by a right-of-center majority, chose to make use of them. Two years later, in April 2014, the same parliamentary majority—still wedded to the politics of austerity—had done away with the photos on the large screens adjacent to the speakers' dais, but virtually all of the other elements of the performance controlled by those actors continued on as before.

However, one important component of the event not under the control of the PSD did change quite fundamentally. The surviving "Captains of April," united in the April 25 Association, had requested the right to speak at the parliamentary event in order to make public their denunciation of the externally imposed austerity policies and—in the view of the Captains—the loss of national sovereignty that the 2011 bailout package represented. Arguing that the Captains had not been part of the program of speakers in the past, and that they had long exercised their "voice" in other ways and venues, the PSD President of the Assembly of the Republic denied their request. This led the Captains to boycott the special session of parliament and to hold an alternative event that same morning on the Largo do Carmo. Mário Soares and several other prominent political leaders supported the Captains, joining in their boycott and in the alternative event they had organized. This was not the only change in commemorative activities that year, but at its core the commemorative session of parliament continued on as before, making use of numerous symbols of the Revolution, celebrating its memory, and offering political leaders of all parties present in the chamber an opportunity to publicly articulate its enduring significance. The changes that took place that year were more evident in the streets.

Indeed, the commemorations in the streets are perhaps even more creative and significant than the parliamentary session. The annual demonstration in the heart of downtown Lisbon, organized by the April 25 Association and supported by parties and movements extending from the Socialists left-ward, succeeds in weaving together memories and symbols of the revolution, implications and slogans for contemporary political life, and representations of the country's national and folk identity. Members of associations of military officers and policemen demonstrate alongside militants in Left and far-left parties. Portuguese residents of rural areas dressed in traditional Alentejan folk outfits participate along with recent immigrants and their supporters. The demonstration typically articulates a mix of goals and principles including distinctively Portuguese ones and others that are thoroughly universalistic. A common slogan, shouted repeatedly year after year, is "Somos muitos mil per continuar Abril" "We are many thousands for continuing with April." Other more or less predictable slogans, honoring the 25th of April and opposing dictatorship, are annually repeated, but every year there are new and fresh slogans added to the mix along with the old ones. Even in reproducing the memory of April and its lessons, this large commemorative endeavor leaves much space for micro-level cultural change and innovation. In 2016 a young demonstrator held aloft a creative sign reading "A Rua esta na Poesia," in effect inverting the message of artist Vieira da Silva's classic revolutionary-era posters which read "A Poesia esta na Rua." The 2016 assertion that the "The Streets are in the Poetry" could be read as suggesting that in difficult economic times the social energy of the revolution can be preserved more easily in the cultural sphere than elsewhere.

Slogans emphasizing the social commitments of the Constitution and that document's roots in the Revolution have also gotten increased play in austerity-era commemorations. Demonstrators in this and other related events have also focused quite directly on their critique of austerity and the Troika, alongside their call for a renewal of national sovereignty in decision-making. The memories of April have served to orient and frame contemporary grievances and demands—a point that has been underscored in other recent research (Baumgarten, 2017; Fernandes, 2017).

New events are regularly added to the list of commemorative activities, and in Lisbon many of them have taken place on the Revolution's symbolically central Largo do Carmo. In 2014 an unofficial social movement event took place on that square late on the evening of April 24. This initiative was organized primarily through a Facebook call for participation under the heading "All rivers flow to *Carmo.*" Among the groups participating in the protest-commemorative "happening" was the anti-austerity social movement "Que se lixe a Troika" (QSLT), roughly translatable as "Screw the Troika." For a period of more than two hours, columns of demonstrators organized by one or another left-wing movement or party entered the square, leading chants there. Many supporters joined in the commemorative demonstration in the plaza itself. The focus of this event was on the effort to link the memory of April, and the contemporary re-dedication to its message, with opposition to externally imposed austerity. The slogans chanted by participants and transmitted by their banners and signs likened austerity to another dictatorship, criticized the Troika, and called for keeping "April" alive and for "another April." The overall undertaking was as much a commemoration as a demonstration,[6] but that duality in and of itself was not really new, even if the form taken *was*. The annual commemorative demonstration in the streets of central Lisbon every April 25 in the afternoon had long mixed these two genres.

The use of the Largo do Carmo for the event was also not new, even though the Internet-era organizing strategy for the event did break new ground. For example, ten years earlier, the square was the scene of two quite different commemorative efforts. In the afternoon and evening of April 23, 2004, immigrant associations gathered there to mark the Revolution's thirtieth anniversary and to collectively pass on its message to a new generation—the young children of the immigrants. For several hours the immigrants listened to songs and commentaries while also mingling with one another and enjoying food and drink. The crowd joined in singing "Grandola"—collectively taking on the Portuguese shared memory of liberation from dictatorship through revolution. At around midnight a large birthday cake was taken onstage and the young children of the immigrants were brought alongside it to sing together "Happy Birthday" to April 25 on the revolution's thirtieth anniversary. The next evening the same plaza was used by the youth group of the right-of-center PSD for its commemorative celebration of April. That event was less marked by revolutionary symbols than the immigrants' gathering one day earlier, but the very presence of the PSD youth group on the Largo do Carmo, the symbolic center of the Carnation Revolution, carried meaning.

The emphasis of those two 2004 commemorative events on young people was not in any sense exceptional. The effort to teach young people the story and meaning of the country's revolutionary liberation from dictatorship has absorbed a great deal of cultural energy, year after year. A long list of books aim at telling the story of April to children. In the most academically distinguished and substantively developed exemplar of the genre, a team led by the social theorist Boaventura de Sousa Santos published a text for use by school teachers, offering numerous ideas about how to transmit the message of April to school children (De Sousa Santos et al., 2004). A key element of the thirtieth anniversary celebrations in 2004 was the painting of a large mural by adolescents. Public opinion research by Portuguese social scientists shows that this massive effort has been quite successful (Costa Lobo, Costa Pinto, and Magalhaes, 2016). In survey work carried out in both 2004 and 2014 these scholars found that a large majority of Portuguese respondents view April 25 positively and identify with its legacy. Crucially, the percentage holding this view remained virtually unchanged in 2014 after ten years that included quite difficult economic times. The long and deep economic crisis had not altered conceptions of the Carnation Revolution and its continuing relevance. Moreover, the identification with April 25 was virtually the same across age cohorts. The attempt to transmit the meaning of the Revolution to people too young to have personally experienced it directly has succeeded, according to the available survey research.

The breadth of cultural efforts involved in telling the story of April is quite staggering, especially for a country of only ten million people. In what has certainly been the most widely viewed cultural representation of the Revolution, the film star Maria de Medeiros directed a lively movie-length reenactment of the key events with personal vignettes mixed into the narrative. Her movie, *Captains of April* (also translated as *April Captains*) was originally released in Portugal in the year 2000, but it has had a long "shelf life" within the country and has been repeatedly shown in movie theaters, in schools, and on national television around the time of the commemorations. In one of the frequently shown promotional trailers for the film, the movie's leading hero, Maia—a fictional adaptation of the historical Captain Salgeiro Maia—admonishes a hierarchical superior in the military who, in the early moments of the uprising in the Santarem barracks, asks him to obey an order to abandon the rebellion. In his emphatic response, Maia insists that sometimes it is necessary to *disobey*. Maia's declaration has been repeated time and again on Portuguese television in advance publicity for the broadcasting of the film and is, of course, also featured in the movie itself. In celebrating and remembering the Revolution, the Portuguese have reminded themselves of the historical and ethical value of disobedience.

Some of the ongoing efforts to remember and reaffirm the meaning of the Revolution have been musical. Songs associated with April 25 and its mobilizational aftermath have been sung in parliament and in the streets during commemorations—as noted earlier. Special concerts of revolutionary-era songs, broadcast on television, have also played a prominent role in the annual tributes to the story of April 1974. A popular and humorous protest-folk musical band, Homens da Luta, has performed politically charged songs in attire, and with red carnations, intended to call to mind April 25 and the commemorations in the streets. Their 2011 song, "A Luta e Alegria"

("The Struggle Is Joy") was, in effect, a musical demonstration against the external imposition of austerity, calling on people to resist through protest movements. In a reflection of the preferences of members of the public who participated in the selection process, this protest song was chosen in 2011 as the country's official representative in the annual Eurovision song contest—held shortly after Portugal was forced to accept the negotiation of a bailout agreement that involved harsh austerity measures. The selection by the Portuguese public of a song that celebrates protest demonstrations stands as a strong reflection of the broader processes analyzed here. The memory of April 25 has been deeply incorporated within the country's popular culture and self-conception.

It seems quite evident that the massive cultural effort involved in telling and *celebrating* the story of April—and in articulating its significance—has played a major role in reproducing the country's inclusionary post-revolutionary democratic practice. Crucially, the commemorations—and related efforts at sustaining the collective memory of the 1974 events—have been characterized by a combination of *breadth* of support and (at least for the most heavily committed actors) *depth* of commitment. Moreover, the commemorative project has effectively spanned the divide between official public institutions and civil society—involving both in the large collective effort. In contrast in Spain, efforts to commemorate crucial episodes in the country's transition to democracy have been as segmented as the country's democratic practice itself. Political elites have commemorated the elections of 1977—the first of the new democratic period—and the approval of the Constitution in a national referendum held on December 6, 1978. The events honoring those two mileposts in the democratic transition have been largely limited to the country's representative institutions. Political and social sectors located outside the circles of power have honored other dates and memories with commemorative activities. For example, the fortieth anniversary of the January 1977 massacre of left-wing labor lawyers in a politically prominent anti-Francoist law office on the Calle Atocha in Madrid was the subject of several commemorative events in 2017 in that city. Among the events was the presentation of a new work of oral history that artfully traces out the interconnections between the lives of three protagonists of the Atocha Street law office, all now prominently involved in politics.[7]

In Spain's multi-national periphery, Catalan and Basque nationalists have mobilized their supporters to honor days and events of historical significance for their movements. These mobilizations of Catalan and Basque nationalists are carried out annually, but clearly participation is limited to those who identify with the nationalist cause, and the dates that are collectively remembered are totally unrelated to the democratic transition of the 1970s. Other transition-related commemorations that have taken place in Spain have been held somewhat sporadically rather than annually. In breadth of involvement and intensity of effort on the part of those involved, Spanish commemorative activities focused on the democratic transition are not in any way comparable to those of Portugal. Moreover, the limited commemorative projects that have emerged in Spain have not been able to effectively span the divide between representative institutions and socio-political action located outside their bounds.

To sum up, shared commemorative symbols, rituals, and events in Portugal help to sustain and reproduce that country's historically rooted inclusionary democratic practice. Widespread participation in the annual commemorations solidifies broad-based identification with the legacies of revolution and reminds political actors of lessons to be learned. The absence of anything similar in Spain, and that country's more compartmentalized collective memory, are associated with an institutionally and hierarchically segmented form of democratic practice. The way the two societies remember and treat memories of their 1970s transitions is congruent with their forms of democratic practice and plays a role in sustaining the underlying logic of that practice in both cases. The Portuguese commemorations are supportive of a way of understanding democracy, and of forms of conduct, that are highly inclusionary—and that span across demarcations that delimit political life in some other democracies. Spanish commemorative endeavors are as segmented as the country's democratic practice and fail to provide any basis for a genuinely broad and expansive understanding of the essence of democracy—capable of drawing together in one cohesive conversation the diverse actors that populate the country's contemporary democracy. Innovative cultural endeavors dealing with the past are easily fitted into this existing logic in both cases and, therefore, innovations—even those of new actors, as we will see in the next section—have failed to fundamentally change either country's prevailing form of democratic practice.

III. Dynamics of Cultural Change in Spanish Politics

Despite the limitations of Spanish democratic practice, the country's political life has been characterized by a recurring capacity for cultural change of various sorts—a theme that merits our attention and analysis. Some instances of cultural innovation, challenging dominant conceptions, have been small in scale, at least initially. The movement to exhume the bodies left in mass graves of the Republic's fallen soldiers (and supporters) during the civil war began in that manner, and localized attempts to handle political challenges in novel ways—as in the case of the Andalusian town of Marinaleda (Fishman and Everson, 2016)—also deserve mention. The first partial breakdown of Spain's dominant form of democratic practice at the system-wide level after the transition's "coda" in 1982 occurred in March 2004 as a result of a major exogenous shock.

The tragic terrorist incident on March 11, 2004, the next to last day of the period legally set aside for campaigning in advance of elections scheduled for March 14, touched off a series of extraordinary political events and mobilizations. The massive loss of life forced an abrupt end to the campaign and brought the country as a whole to a state of collective grief—and concern. The quick and premature end to the campaign closed off institutionalized channels for expressing political sentiments and communicating them to others. Long established ways of appealing to the public in the closing period of an electoral campaign were shut off just when new expressive needs arose and assumed great significance—especially due to the Partido Popular (PP) government's effort to erroneously attribute responsibility for the attack to ETA instead of Al Qaeda. Most observers assumed that attribution of the attack to ETA would benefit the Right electorally, whereas attribution of the attack to Al Qaeda was likely to benefit the Left opposition that had been critical of the government's active support for the American war in Iraq. Political activists improvised two innovative responses intended to critique the government for politically manipulating news of the event: micro-demonstrations within the large official demonstration held in major cities the day after the attack, and new demonstrations against the ruling PP the next day, on the official day of reflection when campaigning was prohibited (Sampedro, 2005, 2008; Fishman, 2007). These un-institutionalized forms of protest attracted great attention—conveying the sense held by millions of Spaniards that the PP had tried to foster an erroneous view of the attack in order to sway voters' choices.

Activists using rapidly improvised tactics were implicitly encouraging other Spaniards to vote for the Socialist candidate, Jose Luis Rodriguez Zapatero. Zapatero's surprise victory on March 14 was in a sense as much a social movement event as an electoral outcome. Many of Zapatero's first-term initiatives at least to some degree attempted to pursue the goal of cultural change, while broadening and deepening Spanish democracy in various ways (Encarnacion, 2008; Field, 2010; Sánchez-Cuenca, 2012). Themes that had been kept off the political agenda were taken up, and existing debates were addressed in new ways. Zapatero's government withdrew Spanish troops from Iraq, legalized same-sex marriage, increased social spending in support of families and individuals, and ultimately passed a Law of Historical Memory that created a legal foundation for removing symbolic tributes to the Francoist past from public places. Zapatero also engaged in dialogue with peripheral nationalists, leading to the marked success of the new 2006 Statute of Autonomy for Catalonia, which seemed to largely resolve the region's status question—until the Statute was declared partially unconstitutional in 2010. In the economy the government introduced some space for policy debate between orthodox and neo-Keynesian perspectives (Ban, 2016), before the pro-austerity U-turn of May 2010. Yet Zapatero's government and its initiatives were essentially treated as illegitimate by the country's main rightist party, the PP (Sánchez-Cuenca, 2012).

The first major systemic attempt to culturally transform the handling of deep questions about democracy, national identity, and many other important themes, including individual sexuality, was met by the effort of institutional insiders to treat the whole episode as politically illegitimate. One could scarcely ask for a clearer example of how an effort at cultural innovation—initially rooted in a large exogenous shock—could produce bitter political conflict, reinforcing the segmented character of the country's democratic practice, instead of a system-wide turn toward inclusion. However, the exclusionary tendencies in the country's democratic practice were now subject to contestation. Partisan political conflict had taken a turn toward relatively bitter cultural disagreement over the bounds of inclusion in the system and thus the nature of questions to be legitimately debated within the sphere of institutionalized politics. By the end of his two terms in office Zapatero had in various ways moved back toward earlier forms of more restrictive democratic practice, as is reflected in material discussed in chapters 3 and 5. However, the larger political system was now the scene of cultural conflict over the legitimate bounds of inclusion in political decision-making.

A new major attempt at cultural change emerged in mid-May 2011, when the movement of the *indignados* occupied the central squares of Madrid, Barcelona, and several other cities, offering a comprehensive critique of Spanish democracy and its May 2010 turn toward the politics of austerity under Zapatero. With an initial basis in "alternative" movements that stressed their autonomy from existing institutions, the *indignados* used Internet-era mobilization techniques to channel widespread existing discontent (Flesher Fominaya, 2015; Anduiza, Cristancho, and Sabucedo, 2014). Both their criticisms and their aspirations were quite broad (Ibarra, 2013; Díez Garcia and Laraña, 2018): In their un-institutionalized movement the 15-M activists sought to change the agenda and direction of the country's political system.

For a time they succeeded. The news media treated this mass protest as extremely important, and the early data in public opinion polling and surveys reported at the time in the news media was strongly supportive. Moreover, the creation of new un-institutionalized spaces for collective expression of grievances quickly gave way to a flowering of new expressive forms—and in that sense to much evidence of the popular sentiments that had long gone unexpressed. Citizens spontaneously wrote political messages and demands on small pieces of paper or cardboard and on stones, walls, and bulletin boards in the occupied plazas. It was almost as if a revolution had taken place but in spatial terms it was largely confined to the central plazas—while they were occupied. In a sense, the success of the 15-M movement served to underscore how much citizen discontent had been marginalized by the predominant Spanish form of democratic practice.

The movement itself sought to institutionalize this partially spontaneous expression, channeling individual demands and aspirations into a voting process, choosing among the main ideas for change that had been put forward by participants. This was an extremely important movement, but several qualifications should be introduced: The new forms of activism and expression were quite significant, but they never represented a full overturning of hierarchies within the country's institutions as had happened in revolutionary Portugal. And this large effort at cultural change was quickly countered by political authorities who managed to "clip the wings" of the new movement, limiting the use of the plazas. However, even without a continuing presence in the country's central plazas, the movement aspired to achieve significant change. The aspirations of the *indignados* partly took the form of a reflexive focus on the movement's own practice and partly centered on the goal of fostering new types of civic engagement and participation (Díez García and Laraña, 2018).

The significance of the 15-M movement should be assessed not only by analyzing its impact on the Spanish political system but also through a consideration of its innovative forms of practice and mobilization. The Spanish *indignados* formed part of a broad cross-national family of movements that organized in response to austerity policies and the political systems that implemented them (della Porta, Massimiliano et.al. 2017; Portos Garcia, 2017), but they were an especially innovative exemplar of the broader family of movements. Spanish social protest has shown a repeated capacity to forge creative tactics whether through humor (Romanos, 2013), the innovative use of public space (Fishman, 1990b; 2012a), or in other ways. And this, in turn, has promoted the usefulness of Spanish examples in the development of protest repertoires in other countries (Baumgarten and Diez Garcia, 2017;

Romanos, 2016a). Although Spain has been a laggard in the culture of democratic inclusion, it has been a leader in the development of innovative forms of protest. Yet for Spanish democracy the unavoidable question has been whether this creative capacity would ultimately be matched by an ability to transform the larger political system.

The 15-M movement led to some change in the country's repertoires of contention but did not manage to end the institutional and hierarchical segmentation of the country's democratic practice. Those features were instead reinforced, albeit in new ways, by the institutional response to the movement. With the 15-M movement, Spanish democratic practice moved further toward a strongly contestatory version of segmentation and exclusion. The voices of protest in the streets now aspired to reconfigure the boundaries of inclusion in decision-making; many mainstream actors inside political institutions construed this aspiration as illegitimate and dangerous. Spanish politics now faced a cultural divide over the breadth of inclusion. For the time being the division was still largely structured by the dividing line between representative institutions and the expression of citizen sentiments outside their bounds, but that would soon change. With the emergence in 2014 of Podemos as a new outsider party and a partial heir of the 15-M movement (Fernandez-Albertos, 2015), there was a new actor attempting to promote large-scale cultural change in the country's political life by entering representative institutions and changing them from within, radically expanding the unwritten boundaries of inclusion. Podemos initially criticized the "regime of 1978," implicitly suggesting that its critique was focused on the Constitution approved that year, but from my perspective their underlying political grievances were essentially cultural ones centered on unwritten assumptions about the boundaries of political inclusion. Yet in exactly the same logic as before, new elements of change ended up accentuating the segmentation of democratic practice—and the tendency of many institutional actors to practice a politics of renewed exclusion. Many major political actors framed Podemos as an essentially illegitimate participant in parliamentary life, as a party not available for the formation of a governing parliamentary majority. This tendency was not limited to the Right but could also be found within a sector of the PSOE. The cultural divide over the boundaries of inclusion now conditioned the internal politics of the Spanish parliament and most especially of the Socialists.

The severe internal divisions experienced by the PSOE after the elections of 2015 and 2016, and the triumph in May 2017 of a bottom-up insurgency in the primary election of Pedro Sánchez as Secretary General, offer another instance of cultural change and conflict. For Sánchez himself this victory was a vindication of past endeavors: He had been forced out as party leader on October 1, 2016, as a result of opposition by old-guard sectors of the party to his alliance strategy in parliamentary discussions on the formation of a new government. Sánchez was adamantly opposed to offering tacit support to continuing government by the PP and was more open than many in the party "apparatus" to collaboration with Podemos and peripheral nationalists. Sánchez seemed willing to expand the boundaries of inclusion as a basis for government by the Socialists in a politically fragmented parliament. This last case once again involves conflict *within* the PSOE, conflict that has systemic implications. This conflict within the PSOE is thoroughly congruent with the distribution of attitudes conveyed by the survey data presented in chapter 3. Both those data and the historical record of internal party debates manifest the existence of a fault line within the PSOE over democratic practice. Ultimately that fault line was to foster governmental change. It took just over one year for the 2017 primary victory of Sánchez to produce major systemic consequences.

In May 2018 a Spanish court issued a ruling that was strongly unfavorable to the PP in a corruption case, explicitly questioning the credibility of Prime Minister Rajoy. Sánchez quickly responded by filing a parliamentary motion of no confidence in the sitting government. In the Spanish system, in order to be successful, motions of no confidence require the votes of an absolute majority of parliamentary deputies in favor of an alternative government. A motion of no confidence is in fact a vote on the proposal to seat a new government, and an absolute majority of all members of parliament is required for such a change in government to take place. The makeup of parliament had been decided by the elections held in June 2016. The Socialists once again had two numerically viable routes to governmental power: winning simultaneous support from Podemos on their left and Ciudadanos on their right or gaining the support of Podemos and virtually all of the peripheral nationalists present in the representative chamber. Ciudadanos quickly made it clear that they would oppose the Socialists' motion. A series of newspaper polls had placed Ciudadanos in the lead in citizen preferences, encouraging the leadership of that party to see itself as a plausible party of government in the near future, essentially displacing the Socialists as the primary alternative to the PP. The Socialists' only route to victory was to be the inclusionary strategy of negotiating a basis for support from Podemos and from peripheral nationalists—including Catalan parties in favor of independence.

On this occasion the inclusionary strategy that treated Podemos and pro-independence Catalan nationalists as legitimate, if temporary, allies in parliament succeeded. On June 1, 2018, the Socialists' motion of no confidence in the government of Mariano Rajoy won a majority of votes and Pedro Sánchez became Prime Minister. Why this coalitional strategy succeeded in 2018 after failing in 2016 is a question that will surely be long debated. Several hypotheses are likely to attract the attention of sustained analysis into this question. The accumulation of new grounds for their dissatisfaction with the PP government likely served to motivate both Podemos and peripheral nationalists. The magnitude of the corruption scandals that continued to emerge, primarily affecting the PP, had served as the public rationale for the motion of no confidence and presumably influenced the decisions of political forces on how to respond. But another factor also may have been decisive: the rise of Ciudadanos in public opinion polling threatened the Socialists with the possible loss of their status as the largest alternative to the PP, presented Podemos with a strong competitor for the support of voters searching for political outsiders to somehow change the system, and offered peripheral nationalists the scenario that they most feared. Ciudadanos was strongly committed to recentralizing initiatives, arguing that they were necessary to guarantee all Spaniards equal treatment in matters of policy and law. All of the forces that voted in favor of the Socialists' motion of no confidence had reason to fear the rise of Ciudadanos; this factor may have served as the "glue" that held together the diverse parliamentary coalition that made Sánchez Prime Minister.

Yet however one explains the Socialists' victory in the parliamentary vote on June 1, 2018, the consequences for Spanish politics and for the themes of this book deserve attention. The parliamentary vote making Sánchez Prime Minister was a de facto institutional step in favor of substantially broadening the inclusionary scope of the system. Podemos and peripheral nationalists, including those actively pursuing independence from Spain, were brought into the circles of conversation and negotiation underpinning the formation of a governing parliamentary majority. Crucially, this turn toward inclusion was operationally accepted by the PSOE as such; on this occasion no one sought to oust Sánchez in order to prevent the change from taking place. At least initially this embrace of increased inclusion has been largely limited to the internal politics of parliament itself and other representative institutions, but it seems likely that consequences will soon emerge in other terrains where political conduct is conditioned by understandings of democratic practice. A system-wide turn toward the form of inclusion that characterizes Portuguese democratic practice seems extremely unlikely. With the successful vote of no confidence, Spain entered partially uncharted territory for the post-Franco political system, but the experiences of the Zapatero government offer some basis for analysis. The new Sánchez government with its foundation in a turn toward increased inclusion is likely to face severe challenges to its legitimacy from at least some of its political adversaries.

American politics, after the country's turbulent turn toward increased inclusion in the 1960s, provides a useful example of how the elimination of old forms of exclusion can change political life. In the United States, political competition between electoral adversaries and cultural conflict over the boundaries of inclusion in the polity have grown increasingly interconnected. In such a context political competition and cultural conflict over the legitimacy of collective actors and forms of political conduct cannot be easily separated. The arguments presented here are not intended to deny the significance of material interests, political ambitions, electoral calculations, and the selection of organizational leaderships in forging the course taken by such conflict. Indeed, struggles over power and interests have clearly played a role in promoting or constraining efforts at cultural change in the Spanish case. Cultural factors do not act alone as if in a context devoid of other causal dynamics. But one cannot make full analytical sense out of the life of democratic polities without incorporating cultural factors into the set of explanatory factors of relevance. Cultural factors help to condition the conduct of actors and the assumptions that guide their interactions with others, magnifying or reducing the strength and the convictions that actors would otherwise hold. Where cultural and political forces manage to put in place and reproduce a broadly accepted inclusionary framework for political conduct, as in Portugal, the consequences are multiple in nature as a great deal of material presented in this book makes clear. Where cultural assumptions about the boundaries of inclusion are subject to ongoing political conflict, a variety of cultural phenomena including messages, codes, and frameworks constitute much of the substance of political life. Efforts to win political battles in polities that suffer deep internal divisions over the boundaries of inclusion inevitably involve a strongly cultural dimension.

Ultimately the direction taken by attempts to promote cultural change or regress is determined by complex historical processes. Critical junctures of the sort emphasized here play a crucial role in shaping the directionality of such processes, but history is not limited to such large-scale "turning points" (Abbott, 2001). Democracy is an open system, but cultures can prove more difficult to change than laws. In the final chapter we turn to the theoretical messages offered by the neighboring countries of the Iberian Peninsula and their significance for democracy elsewhere.

 | # Conclusions

*On the Global Significance of the Iberian
Divide in Political Inclusion*

I. Introduction

What do the arguments of this book add up to, in the first instance for our
analysis of the neighboring countries of the Iberian Peninsula, and more
broadly for our understanding of the state of democracy in the contemporary
world? In the pages that follow I address this large two-part query. I focus
first on the book's contribution to understanding observed patterns of political conduct and socio-economic outcomes in Spain and Portugal. In that
context I consider several explanatory alternatives to the argument proposed
here. I then turn to general implications of the contrasts between Portugal
and Spain on which this book focuses. I take up both normative points of
relevance for our conceptualization of how democracies *should* work and
empirically oriented points related to our theoretical understanding of how
democracies *do* work and how they got to be the way they are. In addressing
these issues I bring several other national cases into the discussion. But before doing any of this I first underscore a central lesson of the research.

Scholarly students of democracy have long understood that normative
conceptions of democracy are multiple in number (Held, 1987; Markoff,
1999). Advocates of democratic government have not achieved full consensus
in their views of what democracy should be, although the Schumpeterian
"minimalist" understanding has won general acceptance as a core basis
for defining such systems even if many democratic theorists think that
this conceptualization is only a starting point. This book contributes a key
finding that is directly parallel to that observation. The Iberian divide in

democratic inclusion clearly demonstrates that political actors and at least to some degree national political systems that qualify as democratic by the Schumpeterian standard also differ in their fundamental understanding of what democracy is all about. Whereas Portuguese political actors are fully persuaded that democracy rests on a deep complementarity between the expression of political views inside official institutions and the articulation of citizen preferences outside the bounds of such institutions, mainstream Spanish actors have tended to believe that democracy necessarily involves the sharp separation between those two arenas of political expression: inside parliament and outside in the streets. In this and related ways Spanish and Portuguese political actors have tended to view democracy in different ways and as a result have often conducted themselves in ways that differ by country—reflecting the power of cognitively embedded frameworks. Thus this book shows that in empirical reality actors really do understand democracy in quite different ways and that such contrasts lead to a wide range of consequences in outcomes of real importance. Democratic practice varies across cases and that variation matters.

I have argued that the Iberian Peninsula contrast in democratic practice has its roots in the polar opposite pathways to democracy of Portugal and Spain in the mid-1970s. I link this effect to the mediating role of cultural legacies of national histories and more concretely of the two countries' democratic transition scenarios. Yet at the same time the discussion of cultural change has acknowledged the possibility that such legacies may be subject either to erosion or at least partial reversals as a result of efforts by actors to promote cultural change. I conceive of culture as a powerful causal force that acts in interaction with other factors but not as an unchanging essence that is unmovable and frozen in place once it takes shape. Considering the broadly comparative and normative implications of this paired comparison it seems useful to first review the evidence in favor of these claims and to weigh alternative explanations.

II. Assessing the Argument on Contrasts between Portugal and Spain

Perhaps the most basic objection that could be raised in response to this book's argument would be to question the claim that numerous ultimate outcomes have proved more favorable in Portugal than in Spain. Given the vast number of indicators on which one could focus it is certainly possible to find ways in which Spain has performed better than Portugal during the forty plus years that have passed after the democratic transitions of the 1970s. The Spanish health system is an undeniable achievement of that country's post-Franco system (Guillén Rodriguez and Cabiedades Miragaya, 1998) and by most objective or subjective indicators can be ranked more highly than Portugal's medical system. The Spanish educational system has also made important achievements, especially in its pursuit of egalitarian guarantees of decent education for students from underprivileged backgrounds (Fernández Mellizo-Soto, 2001). For much of the democratic period Spain performed relatively well on distributional measures of income inequality and for some periods of time Portugal performed less well (Huber and Stephens, 2012). Nonetheless, on balance, Portugal's distributional profile is now clearly more egalitarian than that of Spain. When one examines the totality of the available evidence (Perez and Matsaganis, 2018), it seems clear that Portugal has established a better record than Spain in addressing the interests of low-income sectors. The available evidence seems increasingly favorable to the claim that the Portuguese political system has been more attentive than the Spanish political system to the voices of the poor and the socially marginal.

But what of the possibility that alternative explanations can effectively account for this pattern? Two possible explanations for the form taken by Spanish democratic practice deserve consideration. One hypothesis that merits discussion concerns country size and the relative degree of internal diversity of the two Iberian Peninsula cases. Spain is more than four times larger than Portugal in population and, at least in terms of national identity, also much more internally diverse. The Catalan case, taken up in chapter 6, offers an especially valuable way to assess this concern. After all, the population of Catalonia is slightly smaller than that of Portugal and Catalonia is obviously at least somewhat less internally diverse than Spain taken as a whole. Nonetheless, as was discussed in chapter 6, Catalan political actors have tended to follow the predominant Spanish approach to democratic practice even when they are defending perspectives—such as the pursuit of independence—that are thoroughly at odds with the position of mainstream Spanish actors. Our examination of the Catalan case makes it possible to largely reject the attribution of the contrasts between Portugal and Spain to country size or to the degree of internal heterogeneity of the two cases.

Another possible explanation for central features of Spanish democratic practice concerns the legacies and memories of the country's civil war of 1936–1939. This hypothesis involves a factor of undeniable significance for the individual and collective sensibilities of Spaniards. But as the discussion in chapter 2 suggested, there are strong reasons to believe that the meaning that Spaniards have assigned to memories of the civil war was partly conditioned by the transition to democracy and its "coda" in 1982. If the country had experienced a fundamentally different form of democratization due to a "crisis of failure" for the Franco regime or another scenario leading to the breakdown of both state and regime in the context of political change, the memories of civil war would almost certainly have been reconfigured under quite different circumstances. Thus even though the civil war held indisputable importance for Spanish politics, that fact in no way undercuts the causal importance of the contrasting pathways to democracy of Portugal and Spain in the 1970s.

Two alternative explanations also deserve attention in the Portuguese case, both of them hypotheses that have been recently taken up by Tiago Fernandes in important work. Perhaps the more inclusionary record of Portuguese democracy, when it is compared to the Spanish case, can be accounted for either by broad coalitions between Portuguese Socialists, Communists, and Left Catholics in the period prior to the Carnation Revolution (Fernandes, 2017) or by the greater growth of civil society organizations in democratic Portugal than in Spain during the same period (Fernandes, 2015). Both hypotheses raise issues deserving considerable attention. Explanations of political outcomes that focus on the causal force of coalitional arrangements and on the balance of power in civil society have a long tradition of usefulness in the social sciences. However, in this instance neither hypothesis undercuts the causal relevance of the argument advanced here with its emphasis on cultural legacies of pathways to democracy. In both Iberian Peninsula cases coalitional arrangements such as those emphasized by Fernandes could be found in at least some local or regional contexts, but in both cases the pre-existing coalitional arrangements were subject to re-definition in the context of the challenges and conflicts of the transition period. Political challenges or constraints of the two transitions and emergent cultural understandings helped to condition the rearrangement of coalitional patterns once democratization had taken place. The impact of civil society organizations on political life was also conditioned by the cultural legacies of transition: In Portugal even small and resource-poor organizations have won a hearing from elected office holders, but the same has not been the case in Spain (Fishman, 2017). Moreover, important recent work has shown that the strength of civil society involves more than simple organizational capacity as measured in membership or related resources (Riley and Fernández, 2014).

In comparing the trajectory of post-transition political outcomes in Spain and Portugal there is a solid basis for arguing that civil society organizations and coalitional strategies have exerted a causal impact that operates through their interactions with cultural factors. The empirical record is not supportive of any effort to rely on such factors as a substitute for specifying the causal significance of cultural legacies of historical pathways to democracy. Moreover, important research of Jorge Sola on explanations for Spain's wave after wave of labor market deregulation has underscored the inability of causal approaches that emphasize only civil society strength and coalitional arrangements to adequately account for this arena of policy change (Sola, 2013,). Without recourse to the Iberian divide in democratic practice and its cultural roots in the 1970s experiences of democratization it would be terribly difficult to account for the numerous contrasts between Portugal and Spain that are identified here.

III. Assessing the Implications beyond the Iberian Peninsula

Thus the seemingly most significant alternatives to this book's claims on the origins and consequences of the Iberian divide in political inclusion fail to undercut the case presented here. This leaves us with the need to address the comparative and normative implications of the argument for our understanding of democracy in other national cases. I have argued throughout the book that the implications are indeed quite broad-ranging and that the differences between these cases in democratic practice help to elucidate a major dimension of variation among democracies, a dimension that has the potential to strongly condition the extent to which democracies actually fulfill their theoretical promise to afford all citizens with full political equality.

An important normative and operational issue in the understanding of democracy is of great relevance. Portuguese democratic practice assumes that demonstrations form an important part of the political system and that elected office holders should, in principle, be open to conversation with those engaged in public protest. However, some democratic theorists, in the logic underpinning Spain's segmented democratic practice, have tended to assume that it would be unhealthy to subject elected office holders to strong pressures emanating from voices of discontent in the streets. Clearly, demonstrations in the streets can be organized by political forces across the entire political spectrum, including those who harbor anti-democratic or exclusionary aspirations. What, then, is the basis for assuming that the Portuguese pattern holds democratic advantages? The answer is quite simple: Economically and institutionally powerful actors have at their disposal considerable resources and power that they can readily deploy in the effort to influence elected office holders. Their advantages hold the potential to produce an asymmetric playing field in the polity, one that would effectively prevent relatively poor or socially marginal actors from enjoying the benefits of genuine political equality in the complex interactions leading to policymaking and agenda setting. In that context, demonstrations are a highly important instrument of economically *disadvantaged* sectors. A robust form of political equality, capable of contributing to relatively egalitarian distributional outcomes and other marks of inclusionary politics, is for this reason promoted by a type of democratic practice that conceptualizes demonstrations as a central component of the polity's legitimate conversation.

It is also important to address the potential comparative reach of the approach developed here and to examine implications of the argument within the "critical junctures" framework for the study of causality. This book has argued that large-scale historical processes of change leave in their wake culturally rooted legacies that condition ongoing political life and that—as a result—shape numerous ultimate outcomes. The chain of causality runs from national history to cultural legacies that condition democratic political life and finally a series of societal consequences reflective of the degree of political inclusion put in place by national histories. The elements of national history emphasized here concern the path taken from authoritarianism to democracy in the 1970s, but that emphasis is not intended to exclude the parallel significance of *critical antecedents* or of other historical processes and structures. As David and Ruth Collier argued in their landmark contribution to the critical junctures framework, this approach is best understood as probabilistic. It seeks to identify ways in which the experience of countries during crucial historical turning points significantly increases or decreases the odds of various outcomes later in historical time, acting in conjunction or interaction with other relevant variables (Collier and Collier, 1991). In that sense, the approach is thoroughly Weberian, along with a great deal of contemporary social science.

With this understanding of the critical junctures approach, two major questions come into view: How should we conceptualize the causal interaction between the 1970s transitions to democracy and relevant *antecedent variables* such as Spain's civil war of the 1930s, and how can we combine the insights of this book's approach with those of other approaches—such as power resources theory, to name one major framework that certainly can be called on in conjunction with the democratic practice perspective? New work by political scientists Rachel Beatty Riedel and Kenneth Roberts provides a highly useful analytical instrument to address the first question. Riedel and Roberts (2018) differentiate between two types of critical junctures: those that are generative and those that instead activate certain potentialities of the cases under study. Activating junctures operate in a way that is strongly influenced by the role of critical antecedents; generative junctures, in the framework of Riedel and Roberts, do not. It is quite useful to think of the 1970s transitions as representing, in this sense, an activating juncture. Prior to the 1970s the neighboring countries shared the potential for a range of possible outcomes in the field of democratic practice. The memory of civil war was often called on by Spanish political actors during the transition period but always in ways that were conditioned by the political parameters of the transition process. The civil war mattered, but the way in which it mattered was decisively shaped by the country's transition pathway. With a fundamentally different type of transition the politically relevant collective memory of the civil war would have developed in different ways. For a social science that is genuinely concerned with both the drive to theorize and the commitment to understand empirical reality as it really is, there is no alternative to the search for such interactions—and their incorporation into our explanatory conclusions.

How, then, can one combine the democratic practice approach introduced here with other important theoretical frameworks for the explanation of cross-national variation among democracies? Social science methodology obviously offers various ways to examine the relative predictive or explanatory weight of alternative or complementary explanations and to explore the magnitude of the causal interactions at work. Multiple regression and similar techniques are perhaps the most widely used instrument of analysis; once conceptually defined variables—such as types of democratic practice—have been operationalized and research observations have been coded, conventional quantitative approaches can be fruitfully employed in this and similar cases. Comparative historical analysis is, of course, a classic alternative for examining questions such as how culturally defined forms of democratic practice interact with the organizational strength of civil society entities in shaping macro-political outcomes. Charles Ragin's innovative framework for configurative "qualitative comparative analysis" through the use of "fuzzy sets" (Ragin, 2008) offers another important alternative. Social science thrives on the scholarly interchange between practitioners of alternative methodological techniques, but whether in one way or another the key point is to conceive of the democratic practice approach as one that can and should be employed in conjunction with other explanatory frameworks. Culturally rooted understandings of democracy do not, by themselves, determine the resource endowments or organizational strength of political and social adversaries but forms of democratic practice do shape the willingness of powerful actors to provide a hearing to actors that are resource-poor and organizationally weak. There is much work to be done specifying *how* such interactions operate in the real world of democratic politics.

A large question that requires consideration concerns the types of large-scale historical process that may be able to generate effects at least partially similar to those observable in Portugal—where the culturally rooted dominant form of democratic practice is strongly favorable to enhanced political equality and democratic depth. The contrast between Spain and Portugal is intended to clearly establish the existence of a major dimension of variation across national cases, but it is not designed to permit the formulation of one simple continuum of differentiation on which all cases could theoretically be arrayed. The fundamental argument presented here is that national political histories condition the cultural basis for ongoing democratic practice; the linkage between national history and contemporary democratic practice should be a generalized phenomenon, if the argument is valid. But given the large constellation of factors and collective experiences that configure the history of any one national case, there is no reason to assume that all global variation in democratic practice can be reduced to one sole continuum of differentiation. A paired comparison between two carefully chosen cases can establish the existence of an arena of variation that holds wide political significance, but it cannot be expected to fully elucidate all parameters of variation in democratic practice within the universe of all democracies. In-depth work on more cases is necessary to adequately "fill in the map" of all global variation in democratic practice.

IV. *Comparing the Democratic Practice of Spain and Portugal with Greece*

One of the most obvious comparisons of interest in the search for wider implications of the Iberian Peninsula cases is with Greece. After all, the three countries moved from dictatorship to democracy in close sequence in the 1970s (Fishman, 1990a) and comparisons among them have attracted a great deal of scholarly interest—in various studies including Italy as well in the "mix"—especially after pressures for austerity impacted all of southern Europe beginning in 2010. By now, a great deal of published work has argued that the patterns of contention—the existing forms of social mobilization and protester–power holder interaction—in these countries are rooted in cultural understandings embedded in national histories of regime change (Fishman, 2010, 2011, 2012a; Andronikidou and Kovras, 2012; Kornetis, 2013). The scholarship of Kalyvas (2015: 122–123, 126), Andronikidou and Kovras (2012), and

Mavrogordatos and Mylonas (2011) on the Greek case underscores the fundamentally confrontational nature of protester–power holder interactions in that country. Indeed, much of the academic literature on contemporary social discontent in Greece conceptualizes much protest there as "riots," emphasizing the predominance of violence and disorder. The significance of violent and highly disruptive protest in this case is, in at least a superficial sense, congruent with the polarized character of the country's party system with both neo-Nazis and traditional Communists playing a large role in electoral competition. This pattern raises the question of whether Greece's especially confrontational and oppositional form of democratic practice can be accounted for through the explanatory framework introduced here.

Although it is not possible to address this question in depth here,[1] a brief discussion is useful. From the standpoint of the three 1970s south European transitions to democracy, Greece could be construed to occupy a mid-point between Portugal and Spain, not only in the chronological timing of the political change but also in its trajectory and character. The Greek transition was an instance of clear *ruptura* between the dictatorial regime and the newly established democracy but the process of change was not at all revolutionary. As in Portugal, the military was the institutionally key actor, but in the Greek case the Armed Forces acted through the reassertion of the strictly institutional and professional line of command. Unlike Portugal, there was no inversion of hierarchies and no state crisis.

I suggest that the key to placing Greece in the same comparative framework as Spain and Portugal is to differentiate between two dimensions of the contrast. Of course, Greece also differs from the Iberian Peninsula cases in the "critical antecedents" of democratic transition. The highly clientilistic and partially exclusionary nature of the country's post–World War II democracy (Sotiropoulos, 1996) has influenced the contemporary democracy, but the transition itself merits greater emphasis. One dimension of variation in the study of the south European transitions concerns the degree to which actors were subject to transition-related *constraints* on their actions. On that dimension Portugal and Greece appear fairly similar: their transition scenarios minimized the constraints on the actions of key players, leaving them relatively "unencumbered" if compared to their Spanish counterparts, who, for long periods during the transition, were concerned to reduce the danger of hardline efforts to restore Francoist repression. Self-imposed limitations played a greater role in shaping the initiatives of political actors in Spain than in Greece or Portugal. However, the second dimension of variation places Greece and Spain closer to one another—in a position quite unlike that of Portugal. This spectrum of differentiation concerns the extent to which the transition generated an inversion of hierarchies and an intensification of bottom-up social pressures. In Greece, in the absence of a state crisis and as a result of the predominant role of the military hierarchy itself in producing the end of dictatorship, top-down politics remained much more viable than in Portugal. This third case's combination of disencumbered politics for virtually all political actors with the survival of clientelistic methods used by elites to maintain the capacity for a top-down political style, has generated a type of democratic practice that has been even more confrontational and prone to violence in the streets than in Spain.

It is worth mentioning that Argentina, a distant country that experienced a democratic transition remarkably similar to that of Greece on the two dimensions discussed here, has also been subject to an especially confrontational model of democratic practice. The presence of striking parallels between post-transition Argentina and Greece—despite the large differences between these two cases in economic structure and in prior history—lends added weight to the claims made here. Thus it seems quite plausible to argue that the differences in democratic practice between Greece and the two Iberian Peninsula cases are congruent with variation among the cases in their 1970s pathways from dictatorship to democracy. In the Greek case qualitative and historical evidence supports the claim that important elements of political culture and practice have roots in the history of the transition to democracy and its antecedents (Kornetis, 2013). The differences between Greece and the two cases studied in this book lend at least tentative support to the book's argument, but in the absence of a more in-depth coverage of the Greek case that conclusion has to be seen as merely suggestive.

V. Social Reform Efforts and Social Movements: Alternatives to Revolution?

If the key to Portugal's inclusionary democratic practice lies in the historical intertwining of thorough cultural change with a partial inversion of hierarchies during the country's revolutionary transition to democracy, a reasonable question is whether any non-revolutionary cases share with this country that crucial causal configuration. One possibility that deserves consideration is that of the Scandinavian social democracies in which reform movements largely rooted in the working class—but with a broad coalitional strategy—managed to partially reshape both social hierarchies and cultural competences (Esping-Andersen, 1990). Although the trajectories of the social democratic cases are most conventionally understood to reflect the logic articulated by the power resources and power constellations approach, much in the history of these cases may also reflect a political openness of social democratic government to relatively new and initially weakly organized movements, including those focusing on housing (Stromberg, 1992) or on feminist demands (Ohlander, 1992). The social democratic cases of Nordic Europe may well have some elements in common with the postrevolutionary practice of Portugal. This is just what a configurative approach to social science explanation would lead one to expect. Where historical developments placed alongside one another a movement-based challenge to social hierarchies and a successful program of cultural renewal, important consequences followed.

The early 1970s experience of prominent sociologist Gosta Esping-Andersen as a grass-roots activist offers suggestive evidence that appears to support this view—at least in the case of social democratic Denmark. In response to developmental plans to build a large motorway leading into the very center of Copenhagen with likely serious consequences for the urban environment, Esping-Andersen and two fellow graduate students decided to issue a call for a demonstration of bicycle riders opposed to the construction of the new motorway.[2] Their organizational activities in support of the event were largely limited to announcing their plans in the press, calling on a journalist friend for help in this matter. Much to the surprise of the protest organizers, many thousands of bicycle riders joined in the protest. The police offered friendly treatment to those involved, and the official plans to construct the motorway were withdrawn. A small group of activists had initiated events leading to a significant change in urban and transportation policy. Danish democratic practice followed a pattern similar to that now found in Portugal.

But what of the possibility that social movements *themselves* can change the cultural assumptions and practice underpinning democratic political life even in the absence of a polity-wide majority articulated around a social reform party such as the Social Democrats of Scandinavia? Several quite distinguished authors (Tarrow, 1993; Clemens, 1998; Gamson, 1998; della Porta, 1999; Jasper, 2014) have argued that protest movements can do exactly that, and there is much supporting evidence for the claim. Peace movements, the feminist movement, the civil rights movement, and many others have contributed significantly to long-term processes of cultural change with important ramifications in the meta-political assumptions shaping democratic life. There is perhaps no avenue of wider potential cross-national relevance than this one. The plausible capacity of social movements to contribute to cultural change—and thus possibly to the long-term transformation of a country's predominant form of democratic practice—appears to be the most hopeful scenario for a widespread turn toward the inclusionary form of democratic practice found in Portugal. However, there is one fundamental difficulty with this scenario: Social movements can easily promote the growth of counter-movements, and efforts to generate cultural change can do the same. The polity-wide acceptance of many central legacies of Portugal's Carnation Revolution is extremely difficult to duplicate through social movement-induced cultural change. Thus cultural change of the sort made possible by social protest movements can easily lead to ongoing cultural conflict over democratic practice itself rather than widespread consensus in favor of new and inclusionary approaches to politics. Revolutions are distinctive.

VI. *Post-Revolutionary Polities and Democratic Practice*

To what extent is the pattern of democratic practice found in Portugal emblematic of a widespread post-revolutionary way of "doing" democracy? The first analytical distinction that needs to be posed in order to answer that question concerns the difference between political and social revolutions. Strictly political revolutions are substantially more common than social ones, so the effects should be more widespread if political revolutions are able to put in place consequences as significant for democratic practice as those outlined here for Portugal. Della Porta's important new study of the legacies of revolutionary transitions to democracy (2016) makes the case that political revolutions do, in fact, hold significant implications for the conduct of democratic life. However, the effects outlined do not appear to be as deeply inclusionary or significant as the consequences of social revolution in Portugal. Absent the partial overturning of hierarchies that takes place in social revolutions, it is difficult to see how a political revolution can bring about transformation as deep and wide as found in Portugal.

An interesting case of a democracy rooted in part on political revolutionary origins is the United States, notwithstanding the severe limitations in the *authenticity* of early American democracy or semi-democracy (Dahl, 2002). Samuel Huntington's (1981) theorization of American politics—arguably his best and most insightful book—argues that revolutionary-era principles and discourse have provided the country's democracy with a founding "creed" that is then interpreted and reinterpreted in contrasting ways providing a shared historical rootedness for much of the country's politics, including successive waves of radical efforts to return to the egalitarian essence of some elements of the initial creed. This conceptualization of American politics may help account for certain limited similarities between some chapters of American history and this book's conceptualization of Portugal's post-revolutionary democracy. Despite all of the repression and exclusion to which African Americans were historically subject, when the civil rights movement mobilized masses in the streets and in other crucial venues many politicians responded through "conversation" and then ultimately by enacting legislation that addressed many demands of the movement. At its inclusionary best, American democratic practice—as reflected in the interactions between office holders and protest movements—has been strikingly post-revolutionary and inclusionary. However, such achievements have been contested politically, socially, and culturally. Rogers Smith's (1993) interpretation of American politics as characterized by multiple traditions seems more empirically adequate than a view that places exclusive emphasis on cultural legacies of the polity's political revolutionary origins.

Smith's emphasis on the long history of conflict between quite opposed political traditions in the United States highlights the historical weight in the American case of contention between forces that differ sharply with one another over both culture and politics—especially over the contributions of social movements to political change. The historical treatment of slavery's legacies has constantly been shaped by struggle over competing conceptions of political practice. The American Revolution and its discursive commitment to the principle of equality initially led to a period of anti-hierarchical cultural effervescence with numerous practical consequences (Wood, 2002: 99–101, 120–126). To a far greater extent than is often now recognized, this initial surge of anti-hierarchical thinking and practice contributed to a rapid rise of abolitionism, even in the South (126–129). However, political defenders of slavery quickly responded. The initial surge of egalitarian thinking was soon contested by advocates of one of the deepest forms of exclusion and hierarchical subordination that is humanly imaginable. The defeat of slavery in the 1860s and the victories of the civil rights movement in the 1960s both required episodes of expansive re-interpretation of American democratic practice. Lincoln's discursive return at Gettysburg to the principle that "all men are created equal" in defense of government "of, by and for the people" (Wills, 1992) and John Kennedy's decision to work with Martin Luther King, and his fellow advocates of non-violent civil disobedience in the civil rights movement, both represented efforts to push American democratic practice toward greater inclusion. Obviously, both Lincoln and Kennedy—and their allies—encountered severe conflict from defenders of exclusion. In crucial moments American politics has involved struggle over how to define the essence of the political system and of appropriate political conduct.

American politics continues to be driven by conflict over fundamental understandings about the breadth of inclusion—and over efforts to restore old forms of exclusion. Conflict of this nature often involves disputes about the legitimacy of political actors and forms of action. American democratic practice is often sharply contested. Strongly inclusionary and exclusionary conceptions of the country's political system have co-existed for some time. The election of Donald Trump as president in 2016 renewed the urgency of understanding such conflict and—for those committed to the view that all persons are created equal—of finding effective ways to promote the renewal of inclusionary principles. The 2016 election contributed significantly to new concerns over the authenticity and consolidation of American democracy— or to put the matter somewhat differently, over the danger of democracy's erosion.

The important new book of Levitsky and Ziblatt (2018) on this theme highlights the importance of cultural principles or norms for the functioning and survival of democracy. Levitsky and Ziblatt underscore the significance of mutual tolerance among political adversaries and of institutional restraint or "forbearance" on the part of powerful political elites. Their arguments offer a major contribution to understanding contemporary challenges faced by democracy and in the process they make a strong case for the relevance of cultural factors. Nonetheless their approach may analytically undervalue cultural conflict over the bounds of democratic inclusion, a dimension that stands at the center of this book's theory of democratic practice. Levitsky and Ziblatt focus in extremely useful ways on *elite-level* understandings and practice, an important terrain of analysis. However, the triumph or defeat of political inclusion and equality is also shaped by cultural understandings of how persons located *outside* institutional centers of power ought to interact with the holders of institutional power. Cultural conflicts over the bounds of inclusion—both in the United States and elsewhere—involve much more than disagreement over norms guiding interactions within the political elite. The political revolution that launched independent government in the United States gave birth to a cultural tradition stressing the idea of political equality but did not guarantee its triumph. Much of the contemporary drama of American politics involves conflict over competing understandings of democratic practice.

The greatest parallels with the democratic practice of the Portuguese case are likely found in other historically rare cases of democratizing social revolutions. Yet clearly such cases are very historically uncommon. The Nicaraguan Sandinista Revolution has been interpreted as providing the basis for an emergent democracy (Anderson and Dodd 2009), but after the return of Daniel Ortega to the presidency in 2007 it became increasingly difficult to sustain that claim (Mainwaring and Pérez-Liñán, 2013; Levitsky and Way, 2010). Yet in its most democratic periods, prior to 2007, elements of that country's political practice did appear to carry inclusionary legacies of the system's revolutionary beginnings—for example in the reporting of the news (Viterna, 2007). In the Salvadoran case, the social revolutionary origins of democracy in part of the national territory (Wood, 2003) also seem to have left their mark in elements of democratic practice that are more inclusionary of low-income sectors than in otherwise similar polities. But France offers perhaps the greatest set of parallels. Although the linkage between social revolution and contemporary democracy has been a discontinuous one, in symbolic and cultural terms the elements of continuity have been quite important. The post-revolutionary elements of French democracy have been linked to that country's patterns of contention (Tilly, 1986; Ross, 2007) and predominant approaches to equality and inclusion (Lamont, 2000; Brubaker, 1992). There is a strong basis to argue that where democracy is rooted in a social revolutionary experience, the consequences seem to have much in common with what this book identifies as the Portuguese pattern of democratic practice.

VII. Assessing the Spanish Case

It is also clearly important to assess the broader comparative lessons of the Spanish case and the implications of this book's argument for our understanding of that political system. The claims advanced here may be read by some as a critique of the Spanish transition, but that is not the intent of the book—at least not until we reach the transition's coda and the system's turn toward the right with the virtual elimination of the Unión del Centro Democrático (UCD) and the approach to democracy that party represented. The Spanish transition was almost certainly the only viable pathway to democracy in that country in 1976–1977, and its success required ingenuity as well as a significant dose of courage on the part of crucial political actors (Gunther, Montero, and Botella, 2004). But several decades later it is clear that the cultural legacies of the path followed have introduced difficulties and unfortunate exclusionary tendencies in the predominant form of democratic practice. The new lesson that this book extracts from the Spanish experience concerns unanticipated cultural legacies of political action that was initially intended to promote democratic consolidation in uncertain circumstances. The arguments and evidence presented here provide a strong basis to conclude that the costs of ignoring the cultural dimensions of democratization can be quite high. And the difficulties posed by failing to found democracy on inclusionary principles and understandings are very real ones. Much of the ongoing conflict in Spanish democracy and many of the material problems that large numbers of citizens face have been accentuated by the non-inclusionary elements of the country's long-predominant form of democratic practice. The political energy that has been channeled into efforts to change this pattern is considerable, but the outcome of those efforts, and indeed the future of the political system, remain less than fully clear.

VIII. Final Thoughts

The contrasts between the neighboring countries of the Iberian Peninsula hold not only local but also universal significance. The lessons of the two countries underscore the viability of a culture of inclusion in democracy and the costs of the alternative. Inclusion carries with it many positive consequences. The lessons of these two cases also highlight the explanatory importance of history—and thus the weight of the past in people's lives—and the great speed with which historical patterns can reverse themselves under exceptional circumstances. There is very little in the earlier history of the two countries that would lead one to anticipate the differences that emerged in the wake of their polar opposite pathways to democracy in the 1970s. Granted, the considerably greater diversity and scale of Spain is not new, and that factor interacts with all else—constantly providing Spain with localized "counter-narratives" that in small ways run against the dominant country-wide tendencies. In the end, the story of these two countries— historical "giants" that shaped the modern world in the age of exploration and colonialism—also serves to remind us how very important the actions of individuals can be in crucial moments of historical change and how long their consequences endure.

The story of Portugal and Spain also brings into clear view the extraordinary importance of cultural work and of the taken for granted assumptions that underpin democratic practice. The lessons of "April" taught to countless Portuguese children hold truly universal significance, as does the recurrent inability of many contending Spaniards to join in genuine "conversation" about the polity's future. Historical dynamics such as those that generated these outcomes are of crucial relevance for democracies everywhere. The Iberian divide in political inclusion holds deep lessons for the future of freedom and equality in a world increasingly subject to pressures that constrain the realization of those principles.

Chapter 1

1. I thank Omar Lizardo, Damon Mayrl, and Juan Díez Medrano for important feedback on earlier versions of this definition.

2. For analyses of the decline of Spain's colonial empire, placing that process in comparative perspective, see McCoy, Fradera, and Jacobson (2012).

3. The doctoral dissertation research of Tiago Carvalho at Cambridge University involves the systematic collection of data on protest events in Portugal and Spain.

Chapter 2

1. I argue that these early transitions also likely affected underlying assumptions about politics in countries far removed from the Iberian Peninsula, thereby contributing to the ultimately global scope of the "Third Wave" (Fishman, 2018b).

2. Przeworski et al. (2000) argue that economic development vastly increases the odds that democracy, once established, will survive. Boix and Stokes (2003) argue that development actually increases the probability that democracy will be established. Przeworski et al.'s (2000: 95) calculations gave Portugal in 1974 a 57% chance of being democratic and more developed Spain in 1976 an 85% probability of being democratic.

3. I use the terms "dictatorship," "authoritarian regime," and "authoritarian dictatorship" interchangeably, introducing the variation between these terms for purely stylistic reasons.

4. The most useful general source on the Portuguese revolution in English is Kenneth Maxwell (1995).

5. The posters that the CDS and other parties made use of in the first post–April 25 election campaign were displayed in the Assembly of the Republic in an exposition featured at the time of the 2014 commemoration of the April 25 Revolution. I attended the commemorative session of the parliament on several occasions—including 2014.

6. Interview with José Sobral, Lisbon, June 18, 2008.

7. This pattern of mutual causation is precisely what the Weberian methodological perspective (Fishman, 2007) assumes to be in operation in the social world.

8. Interview with Mário Soares, Lisbon, June 20, 2008.

9. On this point, see Fishman (1990a).

10. Interview with Rodolfo Martín Villa, Madrid, May 21, 2008.

11. For an article denying the historical authenticity of the reported remarks, see "'La calle es mía': La leyenda urbana sobre Fraga que Sánchez se creyó," *ABC*, Internet edition, December 12, 2014, accessed April 21, 2017.

12. Interview with Mário Soares, Lisbon, May 26, 2003.

13. Saramago articulated this criticism on repeated occasions. See the interview that appeared in Barcelona's *El Periódico*, "José Saramago: A veces, los partidos hacen un uso perverso del poder que les otorga el voto," in *Cuadernos del Domingo*, pp. 10–11, *El Periódico*, Internet edition, May 2, 2004, accessed June 12, 2018.

Chapter 3

1. Having taught numerous courses on research methods and as an ardent practitioner of a multi-method and eclectic approach to methodology, I count myself among those who feel such concerns.

2. This was the case fairly early in my research efforts, when I set out to test a preliminary argument I had developed on what I assumed to be the civic self-restraint of Portuguese journalists in reporting political news during the legally imposed "day of reflection" between the end of campaigning and an election itself. On that occasion, as on countless others, I used qualitative interviews and data gathering as a way to test the validity of my argument such as it had developed at the time. One interview on this matter with a highly placed newspaper editor led me to abandon my initial argument, having found it to be incorrect, and to formulate a new one capable of accounting for all of my observations to date. This approach to theory construction based on relatively small *N* fieldwork has been labeled "analytical induction" in the literature on sociological methodology. It is highly compatible with more recent approaches to the use of qualitative interviews in multimethod work (Spillman, 2014).

3. Individuals construct the meaning of existing national borders in quite variant ways. On this point, see Fishman (2006).

4. The article by Mario Soares was published in *La Vanguardia*, print edition, June 30, 2002, p. 31.

5. See *El Pais*, print edition, July 5, 2002, p. 20.

6. In a focus group interview with ten politically active Catalans on July 18, 2002—thematically centered on the adoption of the Euro—I asked the focus group members about this incident, and none of them were aware of the European parliamentary vote condemning the police action.

7. Interview with Francisco Louçã, Lisbon, June 14, 2006.

8. Ibid.

9. By "conversation" I understand not only direct dialogue between actors but also indirect exchanges of views mediated by the communications media or other intervening channels of exchange.

10. There is also a significant nationalist movement in Galicia, and there are smaller nationalist movements in other Spanish regions.

11. In early 2018 several demonstrations of pensioners were able to move beyond police barriers allowing them to move closer the Spanish parliament than has typically been the case. See "Decenas de miles de jubilados se manifiestan en toda España para reclamar pensiones más dignas," *Público*, Internet edition, February 22, 2018, accessed February 22, 2018. Note this is the Spanish *Público*, unrelated to the Portuguese newspaper of the same name.

12. See *El País*, Internet edition, September 22, 2012. Story titled, "Madrid autoriza manifestaciones cerca del Congreso el 25-S", accessed September 23, 2012.

13. See ibid. and "Cifuentes autoriza de forma parcial la convocatoria del 25-S," *El País*, Internet edition, September 23, 2012, accessed September 23, 2012.

14. See, "La Protesta del 25-S en el Congreso acaba con cargas, 64 heridos y 35 detenidos," *El País*, Internet edition, September 26, 2012, accessed May 5, 2017.

15. These declarations of Ignacio González were reported in "Miles de Personas Protestan junto al Congreso en el debate de Prespuestos," *El País*, Internet edition, October 23, 2012, accessed October 23, 2012; and in other media accounts at the time.

16. See "Miles de Personas Protestan junto al Congreso en el debate de Prespuestos," *El País*, Internet edition, October 23, 2012, accessed October 23, 2012.

17. One such exceptional case in Portugal took place in November 2012 on the occasion of a CGTP general strike. See "Sete detidos e 48 feridos nos confrontos junto ao Parlamento, Segundo a PSP," *Público*, Internet edition, November 14, 2012, accessed March 20, 2013.

18. See "Nao fui a primeira pessoa no mundo a abraçar um policía," *Publico* (PT), Internet edition, September 17, 2012, accessed September 17, 2012.

19. I argue at greater length in chapter 6 that democratic practice in Catalonia has tended to follow the pattern that predominates throughout Spain. The Basque Country is another matter and due to considerations of time and space is not taken up here. On Basque contention, see Tejerina, Fernández Sobrado, and Aierdi (1995).

20. See "Detenidos 22 indignados en Barcelona por atacar instituciones del Estado," *El País*, Internet edition, October 3, 2011, accessed October 3, 2011.

21. Interview with Mário Soares, Lisbon, June 20, 2008.

22. The Portuguese *Público*, Internet edition, June 11, 2002; and interview with former president, Jorge Sampaio, Lisbon, February 7, 2008.

23. The text of the remarks delivered by the PSD leader in Maia, Oliveira de Silva, are available at www.scribd.com/doc/38862/Discurso-evocativo-do-25-de-Abril (accessed May 22, 2009). I discuss the broader record of the commemorations in chapter 7.

24. Spain's *Publico*, print edition, June 15, 2011, p. 16.

25. See *El Pais*, Internet edition, February 20, 2012, accessed February 21, 2012.

26. *El Pais*, Internet edition, March 25, 2011, accessed March 25, 2011.

27. I witnessed these events on Portuguese television while on a research trip to the country to follow the presidential election of January 22, 2006.

28. I am grateful to priest Javier Baeza for the information provided in two interviews on this theme, in May 2008 and January 2009. I encountered the immigrants dwelling inside the church on the first of those two interviews.

29. I am grateful to João Ferrão for offering a great deal of information during several interviews, the first on January 13, 2009. I also thank Ferrão for organizing and leading a field visit I made to Cova da Moura.

30. Visit to Cova da Moura, April 28, 2016, accompanied by João Ferrão and two of his collaborators in work on the critical neighborhoods initiative.

31. Interviews with Pedro Soares of the Bloco de Esquerda, Lisbon January 14, 2009, and with João Ferrão, Lisbon, January 13, 2009.

32. Interview with Ada Colau and Adriá Alemany, Barcelona, July 16, 2008. Colau's view on representative elected authority evolved over time, and she went on to be elected mayor of Barcelona in 2015.

33. See the politically engaged scholarship on this question by the lawyer Jaume Asens, "La Presión al Movimiento de las Okupaciones: Del Aparato Policial a los Mass Media," in *¿Dónde Están las Llamas: El Movimiento Okupa, Prácticas y Contextos Sociales*, ed. Ramón Adell Argilés and Miguel Martínez López (Madrid: Los Libros de la Catarata, 2004): 293–338. Asens currently serves as a deputy mayor of Barcelona as this book goes to press.

34. *Público*, print edition, August 27, 2002, p. 39, and August 31, 2002, p. 46.

35. *Público*, Internet edition, June 10, 2008, accessed March 15, 2009.

36. All of these declarations by Spanish political leaders were reported in "Zapatero anuncia 'tolerancia cero' contra los piquetes." *El País*, Internet edition, June 12, 2008, accessed June 12, 2008.

37. "Veintena camioneros recuerdan miembro piquete muerto con marcha en Valladolid," *El Confidencial*, online edition, June 12, 2008, accessed May 5, 2017.

38. See, for example, the discussion in "Ha cultura para todos no primeiro orçamento participativo Portugal," *Público*, Internet edition, September 14, 2017, accessed June 6, 2018. Additional information is available at the government website: https://www.portugal.gov.pt/pt/gc21/comunicacao/noticia?i=20170914-mpma-opp (accessed June 6, 2018).

39. Interview with Enric Bastardes, Barcelona, July 2, 2008.

40. On this matter I have relied on information provided by Enric Bastardes, interviewed July 2, 2008, in Barcelona, and Rodolfo Benito, interviewed May 30, 2008, in Madrid.

41. My interviews with Portuguese journalists included José Manuel Fernandes, at the time director of Portugal's newspaper of record, *Público*, Lisbon, June 12, 2006; with António, Luis Marinho, director of news information at RTP, Lisbon, June 7, 2006; with Arsenio Reis, TSF radio, Lisbon, July 21, 2011; and with journalists in less well-known media outlets.

42. Interview with José Manuel Fernandes, Lisbon, June 12, 2006.

43. Interview with Luis Marinho, Lisbon, June 7, 2006.

44. Enric Bastardes insisted on this point in our interview, Barcelona, July 2, 2008.

45. Interview with Luis Costa, Queluz, February 1, 2008.

46. See note 38.

47. Interview with Sara Fernandes, Lisbon, February 6, 2008.

48. Interview with Elvira, Madrid, May 30, 2008.

49. Interview with María (a pseudonym by request of the respondent), High School Number 1 in a provincial capital south of Madrid, February 29, 2008.

50. See the discussion in "Ministro compromete-se a ouvir os alunos de uma forma mais 'constante,'" *Publico*, Internet edition, May 16, 2017, accessed May 16, 2017.

51. Ibid.

Chapter 4

1. For a discussion of explanations for the superior Basque performance in employment, see Fishman (2012b).

2. The EU15 refers to the fifteen member states that made up the European Union following the 1995 enlargement and prior to the next enlargement of the EU in 2004. Comparative European statistics for that nine-year period of time tend to refer to the EU15. As a "universe" of cases it continues to be useful for comparative social science. The countries making up the EU15 were all western European states. Portugal and Greece were the poorest members of this "club." The member states admitted in the next enlargement included less developed countries in east central Europe.

3. In very interesting recent work Cornel Ban (2016) argues for the central role of ordo-liberalism in the Spanish case.

4. For a distinguished exposition of this perspective, see Rojo (2010).

5. Interview with Emilio Rui Vilar, Lisbon, May 26, 2003.

6. Ibid.

7. Such concerns have been frequently covered in the Spanish press. For press coverage of a survey of SMEs, see *El País*, February 5, 2009, p. 17, and *La Vanguardia*, February 5, 2009, pp. 50–51.

8. Interview with Paulo Pedroso, Lisbon, June 24, 2008. I also previously interviewed Pedroso on June 21, 2007.

9. Information obtained from the two interviews mentioned in the previous endnote.

10. In discussions with Portuguese scholars I have frequently encountered this assumption or hypothesis but never data in its support.

11. The presence of women in the labor force can be measured through two quite different indicators, leading at times to confusion in discussions of the matter. I rely here on women as a percentage of the total labor force. Some discussions focus instead on the percentage of women who participate in the labor force.

12. The possibility that this relationship is endogenous and that welfare state development promotes economic growth obviously also deserves consideration. For an important study that makes this argument, see Valenzuela et al. (2006).

13. Interview with Isabel Guerra, Lisbon, February 8, 2008, and interviews with Joao Ferrao cited in chapter 3.

14. The data are available in Eurostat News Release 70/2012, accessed online June 2013.

15. The most recent PISA data from the 2015 large-scale cross-national study show Portugal to have better results in science, math, and reading than the south European countries with which it is most often compared, Spain, Italy, and Greece. Portugal's results are also higher than those of the United States in all three areas of testing. See the data reported online at: https://read.oecd-ilibrary.org/education/pisa-2015-results-volume-i_9789264266490-en#page46 (accessed June 17, 2018).The summary table of greatest usefulness is found on page 44.

16. The data on musical consumption is from a 2001 Eurobarometer study. The data on citizenship practice is from the 2004 ISSP study.

17. Some effect was also found only in Uruguay, but there it was much smaller in magnitude than in Portugal.

Chapter 5

1. By "regressive effects" I refer to those that augment inequalities.

2. See "Financiamento das empresas e um problema 'urgente do Ministerio da Economia," *Publico*, Internet edition, September 29, 2011, downloaded September 11, 2011.

3. See "CGD quer manter financiamento a economía com depósitos dos clientes," *Publico internet edition*, August 4, 2011. Downloaded August 5, 2011.

4. For press coverage of a survey of Spanish SMEs in which this concern was strongly emphasized by respondents, see the sources cited in chapter 4, note 7.

5. See "Solbes desautoriza a Sebastian: 'Tengo paciencia para rato," *El Pais*, Internet edition, February 5, 2009, downloaded May 10, 2017.

6. See "La financiación sigue sin llegar a las compañías," *El País*, Internet edition, February 2, 2014, downloaded February 4, 2014.

7. See "Gonzalez: 'Cuando las cosas van mal, militancia pura y dura.'" *El Pais*, Internet edition, June 10, 2010, accessed online August 3, 2016. The message of Gonzalez was sent to Zapatero in May of that year and made public in June.

8. See "FMI reconhece que calculous mal o impacto da austeridade na economia," *Público*, Internet edition, October 9, 2012, downloaded October 9, 2012.

9. See "Moody's Warns on Portugal's Bailout Plan," in *Financial Times*, Internet edition, October 5, 2012, downloaded October 5, 2012.

10. See the discussion of this episode in Fishman and Everson (2016).

11. See "Se o Governo recuar é sinal de que ouviu a 'voz do povo', diz Soares," *Público*, Internet edition, September 19, 2012, downloaded September 19, 2012.

12. See the discussion of the OECD study in "España es el pais de la UE con mas porcentaje de trabajadores pobres," *El Pais*, Internet edition, May 10, 2018, accessed May 10, 2018.

13. See note 8, this chapter.

14. The Basque nationalists have been quite willing to offer parliamentary support to right-wing governments in Madrid in exchange for favorable arrangements for the Basque Country when a left-oriented option was not under active consideration.

15. See "Ministro compromete-se a ouvir os alunos de uma forma mais 'constante,'" *Público*, Internet edition, May 16, 2017, downloaded May 16, 2017.

Chapter 6

1. A note on usage: Catalonia is for many a region of Spain, and for many others a nation. Thinking of Catalonia as a nation does not in any way preclude its current status as part of Spain. Indeed, for many residents Catalonia is both a region and a nation. In the text I refer to Catalonia as a region for expositional simplicity and clarity, but as the substantive discussion makes clear, this is not intended to reject or critique the use of the term "nation" to refer to Catalonia. In fact, my own view is that resolution of the status question would be greatly facilitated if Spanish political actors

were willing to conceptualize Catalonia as a nation within Spain. Also for expositional reasons, I use the term "country" to refer to Spain as a whole.

2. I emphasize here the watershed significance of the Catalan parliament's decision on September 6 and 7 to call a referendum despite the opposition of Spanish Courts and the government in Madrid, and to initiate a process of legal detachment or "disconnection" from Spain. However, that September 2017 decision had a rather long pre-history that would require extensive treatment in a monographic examination of the Catalan crisis.

3. My first in-depth encounter with Catalan realities took place during the spring semester of 1973, in the twilight of the Franco dictatorship, when I spent the last semester of high school studying in the School Year Abroad program then located in Barcelona.

4. See the very useful discussion of this underlying logic by Lluís Orriols in "Romper la coalición Independentista," *El País*, Internet edition, September 19, 2017, https://elpais.com/elpais/2017/09/14/opinion/1505379606_862594.html (accessed June 14, 2018).

5. There are those, especially in Podemos and to a lesser extent in the PSOE, who see Spain as a multi-national state.

6. The data from the 2013 survey are available at the following web address: https://www.idescat.cat/cat/idescat/publicacions/cataleg/pdfdocs/eulp2013.pdf (accessed April 1, 2018).

7. See the responses to question 30 in the CIS study, available at: http://datos.cis.es/pdf/Es3202mar_A.pdf (accessed April 27, 2018).

8. During the transition period several previously separate tendencies within the Catalan socialist tradition joined together.

9. As recently as December 2017 a survey by a well-respected public opinion firm reported that two thirds of Catalans place themselves on the left or the center-left. See: https://www.elperiodico.com/es/politica/20171220/elecciones-cataluna-perfil-sentimiento-catalanes-6507534 (accessed May 16, 2018).

10. Convergència changed not only its position on independence but also its name, calling the new party, officially founded in 2016, the Partit Demòcrata Europeu i Català (PDeCAT).

11. The electorate was defined in an especially expansive way in this case partly as a legal tactic intended to differentiate the consultation from elections subject to regulation by Spanish law.

12. See the data mentioned in note 7.

13. The initial call for the creation of the party was issued in 2005, but the founding party congress took place in 2006.

14. The strong opposition to peripheral nationalism of Ciudadanos and its leader, Albert Rivera, has led him to oppose the inclusion of Basque or Catalan nationalist parties in the construction of majority coalitions needed to approve and support governments in Spain's parliamentary system. For a recent example of this position, see "Rivera pide 'sentido de Estado' al PSOE y carga contra el PNV por los Presupuestos," *El País*, Internet edition, April 2, 2018, accessed April 12, 2018.

15. See the coverage in "La carga policial desata la indignación en Barcelona," *El País*, Internet edition, May 27, 2011, accessed May 12, 2018.

16. See, for example, the discussion available at: http://blogs.periodistadigital.
com/opinion.php/2011/06/17/ (accessed May 13, 2018), and http://www.escolar.
net/MT/archives/2011/06/policias-infiltrados-en-las-protestas-de-barcelona.html
(accessed May 13, 2018).

17. On the protests outside the Catalan parliament on June 15, 2015, see the informative article in *La Vanguardia*: http://www.lavanguardia.com/politica/20110615/
54170903036/los-parlamentarios-catalanes-logran-acceder-al-parlament-entre-
pintadas-empujones-y-abucheos.html (accessed May 12, 2018). See also "Detenidos
22 indignados en Barcelona por atacar instituciones del Estado," *El País*, Internet
edition, October 3, 2011, accessed October 3, 2011.

18. On the judicial decision on this case, see the useful coverage in Spain's
Publico: http://www.publico.es/politica/supremo-condena-protesta-parlament-y.html
(accessed May 12, 2018).

19. See "Cuando Puigdemont veía 'lamentables' los piquetes en las huelgas," *El
Periodico de Catalunya*, Internet edition, November 11, 2017, accessed May 13, 2018.

20. The events of this day were extensively covered in the press in Catalonia and to
an only slightly lesser extent in the rest of Spain. See, for example, the discussion in
Spain's most widely read newspaper, *El País*: "Decepción entre los independentistas
concentrados alrededor del Parlament," *El País*, Internet edition, October 10, 2017,
accessed May 14, 2018 (and earlier).

21. See "Un Parlament fracturado declara la independencia tras una votación
secreta," *El Periódico*, Internet edition, October 27, 2017, updated October 30, 2017,
accessed May 14, 2018.

22. See "Saura se escuda en el juez para justificar el desalojo okupa que causó el
caos en Barcelona," *El Mundo*, Internet edition, October 1, 2010.

23. See the description of this 2007 incident at: https://www.20minutos.es/
noticia/236834/0/punzones/mossos/manifestacion/ (accessed May 15, 2018).

24. See the account of this incident provided by the AHDS at: http://barcelona.
indymedia.org/newswire/display/320031/index.php (accessed April 26, 2018).

25. Unió, the longtime electoral ally of Convergència, ran on its own on this occasion as it had adopted a much more moderate position on the status question.

26. The controversies surrounding this parliamentary session were extensively
covered in the press. See for example, "El secesianismo consuma la ruptura," *El País*,
Internet edition, September 7, 2017, accessed April 12, 2018.

27. Opponents of the proposal to hold a referendum have argued that only the
Spanish people as a whole are entitled to vote on Catalonia's status. This view, which
disallows the right of Catalans to express their collective sentiments on the status
question, has tended to close off a relatively easy avenue to resolving the impasse.

28. In one of the strongest polling results in favor of the third way, a January 2018
survey carried out by *El País* indicated that 51% of the Catalan public would vote for
enhanced autonomy, only 26% for full independence, and 17% for the status quo if
all three options were made available in a referendum. See https://elpais.com/elpais/
2018/01/19/media/1516384171_189989.html (accessed January 20, 2018). In one of
the most dramatic examples of the effort of some pro-independence Catalans to
marginalize defenders of the "third way," a candidate highly placed on the Esquerra
Republicana list in December 2017 likened Catalan advocates of the third way to

pro-Nazi Jews. See: https://www.elperiodico.com/es/politica/20171220/antoni-castella-compara-catalanes-tercera-via-con-judios-pronazis-6507538 (accessed May 27, 2018). In the context of the same election campaign, the Catalan Socialist leader Miquel Iceta, a defender of a "third way" approach to resolving the conflict, was harshly criticized by Ciudadanos and others for suggesting that a useful path to reconciliation would be a legal pardon of pro-independence leaders if they are ultimately found guilty of criminal offenses for their actions in support of Catalan sovereignty. See: https://www.eldiario.es/politica/Cs-frivolidad-Iceta-indultos-soberanistas_0_716029271.html (accessed May 27, 2018).

29. I encountered many such cases in a long series of conversations with Catalans during this time period.

30. A prominent Catalan political scientist who is personally opposed to independence reported to me that he personally tested the system by attempting to vote twice, in separate polling stations in Barcelona—against independence on both occasions. On the second attempt he was told that the electronic voter rolls indicated that he had already voted once and could not do so again. Isolated instances of individuals voting more than once surely exist; the conditions for monitoring such matters were more challenging on that day than in routine elections in democracies. But as a general matter the efforts of referendum supporters to prevent double voting from taking place seem to have succeeded.

31. The data are reported in "La Generalitat publica una encuesta sobre el 1-O pese a la intervención," *El País*, Internet edition, February 9, 2018, accessed May 17, 2018.

32. On the Spanish side, those who have complained that Catalan actions constituted a de facto "coup d'état" include the veteran Socialist leader Alfonso Guerra, former PP Prime Minister Jose Maria Aznar, the PP Foreign Minister Alfonso Dastis, and many others including intellectuals. On the Catalan pro-independence side, charges that Spanish governmental actions represent a "coup d'état" have been even more broadly articulated, encompassing not only elite statements but also mass-level routine conversations on the crisis. The important analysis of Sánchez-Cuenca (2018) conceptualizes the problem instead as a constitutional crisis in which elected institutions are thoroughly at odds with one another.

Chapter 7

1. For a discussion of alternative conceptualizations and definitions of subcultures, see Fishman (2004: 25–28).

2. I rely here on my fieldnotes from the commemorative activities—including the special session of the Assembly of the Republic—during the following years: 2004, 2006, 2012, 2014, and 2016. During other years I was able to follow the commemorations from outside Portugal via Portugal's international television broadcasts and other journalistic sources.

3. I thank Jose Soeiro for making available the full text of his April 25 speech.

4. The text of this session of parliament is available electronically at parlamento.pt.

5. Durao Barroso's remarks were covered live on SIC Television. Fieldnotes from April 25, 2004.

6. It was, in any case, clear that this event was both a commemoration and a demonstration, but the point was underscored by the comment of a "bystander." When I left the Largo do Carmo by taxi late on April 24, 2014, the driver referred to the demonstration still taking place as "the commemorations."

7. See the book by Aten, Diaz, and Vega (2017).

Chapter 8

1. I examine this question in greater depth in an essay to appear in a volume edited by Cavallaro and Kornetis (2019).

2. Interview with Gosta Esping-Andersen, January 22, 2018, Barcelona.

REFERENCES

Abbott, A. 2001. *Time Matters: On Theory and Method.* Chicago: University of Chicago Press.

Accornero, G., and P. Ramos Pinto. 2015. "Mild Mannered? Protest and Mobilisation in Portugal under Austerity, 2010–2013." *West European Politics* 38(3): 491–515.

Acevedo, C., P. Campabadal, J. Costa, I. Echevarria, A. Fernández-Savater, D. García Aristegui, G. Martínez, et al. eds. (2012). *CT o la Cultura de la Transición. Crítica a 35 años de cultura española.* Barcelona: Debolsillo.

Adelantado, J., and R. Gomà. 2000. "La política de vivienda." In *Cambios en el Estado del Bienestar: Políticas sociales y desigualdades en España,* edited by José Adelantado, 313–347. Barcelona: Icaria.

Aguilar, P. 1997. "La amnesia y la memoria: Las movilizaciones por la amnistía en la transición a la democracia." In *Cultura y movilización en la Espana contemporánea,* edited by Rafael Cruz and Manuel Pérez Ledesma, 327–357. Madrid: Alianza Editorial.

Aguilar, P. 2002. *Memory and Amnesia: The Role of the Spanish Civil War in the Transition to Democracy.* New York: Berghahn Books.

Aguilar, P. 2013. "Judiciary Involvement in Authoritarian Repression and Transitional Justice: The Spanish Case in Comparative Perspective." *International Journal of Transitional Justice* 7: 245–266.

Aguilar Fernández, P., and L. Payne. 2018. *El resurgir del pasado en España.* Barcelona: Taurus.

Ahlquist, J. S., and M. Levi. 2013. *In the Interest of Others: Organizations and Social Activism.* Princeton, NJ: Princeton University Press.

Alén, J. G., I. Díaz, and R. Vega. 2017. *Cristina, Manuela y Paca: Tres vidas cruzadas, entre la justicia y el compromiso.* Barcelona: Peninsula.

Alexander, J. C. 2006. *The Civil Sphere.* Oxford, UK: Oxford University Press.

Allard, A. 2005. "Measuring Job Security over Time: In Search of a Historical Indicator for EPL (Employment Protection Legislation)." *Instituto de Empresa Working Paper* WP05-17.

Almond, G., and S. Verba. 1963. *The Civic Culture: Political Attitudes and Democracy in Five Nations*. Princeton, NJ: Princeton University Press.

Alonso, S. 2012. *Challenging the State: Devolution and the Battle for Partisan Credibility*. Oxford, UK: Oxford University Press.

Altman, D. 2011. *Direct Democracy Worldwide*. New York: Cambridge University Press.

Altman, D., and A. Pérez-Liñán. 2002. "Assessing the Quality of Democracy: Freedom, Competitiveness and Participation in Eighteen Latin American Countries." *Democratization* 9(2): 85–100.

Álvarez, J., J. M. Echavarren, and X. Coller. 2017. "Bound by Blood: The Ethnic and Civic Nature of Collective Identities in the Basque Country, Catalonia and Valencia." *Nations and Nationalism* 24(2): 412–431.

Alvarez-Junco, J. 2001. *Mater Dolorosa: La idea de España en el siglo XIX*. Barcelona: Taurus.

Alves, M. L., and G. Allegretti. 2012. "(In) Stability, a Key Element to Understand Participatory Budgeting: Discussing Portuguese Cases." *Journal of Public Deliberation* 8(2): 1–19.

Amat, J. 2017. *La confabulació dels irresponsables*. Barcelona: Anagrama.

Ana Matias, A. R., and R. do Carmo. 2015. "Desigualdades de rendimentos: Tendencias recentes em Portugal." In *Governar com a Troika: Politicas publicas em tempo de austeridade*, edited by P. Adao e Silva and M. Lourdes Rodrigues, 447–455. Coimbra: Almedina.

Ancelovici, M. 2015. "Crisis and Contention in Europe: A Political Process Account of Anti-Austerity Protests." In *Europe's Prolonged Crisis: The Making or the Unmaking of a Political Union*, edited by V. Guiraudon, C. Ruzza, and H. J. Trenz. London: Palgrave Macmillan.

Anderson, L. E., and L. C. Dodd. 2009. *Learning Democracy: Citizen Engagement and Electoral Choice in Nicaragua, 1990–2001*. Chicago: University of Chicago Press.

Andronikidou, A., and I. Kovras. 2012. "Cultures of Rioting and Anti-Systemic Politics in Southern Europe." *West European Politics* 35(4): 707–725.

Anduiza, E., C. Cristancho, and J. M. Sabucedo. 2014. "Mobilization through Online Social Networks: The Political Protest of the Indignados in Spain." *Information, Communication and Society* 17(6): 750–764.

Asens, J. 2004. "La presión al Movimiento de las Okupaciones: Del apartato policial a los mass media." In *¿Dónde están las llamas: El Movimiento Okupa: Prácticas y contextos sociales*, edited by R. A. Argilés and M. M. López, 293–338. Madrid: Los Libros de la Catarata.

Asensio Menchero, M. 2001. *El Proceso de la reforma del sector público en el sur de Europa: Estudio comparativo de España y Portugal*. Madrid: Instituto Juan March.

Associaçao 25 April. 1996. *25 de Abril, 20 anos 1974–1994*. Lisbon: Associaçao 25 de Abril.

Astudillo, J. 2001. "Without Unions, but Socialist: The Spanish Socialist Party and Its Divorce from Its Union Confederation (1982–96)." *Politics and Society* 29(2): 273–296.

Baiocchi, G. 2005. *Militants and Citizens: The Politics of Participatory Democracy in Porto Alegre*. Stanford, CA: Stanford University Press.

Baiocchi, G., and E. Ganuza. 2017. *Popular Democracy: The Paradox of Participation.* Stanford, CA: Stanford University Press.

Balfour, S. 1989. *Dictatorship, Workers, and the City: Labour in Greater Barcelona since 1939.* Oxford, UK: Clarendon Press.

Ban, C. 2016. *Ruling Ideas: How Global Neoliberalism Goes Local.* Oxford, UK: Oxford University Press.

Barreto, A., C. V. Preto, M. J. V. Rosa, M. C. Lobo, and P. Chitas. 2000. *A situaçao social en Portugal, 1960–1999.* Vol. 2. Lisbon: Imprensa de Ciencias Sociais.

Basta, K. 2018. "The Social Construction of Transformative Political Events." *Comparative Political Studies* 51(10): 1243–1278.

Baumgarten, B. 2013. "Geraçao à Rasca and Beyond: Mobilizations in Portugal after 12 March 2011." *Current Sociology* 61(4): 457–473.

Baumgarten, B. 2017. "The Children of the Carnation Revolution? Connections between Portugal's Anti-Austerity Movement and the Revolutionary Period 1974/5." *Social Movement Studies* 16(1): 51–63.

Baumgarten, B., and R. Díez García. 2017. "More than a Copy Paste: The Spread of Spanish Frames and Events to Portugal." *Journal of Civil Society* 13(3): 247–266.

Bearman, P. S. 1993. *Relations into Rhetorics.* New Brunswick, NJ: Rutgers University Press.

Benet, J. 1995. *L'intent franquista de genocide cultural contra Catalunya.* Barcelona: Edicions l'Abadia de Montserrat, 1995.

Berezin, M. 1994. "Cultural Form and Political Meaning: State-Subsidized Theater, Ideology, and the Language of Style in Fascist Italy." *American Journal of Sociology* 99(5): 1237–1286.

Berezin, M. 1997. "Culture and Politics: A Less Fissured Terrain." *Annual Review of Sociology* 23: 361–383.

Berezin, M. 2015. "Culture, Sociology Of." In *International Encyclopedia of the Social and Behavioral Sciences,* 2nd ed., vol. 5, edited by J. D. Wright, 617–621. Oxford, UK: Elsevier.

Bermeo, N. 1986. *The Revolution within the Revolution.* Princeton, NJ: Princeton University Press.

Bermeo, N. 1987. "Redemocratization and Transition Elections: A Comparison of Spain and Portugal." *Comparative Politics* 19: 213–230.

Bermeo, N. 1998. "Learning from the Portuguese Experience: Some Quick Conclusions about Some Long Processes." In *Modern Portugal,* edited by A. Costa Pinto, 270–274. Palo Alto, CA: Society for the Promotion of Science and Scholarship.

Bermeo, N. 2001. "Conclusion: Unemployment, the New Europe and the Old Inequalities." In *Unemployment in the New Europe,* edited by N. Bermeo, 329–354. Cambridge, UK: Cambridge University Press.

Bermeo, N. 2007. "War and Democratization: Lessons from the Portuguese Experience." *Democratization* 14(3): 388–406.

Bermeo, N., and L. M. Bartels. 2014. *Mass Politics in Tough Times: Opinions, Votes and Protest in the Great Recession.* Oxford, UK: Oxford University Press.

Blanchard, O., and J. Jimeno. 1995. "Structural Unemployment: Spain versus Portugal." *American Economic Review* 85(2): 212–218.

Blyth, M. 2013. *Austerity: The History of a Dangerous Idea*. Oxford, UK: Oxford University Press.

Boix, C. 1998. *Political Parties, Growth and Equality: Conservative and Social Democratic Strategies in the World Economy*. Cambridge, UK: Cambridge University Press.

Boix, C., and S. C. Stokes. 2003. "Endogenous Democratization." *World Politics* 55(4): 517–549.

Bonet, E., I. Martín, and J. R. Montero. 2006. "Las actitudes políticas de los españoles." In *Ciudadanos, asociaciones y participación en España*, edited by J. R. Montero, J. Font, and M. Torcal, 105–132. Madrid: Centro de Investigaciones Sociológicas.

Bourdieu, P. 1990. *The Logic of Practice*. Stanford, CA: Stanford University Press.

Bover, O., P. Garcia-Perea, and P. Portugal. 2000. "Labour Market Outliers: Lessons from Portugal and Spain." *Economic Policy* 15(31): 381–428.

Brady, H. E., D. Collier, and J. Seawright. 2010. "Refocusing the Discussion of Methodology." In *Rethinking Social Inquiry*, edited by H. E. Brady and D. Collier, 15–31. Lanham, MD: Rowman & Littlefield.

Branco, R. 2017. Review of the book *The Left Divided: The Development and Transformation of Advanced Welfare States*, by S. E. Watson. Análise Social, (222): 204–214.

Brito, M., and F. Carreira da Silva. 2010. *O momento constituinte—Os direitos sociais na constituiçao*. Coimbra: Almedina.

Brubaker, R. 1992. *Citizenship and Nationhood in France and Germany*. Cambridge, MA: Harvard University Press.

Buendía, L. 2018. "A Perfect Storm in a Sunny Economy: A Political Economy Approach to the Crisis in Spain." *Socio-Economic Review* 0(0): 1–20.

Burgess, K. 2004. *Parties and Unions in the New Global Economy*. Pittsburgh: University of Pittsburgh Press.

Burt, R. S. 2005. *Brokerage and Closure*. Oxford, UK: Oxford University Press.

Cabral, M. V. 2003. "O exercício da cidadania política em perspectiva histórica (Portugal e Brasil)." *Revista Brasileira de Ciencias Sociais* 18(51): 31–60.

Cabral, M. V. 2006. "Class Effects and Societal Effects: Elite and Working Class Attitudes towards Political Citizenship from a European Comparative Perspective." *Portuguese Journal of Social Science* 5(3): 159–178.

Cabral, M. V., F. C. da Silva, and T. Saraiva. 2008. *Cidade e cidadania*. Lisbon: Imprensa de Ciencias Sociais.

Cameron, D. 2001. "Unemployment, Job Creation, and Economic and Monetary Union." In *Unemployment in the New Europe*, edited by N. Bermeo, 7–51. Cambridge, UK: Cambridge University Press.

Candeias, A., A. L. Paz, M. Rocha, and A. Novoa. 2007. *Alfabetizaçao e escola em Portugal nos séculos XIX e XX*. 2nd ed. Lisbon: Fundaçao Calouste Gulbenkian.

Capoccia, G., and D. Ziblatt. 2010. "The Historical Turn in Democratization Studies: A New Research Agenda for Europe and Beyond." *Sage Journals* 43(8–9): 931–968.

Cardoso, D., and R. Branco. 2017. "Labour Market Reforms and the Crisis in Portugal: No Change, U-Turn or New Departure?" *IPRI-NOVA Working Paper* 56/2017.

Casanova, J. 2010. *The Spanish Republic and Civil War*. Cambridge, UK: Cambridge University Press.

Casanova, J. 2013. *A Short History of the Spanish Civil War*. London and New York: Tauris.

Casanova, J., and C. G. Andrés. 2014. *Twentieth-Century Spain: A History*. Cambridge, UK: Cambridge University Press.

Castells, M. 1983. "The Making of an Urban Social Movement: The Citizens Movement in Madrid toward the End of the Franquist Era." In *The City and the Grassroots: A Cross-Cultural Theory of Urban Social Movements*, edited by M. Castells, 213–287. Berkeley: University of California Press.

Castro Caldas, J. 2013. *The Impact of Anti-Crisis Measures and the Social and Employment Situation: Portugal*. Study for the European Economic and Social Committee, EESC 2013 31-EN. Brussels: European Union.

Cavallaro, M. E., and K. Kornetis. 2019. *Rethinking South European Democratization in Spain, Greece and Portugal: Lost in Transition?* London: Palgrave.

Chhibber, P., and M. Torcal. 1997. "Elite Strategy, Social Cleavages, and Party Systems in a New Democracy." *Comparative Political Studies* 30(1): 27–54.

Clemens, E. S. 1998. "To Move Mountains: Collective Action and the Possibility of Institutional Change." In *From Contention to Democracy*, edited by M. G. Giugni, D. McAdam, and C. Tilly, 109–123. Lanham, MD: Rowman & Littlefield.

Coppedge, M., J. Gerring, D. Altman, M. Bernhard, S. Fish, A. Hicken, H. A. Semetko, et al. 2011. "Conceptualizing and Measuring Democracy: A New Approach." *Perspectives on Politics* 9(2): 247–267.

Coller, X. 2006. "Collective Identities and Failed Nationalism. The Case of Valencia in Spain." *Pôle Sud* 25: 107–136.

Coller, X., A. Jaime, and F. Mota. 2017. "El Poder Político en España." *Revista Española de Sociología*. Online First edition.

Coller, X., A. Jaime, and F. Mota. 2016. *Poder político en España: Parlamentarios y ciudadanía*. Madrid: Centro de Investigaciones Sociológicas.

Collier, D., and G. K. Munck. 2017. "Building Blocks and Methodological Challenges: A Framework for Studying Critical Junctures." *Qualitative and Multi-Method Research* 15(1): 2–9.

Collier, R. B., and D. Collier. 1991. *Shaping the Political Arena*. Princeton, NJ: Princeton University Press.

Colomer, J. M. 1990. *El arte de la manipulación política*. Barcelona: Anagrama.

Colomer, J. M. 1995. *Game Theory and the Transition to Democracy: The Spanish Model*. Cheltenham, UK: Edward Elgar.

Constâncio, V. 2008. "The Portuguese Economy: Achievements and Challenges." In *Challenges Ahead for the Portuguese Economy*, edited by F. Franco, 53–68. Lisbon: Imprensa de Ciências Sociais ICS.

Cook, K., R. Hardin, and M. Levi. 2005. *Cooperation without Trust?* New York: Russell Sage Foundation.

Cordero, G., A. Jaime-Castillo, and X. Coller. 2016. "Selecting Candidates in Multilevel Democracies." *American Behavioral Scientist* 60(7): 773–780.

Costa Lobo, M., A. Costa Pinto, and P. Magalhaes. 2016. "Portuguese Democratisation Forty Years On: Its Meaning and Enduring Legacies." *South European Society and Politics* 21(2): 163–180.

Costa Pinto, A. 2001. "Settling Accounts with the Past in a Troubled Transition to Democracy: The Portuguese Case." In *The Politics of Memory: Transitional Justice in Democratizing Societies*, edited by A. Barahona de Brito, C. Gonzaléz-Enríquez, and A. P. Aguilar, 65–91. Oxford, UK: Oxford University Press.

Costa Pinto, A. 2006. "Authoritarian Legacies, Transitional Justice and State Crisis in Portugal's Democratization." *Democratization* 13(2): 173–204.

Crozier, M., S. P. Huntington, and J. Watanuki. 1975. *The Crisis of Democracy: On the Governability of Democracies*. New York: New York University Press.

Dahl, R. 1971. *Polyarchy: Participation and Opposition*. New Haven, CT: Yale University Press.

Dahl, R. 1998. *On Democracy*. New Haven, CT: Yale University Press.

Dahl, R. 2002. *How Democratic Is the American Constitution?* New Haven, CT: Yale University Press.

Dahl, R. 2006. *On Political Equality*. New Haven, CT: Yale University Press.

De Lucena, M. 1979. "The Evolution of Portugese Corporatism under Salazar and Caetano." In *Contemporary Portugal: The Revolution and its Antecedents*, edited by L. S. Graham and H. M. Makler, 47–88. Austin: University of Texas Press.

De Souza, F. F., and R. Cruz. 1995. *O processo de privatizações em Portugal*. Porto: Associação Industrial Portuense.

De Sousa Santos, B. 1990. *O Estado e a Sociedade em Portugal (1974–1988)*. Porto: Ediçoes Afrontamento.

De Sousa Santos, B. 2005. *Democratizing Democracy: Beyond the Liberal Democratic Canon*. New York: Verso.

Della Porta, D. 1999. "Protest, Protesters and Protest Policing." In *How Social Movements Matter*, edited by M. Giugni, D. McAdam, and C. Tilly, 66–96. Minneapolis: University of Minnesota Press.

Della Porta, D. 2013. *Can Democracy Be Saved?* Oxford, UK: Polity Press.

Della Porta, D. 2016. *Where Did the Revolution Go?* Cambridge, UK: Cambridge University Press.

Della Porta, D., A. Massimiliano, T. Fernandes, F. O'Connor, E. Romanos, and M. Vogiatzoglou. 2017. *Late Neoliberalism and Its Discontents in the Economic Crisis: Comparing Social Movements in the European Periphery*. Cham, Switzerland: Palgrave Macmillan.

Della Porta, D., A. Massimiliano, T. Fernandes, F. O'Connor, E. Romanos, and M. Vogiatzoglou. 2018. *Legacies and Memories in Movements: Justice and Democracy in Southern Europe*. Oxford, UK: Oxford University Press.

Della Porta, D., F. O'Connor, M. Portos García, and A. Subirats Ribas. 2017. *Social Movements and Referendums from Below: Direct Democracy in the Neoliberal Crisis*. Bristol UK: Policy Press.

Diamond, L., and L. Morlino, eds. 2005. *Assessing the Quality of Democracy*. Baltimore, MD: Johns Hopkins University Press.

Diamond, L., and M. F. Plattner, eds. 2001. *The Global Divergence of Democracies*. Baltimore, MD: Johns Hopkins University Press.

Diário de Noticias. 2004. *A poesia está na rua: 25 de Abril. 30 anos. 100 Cartazes*. Lisbon: Diário de Noticias.

Díez García, R., and E. Laraña. 2018. *Democracia, Dignidad y Movimientos Sociales: El Surgimiento de la Cultura Cívica y la Irrupción de los 'Indignados' en la Vida Pública*. Madrid: Centro de Investigaciones Sociológicas.

Diez Medrano, J. 1995. *Divided Nations: Class, Politics, and Nationalism in the Basque Country and Catalonia*. Ithaca, NY: Cornell University Press.

Diez Medrano, J. 2003. *Framing Europe: Attitudes to European Integration in Germany, Spain and the United Kingdom*. Princeton, NJ: Princeton University Press.

Doz Orrit, J. 1995. "Problems of Implementation in Spanish Educational Reform." In *Educational Reform in Democratic Spain*, edited by O. Boyd-Barrett and P. O'Malley, 79–93. London: Routledge.

Druliolle, V. 2015. "Recovering Historical Memory: A Struggle against Silence and Forgetting? The Politics of Victimhood in Spain" *International Journal of Transitional Justice* 9: 316–335.

Durán Muñoz, R. 2000. *Contención y transgresión: Las movilizaciones sociales y el estado en las transiciones española y portuguesa*. Madrid: Centro de Estudios Políticos y Constitucionales.

Dutt, A. K., and J. Ros. 2007. "Aggregate Demand Shocks and Economic Growth." *Structural Change and Economic Dynamics* 18(1): 75–99.

Edles, L. D. 1998. *Symbol and Ritual in the New Spain: The Transition to Democracy after Franco*. Cambridge, UK: Cambridge University Press.

Eliasoph, N. 1998. *Avoiding Politics: How Americans Produce Apathy in Everyday Life*. Cambridge, UK: Cambridge University Press.

Emirbayer, M., and J. Goodwin. 1994. "Network Analysis, Culture and the Problem of Agency." *American Journal of Sociology* 99(6): 1411–1454.

Encarnacion, O. 2008. *Spanish Politics: Democracy after Dictatorship*. Cambridge, UK: Polity Press.

Encarnación, O. 2014. *Democracy without Justice in Spain: The Politics of Forgetting*. Philadelphia: University of Pennsylvania Press.

Escudero Alday, R. 2016. *Memoria historica y democracia en España: La brecha de la transición*. Mexico, DF: Editorial Fontamara.

Esping-Andersen, G. 1990. *The Three Worlds of Welfare Capitalism*. Princeton, NJ: Princeton University Press.

Esping-Andersen, G. 1994. "Budgets and Democracy: Towards a Welfare State in Spain and Portugal, 1960–1986." In *Developing Democracy*, edited by I. Budge and D. McKay, 112–127. London: Sage.

Esping-Andersen, G. 1999. *Social Foundations of Postindustrial Economies*. Oxford, UK: Oxford University Press.

Esping-Andersen, G. 2000. "Who Is Harmed by Labor Market Regulations?" In *Why Deregulate Labor Markets?*, edited by G. Esping-Andersen and M. Regini, 66–98. Oxford, UK: Oxford University Press.

Esping-Andersen, G. 2007. "Sociological Explanations of Changing Income Distributions." *American Behavioral Scientist* 50(5): 639–658.

Esping-Andersen, G., and F. C. Billari. 2015. "Re-Theorizing Family Demographics." *Population and Development Review* 41(1): 1–31.

Esping-Andersen, G., and M. Regini, eds. 2000. *Why Deregulate Labor Markets?* Oxford, UK: Oxford University Press.

Etchemendy, S. 2011. *Models of Economic Liberalization*. Cambridge, UK: Cambridge University Press.

Eurofund. 2017. https://www.eurofound.europa.eu/.

Eurostat. 2001. *Enterprises in Europe: Sixth Report.* Luxembourg: Office of Official Publications of the European Communities.

Ewing, T, ed. 2005. *Revolution and Pedagogy.* New York: Palgrave Macmillan.

Fernandes, T., ed. 2017. *Variedades de democracia na Europa do sul 1968–2016: Uma comparaçao entre Espanha, França, Grécia, Itália e Portugal.* Lisbon: Imprensa de Ciencias Socias.

Fernandes, T. 2006. *Nem ditadura nem Revoluçao: A ala liberal e o Marcelismo (1968–1974).* Lisbon: Dom Quixote.

Fernandes, T. 2015. "Rethinking Pathways to Democracy: Civil Society in Portugal and Spain, 1960s–2000s." *Democratization* 22(6): 1074–1104.

Fernández Enguita, M. 1987. *Reforma educativa, desigualdad social e inserción institucional: La enseñanza secundaria en Espana.* Barcelona: Editorial Laia.

Fernández Enguita, M. 1993. *La profesión docente y la comunidad escolar: Crónica de un desencuentro.* Madrid: Ediciones Morata.

Fernández Mellizo-Soto, M. 2001. *Socialismo, igualidad en la educación y democracia: La experiencia de González y Mitterand.* Madrid: Instituto Juan March de Estudios e Investigaciones.

Fernández-Albertos, J. 2012. *Democracia intervenida: Políticas económicas en la gran recesión.* Madrid: Los Libros de la Catarata.

Fernández-Albertos, J. 2015. *Los votantes de podemos: Del partido de los indignados al partido de los excluidos.* Madrid: La Catarata.

Ferreira, V. 1998. "Engendering Portugal: Social Change, State Politics, and Women's Mobilization." In *Modern Portugal*, edited by A. Costa Pinto, 162–188. Palo Alto, CA: Society for the Promotion of Science and Scholarship.

Field, B., ed. 2010. *Spain's "Second Transition"? The Socialist Government of Jose Luis Rodriguez Zapatero.* London: Routledge.

Fishman, R. M. 1990a. "Rethinking State and Regime: Southern Europe's Transition to Democracy." *World Politics* 42: 422–440.

Fishman, R. M. 1990b. *Working-Class Organization and the Return to Democracy in Spain.* Ithaca, NY: Cornell University Press.

Fishman, R. M. 2004. *Democracy's Voices: Social Ties and the Quality of Public Life in Spain.* Ithaca, NY: Cornell University Press.

Fishman, R. M. 2005. "Legacies of Democratizing Reform and Revolution: Portugal and Spain Compared." *Instituto de Ciencias Sociais, Lisboa.* Working paper 1-05: 1–44.

Fishman, R. M. 2006. "Identity, Social Practice and Currency Change: Catalonia in the Year of the Euro." In *The Year of the Euro*, edited by R. M. Fishman and A. M. Messina, 81–96. Notre Dame, IN: University of Notre Dame Press.

Fishman, R. M. 2007. "On Being a Weberian (after Spain's 11–14 March): Notes on the Continuing Relevance of the Methodological Perspective Proposed by Weber." In *Max Weber's "Objectivity" Reconsidered*, edited by L. Mcfalls, 261–289. Toronto: University of Toronto Press.

Fishman, R. M. 2009. "On the Costs of Conceptualizing Social Ties as Social Capital." In *Social Capital: Reaching Out, Reaching In*, edited by V. O. Bartkus and J. H. Davis, 66–83. Northampton, MA: Edward Elgar.

Fishman, R. M. 2010. "Rethinking the Iberian Transformations: How Democratization Scenarios Shaped Labor Market Outcomes." *Studies in Comparative International Development* 45: 281–310.

Fishman, R. M. 2011a. "Democratic Practice after the Revolution: The Case of Portugal and Beyond." *Politics and Society* 39(2): 233–267.

Fishman, R. M. 2011b. "Portugal's Unnecessary Bailout." *New York Times*, April 12.

Fishman, R. M. 2012a. "On the Significance of Public Protest in Spanish Democracy." In *Democràcia, política i societat: Homenatge a Rosa Virós*, edited by J. Jordana, V. Navarro, F. Pallarés, and F. Requejo, 351–366. Barcelona: Universitat Pompeu Fabra and Avenç.

Fishman, R. M. 2012b. "Anomalies of Spain's Economy and Economic Policy-Making." *Contributions to Political Economy* 31(1): 67–76.

Fishman, R. M. 2013. "The Iberian Divergence in Political Inclusion." In *Ciencias sociais: Vocaçao e profissao. Homenagem a Manuel Villaverde Cabral*, edited by P. A. da Silva, and F. C. da Silva. Lisbon: Imprensa de Ciencias Sociais.

Fishman, R. M. 2016. "Rethinking Dimensions of Democracy for Empirical Analysis: Authenticity, Quality, Depth and Consolidation." *Annual Review of Political Science* 19: 289–309.

Fishman, R. M. 2017. "How Civil Society Matters in Democratization: Setting the Boundaries of Post-Transition Political Inclusion." *Comparative Politics* 49(3): 391–409.

Fishman, R. M. 2018a. "What 25 April Was and Why It Mattered." *Portuguese Studies* 34(1): 20–34.

Fishman, R. M. 2018b. "What Made the Third Wave Possible? Historical Contingency and Meta-Politics in the Genesis of Worldwide Democratization." *Comparative Politics* 50(4): 607–626.

Fishman, R. M., and D. W. Everson. 2016. "Mechanisms of Social Movement Success: 'Conversation,' Displacement and Disruption." *Revista Internacional de Sociología* 74(4): 1–10.

Fishman, R. M., and O. Lizardo. 2013. "How Macro-Historical Change Shapes Cultural Taste: Legacies of Democratization in Spain and Portugal." *American Sociological Review* 78(2): 213–239.

Fishman, R. M., and A. M. Messina, eds. 2006. *The Year of the Euro: The Cultural, Social and Political Import of Europe's Common Currency*. Notre Dame, IN: University of Notre Dame Press.

Fishman, R. M., and M. Villaverde Cabral. 2016. "Socio-Historical Foundations of Citizenship Practice: After Social Revolution in Portugal." *Theory and Society* 45: 531–553.

Flesher Fominaya, C. 2007. "Autonomous Movements and the Institutional Left: Two Approaches in Tension in Madrid's Anti-Globalization Movement." *South European Society and Politics* 12(3): 335–358.

Flesher Fominaya, C. 2015. "Debunking Spontaneity: Spain's 15-M Indignados as Atonomous Movement." *Social Movement Studies* 14(2): 142–163.

Font, J., and C. Navarro. 2013. "Personal Experience and the Evaluation of Participatory Instruments in Spanish Cities." *Public Administration* 91(3): 616–631.

Foweraker, J. 1989. *Making Democracy in Spain: Grass-Roots Struggle in the South, 1955–1975*. Cambridge, UK: Cambridge University Press.

Freire Costa, L., P. Lains, and S. M. Miranda. 2016. *An Economic History of Portugal 1143–2010*. Cambridge, UK: Cambridge University Press.

Fung, A., and E. O. Wright. 2003. *Deepening Democracy: Institutional Innovations in Empowered Participatory Governance*. London: Verso.

Gamson, W. A. 1998. "Social Movements and Cultural Change." In *From Contention to Democracy*, edited by M. G. Giugni, D. McAdam, and C. Tilly, 57–77. Lanham, MD: Rowman & Littlefield.

García-Albacete, G. 2014. *Young People's Political Participation in Western Europe*. London: Palgrave Macmillan.

Giugni, M., D. McAdam, and C. Tilly. 1998. *From Contention to Democracy*. Lanham, MD: Rowman & Littlefield.

Glatzer, M. 2000. "Rigidity and Flexibility: Patterns of Labour Market Policy Change in Portugal and Spain, 1981–1996." In *Unemployment in Southern Europe: Coping with the Consequences*, edited by N. Bermeo, 90–110. London: Frank Cass.

Golob, S. R. 2008. "Volver: The Return of/to Transitional Justice Politics in Spain." *Journal of Spanish Cultural Studies* 9(2): 127–141.

Gómez Fortes B. 2009. *O controlo politico dos processos constituintes: Os casos de Espanha e Portugal*. Lisbon: Imprensa de Ciências Sociais.

Gómez Rosa, F. 2007. "La unión militar democrática en la transición política." Doctoral thesis, Universidad Complutense, Madrid.

Gonzalez Martin, D., and O. Martin Garcia. 2009. "In Movement: New Players in the Construction of Democracy in Spain, 1962–1977." *Political Power and Social Theory* 20: 39–68.

Goodwin, J. 2001. *No Other Way Out*. New York: Cambridge University Press.

Gould, A. C. 2009. "Muslim Elites and Ideologies in Portugal and Spain." *West European Politics* 32(1): 55–76.

Guillén Rodríguez, A. M., and L. Cabiedes Miragaya. 1998. "La política sanitaria: Análisis y perspectivas del sistema nacional de salud." In *Políticas Públicas en España: Contenidos, Redes de Actores y Niveles de Gobierno*, edited by R. Gomà and J. Subirats, 176–199. Barcelona: Ariel.

Guillen, A., S. Alvarez, and P. A. E. Silva. 2003. "Redesigning the Spanish and Portuguese Welfare States: The Impact of Accession into the European Union." In *Spain and Portugal in the European Union: The First Fifteen Years*, edited by S. Royo, P. C. Manuel, 231–268. London: Routledge.

Gunther, R. 1992. "Spain: The Very Model of Modern Elite Settlement." In *Elites and Democratic Consolidation in Latin America and Southern Europe*, edited by J. Higley, and R. Gunther, 38–80. Cambridge, UK: Cambridge University Press.

Gunther, R, J. R. Montero, and J. Botella. 2004. *Democracy in Modern Spain*. New Haven, CT: Yale University Press.

Gunther, R., G. Sani, and G. Shabad. 1986. *Spain after Franco: The Making of a Competitive Party System*. Berkeley: University of California Press.

Hagopian, F. 1990. "'Democracy by Undemocratic Means'? Elites, Political Pacts, and Regime Transition in Brazil." *Sage Journals* 23(2): 147–170.

Hall, P., and M. Lamont, eds. 2009. *Successful Societies*. Cambridge, UK: Cambridge University Press.

Hall, P., and M. Lamont, eds. 2013. *Social Resilience in the Neoliberal Era*. Cambridge, UK: Cambridge University Press.

Hamann, K. 2012. *The Politics of Industrial Relations: Labor Unions in Spain*. London: Routledge.

Hammond, J. L. 1988. *Workers' and Neighborhood Movements in the Portuguese Revolution*. New York: Monthly Review Press.

Held, D. 1987. *Models of Democracy*. Cambridge, UK: Polity Press.

Heller, P. 2000. "Degrees of Democracy: Some Comparative Lessons from India." *World Politics* 52(4): 484–519.

Helmke, G., and S. Levitsky, eds. 2006. *Informal Institutions and Democracy: Lessons from Latin America*. Baltimore, MD: Johns Hopkins University Press.

Herrera, A., and J. Markoff. 2011. "Rural Movements and the Transition to Democracy in Spain." *Mobilization* 16(4): 489–509.

Hopkin, J. 1999. *Party Formation and Democratic Transition in Spain: The Creation and Collapse of the Union of Democratic Centre*. Basingstoke, UK: Macmillan.

Huber, E., and J. D. Stephens. 2012. *Democracy and the Left: Social Policy and Inequality in Latin America*. Chicago: University Chicago Press.

Hunter, W. 1997. *Eroding Military Influence in Brazil: Politicians against Soldiers*. Chapel Hill: University of North Carolina Press.

Huntington, S. P. 1968. *Political Order in Changing Societies*. New Haven, CT: Yale University Press.

Huntington, S. P. 1981. *American Politics: The Promise of Disharmony*. Cambridge, MA: Harvard University Press.

Huntington, S. P. 1991. *The Third Wave: Democratization in the Late Twentieth Century*. Norman: University of Oklahoma Press.

Ibarra, P. 2013. "15-M: Breves reflexiones sobre origenes y retos." Paper presented at "Los Movimientos Sociales y la Nueva Ola de Indignacion." Escuela de Verano de la Universidad Complutense, El Escorial, July 15–17.

Ikegami, E. 2005. *Bonds of Civility: Aesthetic Networks and the Political Origins of Japanese Culture*. New York: Cambridge University Press.

Jackson, G. 1965. The *Spanish republic and the Civil War, 1931–1939*. Princeton, NJ: Princeton University Press.

Jalali, C. 2007. *Partidos e Democracia em Portugal: 1974–2005*. Lisbon: Imprensa de Ciencias Sociais.

Jasper, J. 2014. *Protest: A Cultural Introduction to Social Movements*. Cambridge, UK: Polity Press.

Jiménez, M. 2007. "Mobilizations against the Iraq War in Spain: Background, Participants and Electoral Implications." *South European Society and Politics* 12(3): 399–420.

Jimenez Sanchez, M. 2011. *La normalización de la protesta: El caso de las manifestaciones en España (1980–2008)*. Madrid: Centro de Investigaciones Sociológicas.

Johannsen, R. W. 1965. *The Lincoln-Douglas Debates*. New York: Oxford University Press.

Johnston, 1991. *Tales of Nationalism: Catalonia, 1939–1979*. New Brunswick, NJ: Rutgers University Press.

Jordana, J. 2002. "The Persistence of Telecommunication Policies in National States: Portugal and Spain in the European Arena." In *Governing the New Telecommunications Information Society in Europe*. Cheltenham, UK: Edward Elgar.

Juliá, Santos. 2003. "Echar al Olvido: Memoria y Amnistía en la Transición a la Democracia." *Claves de Razón Práctica* 129: 14–25.

Kadivar, A. 2018. "Mass Mobilization and the Durability of New Democracies." *American Sociology Review* 83(2): 390–417.

Kalyvas, S. 2015. *Modern Greece: What Everyone Needs to Know*. New York: Oxford University Press.

Karl, T. L. 1990. "Dilemmas of Democratization in Latin America." *Comparative Politics* 23(1): 1–21.

Karl, T. L., and P. C. Schmitter. 1991. "Modes of Transition in Latin America." *Southern and Eastern Europe. International Social Science Journal* 43(2): 269–284.

Kornetis, K. 2013. *Children of the Dictatorship: Student Resistance, Cultural Politics and the "Long 1960s" in Greece*. New York and Oxford, UK: Berghahn Books.

Korpi, W., and M. Shalev. 1979. "Strikes, Industrial Relations and Class Conflict in Capitalist Societies." *British Journal of Sociology* 30: 164–187.

L'Institut Catala D'Estudis Politics I Socials. 1973. *Catalunya sota el Règim Franquista: Informe sobre la persecució de la llengua i la cultura de Catalunya pel Règim Franquista*. Paris: Edicions Catalanes de París.

Lamont, M. 1992. *Money, Morals and Manners: The Culture of the French and American Upper-Middle Class*. Chicago: University of Chicago Press.

Lamont, M. 2000. "The Rhetorics of Racism and Anti-Racism in France and the United States." In *Rethinking Comparative Cultural Sociology: Repertoires of Evaluation in France and the United States*, edited by M. Lamont and L. Thevenot, 25–55. Cambridge, UK: Cambridge University Press.

Lamont, M., and V. Molnar. 2002. "The Study of Boundaries in the Social Sciences." *Annual Review of Sociology* 28: 167–195.

Lee, C. W. 2015. *Do-It-Yourself Democracy: The Rise of the Public Engagement Industry*. Oxford, UK: Oxford University Press.

Levitsky, S., and L. A. Way. 2010. *Competitive Authoritarianism: Hybrid Regimes after the Cold War*. Cambridge, UK: Cambridge University Press.

Levitsky, S., and D. Ziblatt. 2018. *How Democracies Die*. New York: Crown.

Linz, J. J. 1964. "An Authoritarian Regime: The Case of Spain." In *Cleavages, Ideologies and Party Systems*, edited by E. Allardt and Y. Littunen, 291–342. Helsinki: Transactions of the Westermarck Society.

Linz, J. J. 1973. "Early State-Building and Late Peripheral Nationalism against the State." In *Building States and Nations, Vol. 2. Analyses by Region*, edited by S. N. Eisenstadt and S. Rokkan, 32–116. Beverly Hills, CA: Sage.

Linz, J. J., 1975. "Totalitarian and Authoritarian Regimes." In *Handbook of Political Science, Vol. 3. Macropolitical Theory*, edited by N. Polsby and F. Greenstein, 175–411. Reading, MA: Addison Wesley.

Linz, J. J. 1977. "Spain and Portugal: Critical Choices." In *Western Europe: The Trials of Partnership*, edited by David S. Landes, 232–296. Lexington, MA: Heath.

Linz, J. J. 1978. *The Breakdown of Democratic Regimes: Crisis, Breakdown and Reequilibration*. Baltimore, MD: Johns Hopkins University Press.

Linz, J. J., et al. 1981. *Informe sociológico sobre el cambio político en España, 1975–1981. Informe FOESSA V. 1*. Madrid: Euramerica.

Linz, J. J., and A. Stepan. 1996. *Problems of Democratic Transition and Consolidation: Southern Europe, South America, and Post-Communist Europe*. Baltimore, MD: Johns Hopkins University Press.

Linz, J. J., and J. R. Montero. 1986. *Crisis y cambio: Electores y partidos en la España de los años ochenta*. Madrid: Centro de Estudios Políticos y Constitucionales.

Lisi, M. 2015. *Party Change, Recent Democracies, and Portugal: Comparative Perspectives*. Lanham, MD: Lexington Books.

Lizardo, O. 2004. "The Cognitive Origins of Bourdieu's Habitus." *Journal for the Theory of Social Behaviour* 34(4): 375–401.

Lizardo, O. 2017. "Improving Cultural Analysis: Considering Personal Culture in Its Declarative and Nondeclarative Modes." *American Sociological Review* 82: 88–115.

Lizardo, O., and M. Strand. 2010. "Skills, Toolkits, Contexts, and Institutions: Clarifying the Relationship between Different Approaches to Cognition in Cultural Sociology." *Poetics* 38(2): 205–228.

Loff, M. 2014. "Estado, democracia e memoria: Políticas públicas e batalhas pela memoria da ditadura portuguesa (1974–2014). In *Ditaduras e revoluçao: Democracia e políticas da memoria*, edited by M. Loff, L. Soutelo, and F. Piedade, 23–143. Coimbra: Almedina.

López, Julia. 2017. "Diminishing Unions' Agency: Weakening Collective Bargaining and Criminalizing Picketing in the Spanish Case." *Comparative Labor Law and Policy Journal* 38(2): 169–186.

López, Jaume. 2017. *Referéndums: Una immersion rápida*. Barcelona: Ediciones Tibidabo.

Loxton, J., and S. Mainwaring. 2018. *Life after Dictatorship: Authoritarian Successor Parties Worldwide*. Cambridge, UK: Cambridge University Press.

Machado Pais, J. 1999. *Consciencia histórica e identidade: Os jovens portugueses num contexto europeu*. Oeiras: Celta.

Magalhaes, P. C. 2003. *The Limits of Judicialization: Legislative Politics and Constitutional Review in the Iberian Democracies*. PhD dissertation, Ohio State University.

Magalhaes, P. C. 2013. "Explaining the Constitutionalization of Social Rights: Portuguese Hypotheses and a Cross-National Test." In *The Social and Political Foundations of Constitutions*, edited by D. Galligan and M. Versteeg. Cambridge, UK, and New York: Cambridge University Press.

Magone, J. M. 2001. *Iberian Trade Unionism: Democratization under the Impact of the European Union*. New Brunswick, NJ: Transaction.

Mahoney, J., and D. Rueschemeyer. 2003. *Comparative Historical Analysis in the Social Sciences*. Princeton, NJ: Princeton University Press.

Mahoney, J., and K. Thelen. 2009. *Explaining Institutional Change: Ambiguity, Agency, and Power*. New York: Cambridge University Press.

Mainwaring, S., and A. Pérez-Liñán. 2005. "Latin American Democratization since 1978: Democratic Transitions, Breakdowns and Erosions." In *The Third Wave of*

Democratization in Latin America: Advances and Setbacks, edited by F. Hagopian and S. Mainwaring, 14–54. Cambridge, UK: Cambridge University Press.

Mainwaring, S., and A. Pérez-Liñán. 2013. *Democracies and Dictatorships in Latin America: Emergence, Survival, and Fall.* New York: Cambridge University Press.

Makler, H. M. 1979. "The Portuguese Industrial Elite and its Corporative Relations: A Study of Compartmentalization in an Authoritarian Regime." In *Contemporary Portugal: The Revolution and Its Antecedents*, edited by L. S. Graham and H. M. Makler, 123–160. Austin: University of Texas Press.

Manuel, P. 1995. *Uncertain Outcome: The Politics of the Portuguese Transition to Democracy.* Lanham, MD: University Press of America.

Maravall, J. M. 1978. *Dictatorship and Political Dissent: Workers and Students in Franco's Spain.* London: Tavistock.

Maravall, J. M. 1982. *The Transition to Democracy in Spain.* New York: St. Martin's.

Maravall, J. M. 1993. "Politics and Policy: Economic Reforms in Southern Europe." In *Economic Reforms in New Democracies: A Social-Democratic Approach*, edited by L. C. Bresser-Pereira, J. M. Maravall, and A. Przeworski, 77–131. Cambridge, UK: Cambridge University Press.

Maravall, J. M. 1995. "The Pre-History of Educational Reform in Spain." In *Educational Reform in Democratic Spain*, edited by O. Boyd-Barret and P. O'Malley, 41–52. New York: Routledge.

Markoff, J. 1996. *Waves of Democracy: Social Movements and Political Change.* Thousand Oaks, CA: Pine Forge Press.

Markoff, J. 1999. "Where and When Was Democracy Invented?" *Comparative Studies in Society and History* 41(4): 660–690.

Martínez, G. 2016. *La gran ilusion: Mito y realidad del proceso indepe.* Madrid: Debate.

Mateus, A. 1998. *Economia Portuguesa.* Lisbon: Verbo.

Matsaganis, M., and C. Leventi. 2014. "The Distributional Impact of Austerity and the Recession in Southern Europe." *South European Society and Politics* 19(3): 393–412.

Mavrogordatos, G., and H. Mylonas. 2011. "Greece." *European Journal of Political Research* 50: 985–990.

Maxwell, K. 1995. *The Making of Portuguese Democracy.* Cambridge, UK: Cambridge University Press.

McAdam, D, S. Tarrow, and C. Tilly. 2001. *Dynamics of Contention.* Cambridge, UK: Cambridge University Press.

McCoy, Fradera, and Jacobson, eds. 2012. *Endless Empire: Spain's Retreat, Europe's Eclipse, America's Decline.* Madison, WI: University of Wisconsin Press.

McDonough, P., S. H. Barnes, and A. Lopez Pina. 1998. *Dynamics of Democratization in Spain.* Ithaca, NY: Cornell University Press.

Mershon, C. 2002. *The Costs of Coalition.* Stanford, CA: Stanford University Press.

Miley, T. J. 2006. *Nacionalismo y Política Lingüística: El Caso de Cataluña.* Madrid: Centro de Estudios Políticos y Constitucionales.

Miley, T. J. 2017. "Austerity Politics and Constitutional Crisis in Spain." *European Politics and Society* 18(2): 263–283.

Mische, A. 2008. *Partisan Publics.* Princeton, NJ: Princeton University Press.

Molinero, C., and P. Ysás. 2017. *De la hegemonía a la autodestrucción: El Partido Comunista de España (1956–1982).* Barcelona: Critica.

Montero, J. R., K. Calvo, and Á. Martínez. 2008. "El voto religioso en España y Portugal." *Revista Internacional de Sociología* 66(51): 19–54.

Morel, L. 2007. "The Rise of 'Politically Obligatory' Referéndums: The 2005 French Referendum in Comparative Perspective." *Western European Politics* 30(5): 1041–1067.

Morgenstern de Finkel, S. 1995. "The Teachers' Centres." In *Educational Reform in Democratic Spain*, edited by O. Boyd-Barrett and P. O'Malley, 178–187. London: Routledge.

Morlino, L. 1998. *Democracy between Consolidation and Crisis: Parties, Groups and Citizens in Southern Europe*. Oxford, UK: Oxford University Press.

Morlino, L. 2012. *Changes for Democracy: Actors, Structures, Processes*. Oxford, UK: Oxford University Press.

Muñoz, J. 2012. *La construccion politica de la identidad espanola: ¿Del nacional-catolicismo al patriotismo democrático?* Madrid: Centro de Investigaciones Sociológicas.

Muñoz, J., and R. Tormos. 2015. "Economic Expectations and Support for Secession in Catalonia: Between Causality and Rationalization." *European Political Science Review* 7: 315–341.

Navarro, V. 2006. *El subdesarrollo social de españa: Causas y consecuencias*. Barcelona: Anagrama.

Nello, O. 2015. *La ciudad en movimiento: Crisis social y respuesta ciudadana*. Madrid: Diaz & Pons.

O'Donnell, G. 2010. *Democracy, Agency, and the State: Theory with Comparative Intent*. Oxford, UK: Oxford University Press.

O'Donnell, G., P. Schmitter, and L. Whitehead. 1986. *Transitions from Authoritarian Rule*. Baltimore, MD: Johns Hopkins University Press.

O'Donnell, G., and J. Vargas Cullell. 2004. *The Quality of Democracy: Theory and Applications*. Notre Dame, IN: University of Notre Dame Press.

O'Malley, P. 1995. "Education as Resistance: The 'Alternativa.'" In *Educational Reform in Democratic Spain*, edited by O. Boyd-Barrett and P. O'Malley, 32–40. London: Routledge.

OECD. 2000. *OECD Historical Statistics 1970–1999*. Paris: OECD.

Ohlander, A. S. 1992. "The Invisible Child? The Struggle over Social Democratic Family Policy." In *Creating Social Democracy: A Century of the Social Democratic Labor Party in Sweden*, edited by K. Misgeld, K. Molin, and K. Amark, 213–236. University Park: Pennsylvania State University Press.

Orwell, G. 1952(1938). *Homage to Catalonia*. London: Secker and Warburg.

Palacios Cerezales, D. 2003. *O Poder Caiu na Rua*. Lisbon: Imprensade Ciencias Sociais.

Pallarès, F. 1991. "El estado autonómico y sistema de partidos: Una aproximación electoral." *Revista de Estudios Políticos* (Nueva Época) 71: 281–323.

Patterson, O. 2014. "Making Sense of Culture." *Annual Review of Sociology* 40: 1–30.

Payne, S. G. 1961. *Falange: A History of Spanish Fascism*. Stanford, CA: Stanford University Press.

Pérez-Díaz, V. M. 1993. *The Return of Civil Society: The Emergence of Democratic Spain*. Cambridge, MA: Harvard University Press.

Perez, S. 1997. *Banking on Privilege: The Politics of Spanish Financial Reform*. Ithaca, NY: Cornell University Press.

Perez, S. A., and M. Matsaganis. 2018. "The Political Economy of Austerity in Southern Europe." *New Political Economy* 23(2): 192–207.

Perrin, A. 2006. *Citizen Speak: The Democratic Imagination in American Life*. Morality and Society Series. Chicago: University of Chicago Press.

Pierson, P. 2004. *Politics in Time: History, Institutions and Social Analysis*. Princeton, NJ: Princeton University Press.

Polavieja, J. G. 2015. "Capturing Culture: A New Method to Estimate Exogenous Cultural Effects Using Migrant Populations." *American Sociological Review* 80(1): 166–191.

Portos Garcia, M. 2017. "Voicing Outrage, Contending with Austerity: Mobilization in Spain under the Great Recession." Doctoral dissertation, European University Institute, Florence.

Prados de la Escosura, L. 2017. *Spanish Economic Growth*. London: Palgrave Macmillan.

Preston, P. 2012. *The Spanish Holocaust*. New York: Harper Press.

Przeworski, A., M. E. Álvarez, J. A. Cheibub, and F. Limongi. 2000. *Democracy and Development: Political Institutions and Well-Being in the World, 1950–1990*. New York: Cambridge University Press.

Putnam, R. 1993. *Making Democracy Work: Civic Traditions in Modern Italy*. Princeton, NJ: Princeton University Press.

Radcliff, P. 2011. *Making Democratic Citizens in Spain: Civil Society and the Popular Origins of the Transition, 1960–78*. London: Palgrave Macmillan.

Radcliff, P. 2017. "Unsettling the Iberian Transitions to Democracy of the 1970s." In *The Routledge Companion to Iberian Studies*, edited by J. Muñoz-Basols, L. Lonsdale, and M. Delgado, 450–461. London: Routledge.

Ragin, C. 1987. *The Comparative Method: Moving beyond Qualitative and Quantitative Strategies*. Berkeley: University of California Press.

Ragin, C. 2008. *Redesigning Social Inquiry: Fuzzy Sets and Beyond*. Chicago: University of Chicago Press.

Ramos Pinto, P. 2013. *Lisbon Rising: Urban Social Movements in the Portuguese Revolution, 1974–75*. Manchester, UK: Manchester University Press.

Requejo, F. 2017. *El tren de les 17:14*. Barcelona: Tibidabo Edicions.

Riedl, R. B., and K. Roberts. 2018. "Critical Junctures' Locus of Attribution and Institutional Legacies: Insights from Party System Development in Africa and Latin America" *Unpublished manuscript*.

Riley, D., and J. J. Fernández. 2014. "Beyond Strong and Weak: Rethinking Postdictatorial Civil Societies." *American Journal of Sociology* 120(2): 432–503.

Roberts, K. M. 1998. *Deepening Democracy? The Modern Left and Social Movements in Chile and Peru*. Palo Alto, CA: Stanford University Press.

Rodon, T., and L. Orriols, eds. 2014. *Cataluña en la encrucijada: Las elecciones de 2012*. Madrid: Marcial Pons.

Rodrigues, M., and P. Adao e Silva, eds. 2015. *Governar com a troika: Politicas publicas em tempo de austeridade*. Coimbra: Almedina.

Rojo, L. A. 2010. "Spain's Membership of EMU: Lessons for 2009." In *Spain and the Euro: The First Ten Years*, edited by J. Jimeno, 27–30. Madrid: Bank of Spain.

Romanos, E. 2013. "Humor in the Streets: The Spanish Indignados." *Perspectives on Europe* 43(2): 15–20.

Romanos, E. 2016a. "From Tahir to Puerta del Sol to Wall Street: The Transnational Diffusion of Social Movements in Comparative Perspective." *Revista Española de Investigaciones Sociológicas* 154: 103–118.

Romanos, E. 2016b. "Immigrants as Brokers: Dialogical Diffusion from Spanish Indignados to Occupy Wall Street." *Social Movement Studies* 15(3): 247–262.

Romanos, E. 2017. "Late Neoliberalism and Its Indignados: Contention in Austerity Spain." In *Late Neoliberalism and Its Discontents in the Economic Crisis*, edited by D. Della Porta, et al., 131–167. Cham, Switzerland: Palgrave Macmillan.

Rosenbluth, F., and I. Shapiro. 2018. *Responsible Parties: Saving Democracy from Itself*. New Haven, CT: Yale University Press.

Ross, G. 2007. "Do Certain Revolutions Promote Certain Kinds of Democracy? Legacies of the French Revolution in Contemporary French Political Culture." Paper, annual meeting of the American Sociological Association, August 2007, New York.

Rowe, K., I. Lago, and S. Lago. 2014. "The Partisan Consequences of Turnout Revisited." *Comparative European Politics* 13(4): 514–534.

Royo, S. 2000. *From Social Democracy to Neoliberalism: The Consequences of Party Hegemony in Spain, 1982–1996*. New York: St. Martin's Press.

Royo, S. 2002. *"A New Century of Corporatism?" Corporatism in Southern Europe— Spain and Portugal in Comparative Perspective*. Westport, CT: Praeger.

Royo, S. 2008. *Varieties of Capitalism in Spain: Remaking the Spanish Economy for the New Century*. New York: Palgrave Macmillan.

Royo, S. 2013. "How Did the Spanish Financial System Survive the First Stage of the Global Crisis?" *Governance* 26(4): 631–656.

Royo, S., and P. C. Manuel. 2003. *Spain and Portugal in the European Union: The First Fifteen Years*. London: Routledge.

Sampaio, J. 2006. *Portugueses*. Lisbon: Imprensa Nacional—Casa da Moeda.

Sampedro Blanco, V. 1997. "The Media Politics of Social Protest." *Mobilization: An International Quarterly* 2(2): 185–205.

Sampedro Blanco, V. 2004. "Nunca mais: La marea, el dique y el bunquer." In *La red en la calle: Cambios en la movilizacion. Anuario de Movimientos Sociales 2003*, edited by E. Grau and P. Ibarra. Barcelona: Icaria.

Sampedro, V. 2005. *13-M: Multitudes Online*. Madrid: Catarata.

Sampedro, V. 2008. *Medios y Elecciones 2004: Telivisión y Urnas. Campaña Electoral*. Madrid: Editorial Universitaria Ramón Areces.

Sánchez Cervelló, J. 1993. *A revolução portuguesa e a sua influência na transição espanhola*. Lisbon: Assírio e Alvim.

Sánchez-Cuenca, I. 2001. *ETA contra el estado: Las estrategias del terrorismo*. Barcelona: Tusquets.

Sánchez-Cuenca, I. 2012. *Años de cambio, años de crisis: Ocho años de gobiernos socialistas, 2004–2011*. Madrid: La Catarata.

Sánchez-Cuenca, I. 2014a. *Atado y mal atado: El suicidio institucional del franquismo y el surgimiento de la democracia*. Madrid: Alianza Editorial.

Sánchez-Cuenca, I. 2014b. *La impotencia democratica*. Madrid: Catarata.

Sánchez-Cuenca, I. 2018. *La confusión nacional*. Madrid: La Catarata.

Sartori, G. 1987. *The Theory of Democracy Revisited. Part One: The Contemporary Debate.* Chatham, NJ: Chatham House.

Sartorius, N. 1977. *El sindicalismo de nuevo tipo: Ensayos sobre Comisiones Obreras.* Barcelona: Laia.

Schedler A. 2001. "What Is Democratic Consolidation?" In *The Global Divergence of Democracies*, edited by L. Diamond and M. F. Plattner, 149–164. Baltimore, MD: Johns Hopkins University Press.

Schmitter, P. C. 1975. "Liberation by Golpe: Retrospective Thoughts on the Demise of Authoritarian Rule in Portugal." *Armed Forces and Society* 2(1): 5–33.

Schmitter, P. C. 1979. "The Regime D'Exception That Became the Rule: Forty-Eight Years of Authoritarian Domination in Portugal." In *Contemporary Portugal: The Revolution and Its Antecedents*, edited by L. S. Graham and H. Mackler, 3–46. Austin: University of Texas Press.

Schmitter, P. C. 1995. "Organized Interests and Democratic Consolidation in Southern Europe." In *The Politics of Democratic Consolidation: Southern Europe in Comparative Perspective*, edited by R. Gunther, P. N. Diamandouros, and H.-J. Puhle, 284–314. Baltimore, MD: Johns Hopkins University Press.

Schmitter, P. C. 1999. *Portugal do autoritarismo a democracia.* Lisbon: Imprensa de Ciencias Sociais.

Schwartzman, K. C. 1989. *The Social Origins of Democratic Collapse: The First Portuguese Republic in the Global Economy.* Lawrence: University Press of Kansas.

Serra Ramoneda, A. 2011. *Los errores de las cajas: Adios al modelo de las cajas de ahorro.* Barcelona: Ediciones Invisibles.

Serrano, E. 2006. *Para compreender o jornalismo.* Coimbra: Minerva.

Sewell, W. H. 1996. "Historical Events as Transformations of Structures: Inventing Revolution at the Bastille." *Theory and Society* 25(6): 841–881.

Sewell, W. H. 2005. *Logics of History.* Chicago: University of Chicago Press.

Shapiro, I. 2003. *The State of Democratic Theory.* Princeton, NJ: Princeton University Press.

Shapiro, I. 2016. *Politics against Domination.* Cambridge, MA: Harvard University Press.

Silva Lopes, J. da. 2003. "The Role of the State in the Labour Market: Its Impact on Employment and Wages in Portugal as Compared with Spain." *South European Society and Politics* 8(1–2): 269–286.

Silva, M., X. Pintado, J. Salgueiro, A. Pinto Barbosa, M. Murteira, J. S. Lopes, M. P. Barbosa, J. Nunes, A. S. Lopes, T. Cardoso, E. Catroga, M. Morgado, et al. 2007. *Memorias de economistas.* Lisbon: Exame.

Skocpol, T. 1979. *States and Social Revolution.* New York: Cambridge University Press.

Slater, D., and E. Simmons. 2010. "Informative Regress: Critical Antecedents in Comparative Politics." *Comparative Political Studies* 43(7): 886–917.

Small, M. L. 2009. "'How Many Cases Do I Need?' On Science and the Logic of Case Selection in Field Based Research." *Ethnography* 10(1): 5–38.

Smith, R. 1993. "Beyond Tocqueville, Myrdal, and Hartz: The Multiple Traditions in America." *American Political Science Review* 87(3): 549–566.

Sola Espinosa, J. 2013. "La desregulación laboral en España, 1984–1997: Recursos de poder y remercantilizacion del trabajo." Doctoral thesis, Madrid: Universidad Complutense.

Somers, M. 2008. *Genealogies of Citizenship*. Cambridge, UK: Cambridge University Press.

Sotiropoulos, D. 1996. *Populism and Bureaucracy: The Case of Greece under PASOK*. Notre Dame, IN: University of Notre Dame Press.

Spillman, L. 1997. *Nation and Commemoration: Creating National Identities in the United States and Australia*. Cambridge, UK: Cambridge University Press.

Spillman, L. 2014. "Mixed Methods and the Logic of Qualitative Inference." *Qualitative Sociology* 37(2): 189–205.

Stallings, B. 2006. *Finance for Development: Latin America in Comparative Perspective*. Washington, DC: Brookings Institution Press.

Stamatov, P. 2000. "The Making of a 'Bad' Public: Ethnonational Mobilization in Post-Communist Bulgaria." *Theory and Society* 29(4): 549–572.

Steinmetz, G. 1999. "Introduction: Culture and the State." In *State/Culture: State Formation after the Cultural Turn*, edited by G. Steinmetz. Ithaca, NY: Cornell University Press.

Stepan, A. 1986. "Paths toward Redemocratization: Theoretical and Comparative Considerations." In *Transitions from Authoritarian Rule: Comparative Perspectives*, edited by G. O'Donnell, P. Schmitter, and L. Whitehead, 64–84. Baltimore, MD: Johns Hopkins University Press.

Stepan, A., J. Linz, and Y. Yadav. 2011. *Crafting State-Nations: India and Other Multinational Democracies*. Baltimore, MD: Johns Hopkins University Press.

Stephens, J. D. 1979. *The Transition from Capitalism to Socialism*. London: Macmillan.

Stinchcombe, A. 1968. *Constructing Social Theories*. New York: Harcourt Brace & World.

Stoer, S. 1982. *Educaçao, estado e desenvolvimento em Portugal*. Lisbon: Livros.

Stoer, S. 1983. *The April Revolution and the Contribution of Education to Changing "Portuguese Realities."* PhD thesis, Open University.

Stoer, S. 1986. *Educaçao e mudança social em Portugal: 1970–1980: Uma decada de transiçao*. Porto: Afrontamento.

Stoleroff, A. 2013. "Employment Relations and Unions in Public Administration in Portugal and Spain: From Reform to Austerity." *European Journal of Industrial Relations* 19(4): 309–323.

Stromberg, T. 1992. "The Politicization of the Housing Market: The Social Democrats and the Housing Question." In *Creating Social Democracy: A Century of the Social Democratic Labor Party in Sweden*, edited by K. Misgeld, K. Molin, and K. Amark, 237–269. University Park: Pennsylvania State University Press.

Swidler, A. 1986. "Culture in Action: Symbols and Strategies." *American Sociological Review* 51(2): 273–286.

Swidler, A. 2001. *Talk of Love: How Culture Matters*. Chicago: Chicago University Press.

Tarrow, S. 1993. "Social Protest and Policy Reform: May 1968 and the Loi d'Orientation." *Comparative Political Studies* 25(4): 579–607.

Tarrow, S. 2010. "The Strategy of Paired Comparison: Toward a Theory of Practice." *Comparative Political Studies* 43: 230–259.

Tarrow, S. 2012. *Strangers at the Gates: Movements and States in Contentious Politics.* Cambridge, UK: Cambridge University Press.

Tejerina, B., J. M. Fernández Sobrado, and X. Aierdi. 1995. *Sociedad Civil Protesta y Movimientos Sociales en el País Vasco: Los Límites de la Teoría de la Movilización de Recursos.* Vitoria–Gasteiz: Servicio Central de Publicaciones del Gobierno Vasco.

Thompson, M. 2003. *Democratic Revolutions: Asia and Eastern Europe.* London: Routledge.

Threlfall, M. 2008. "Reassessing the Role of Civil Society Organizations in the Transition to Democracy in Spain." *Democratization* 15(5): 930–951.

Tilly, C. 1978. *From Mobilization to Revolution.* Reading, MA: Addison-Wesley.

Tilly, C. 1986. *The Contentious French.* Cambridge, MA: Harvard University Press.

Tilly, C. 1995. *Popular Contention in Great Britain.* Cambridge, UK: Harvard University Press.

Tilly, C. 2004. *Contention and Democracy in Europe, 1650–2000.* Cambridge, UK: Cambridge University Press.

Tilly, C. 2006. *Regimes and Repertoires.* Chicago: University of Chicago Press.

Torcal, M. 2014. "The Decline of Political Trust in Spain and Portugal: Economic Performance or Political Responsiveness?" *American Behavioral Scientist* 58(12): 1542–1567.

Valenzuela, J. S. 1990. "Democratic Consolidation in Post-Transitional Settings: Notion, Process, and Facilitating Conditions." *Kellogg Institute Working Paper* 150.

Valenzuela, J. S. 1991. "Labor Movements and Political Systems: A Conceptual and Typological Analysis." *Kellogg Institute Working Paper* 167.

Valenzuela, J. S. 2006. "Los Derechos Humanos y la Redemocratización en Chile." In *Chile: política y modernización democrática*, edited by M. Alcántara Saéz and L. M. Ruiz Rodríguez, 269–312. Barcelona: Edicions Belaterra.

Valenzuela, J. S., E. Tironi, and T. R. Scully. 2006. *El eslabon perdido: Familia, modernizacion y bienestar en Chile.* Santiago de Chile: Aguilar.

Vallès, J. M. 2017. "¿Cinquanta-cinquanta o trenta-quaranta-trenta?" *Revista de reflexió y crítica política d'esquerres, ecologista i feminista.* Internet edition. November 2017.

van Deth, J., J. R. Montero, and A. Westholm. 2007. *Citizenship and Involvement in European Democracies: A Comparative Analysis.* Routledge.

Vespeira de Almeida, S. 2007. "Campanhas de dinamizaçao cultural e acçao civica do MFA: Uma etnografia retrospective." *Arquivos da Memoria*, N2 (Nova Serie).

Vicens, L., and X. Tedó. 2017. *Operació urnes.* Barcelona: Columna CAT.

Vieira, M. M. 2007. "Recém-chegados a Universidade." In *Escola, Jovens e Media*, edited by M. M. Vieira, 137–162. Lisbon: Imprensa de Ciencias Sociais.

Vieira, M. B., and F. C. da Silva. 2010. *O momento constituinte: Os direitos sociais na Constituição.* Coimbra: Almedina.

Vilajosana, J. M. 2014. "The Democratic Principle and Constitutional Justification of the right to decide." *Catalan Social Sciences Review* 4: 57–80.

Villaverde Cabral, M., J. Vala, and A. Freire. 2003. *Desigualdades sociais e percepções de justiça.* Lisbon: Imprensa de Ciencias Sociais.

Viterna, J. 2007. "Revolutionaries, Politicians, and Revolutionary Politics: The Enduring Legacies of Revolution for Central American Democracies." Paper presented at the annual meeting of the American Sociological Association, New York, August 2007.

Viterna, J. 2013. *Women in War: The Micro-Processes of Mobilization in El Salvador.* Oxford, UK: Oxford University Press.

Watson, S. 2015. *The Left Divided.* Oxford, UK: Oxford University Press.

Weyland, K. 2014. *Making Waves: Democratic Contention in Europe and Latin America since the Revolutions of 1848.* New York: Cambridge University Press.

Wheeler, D. L. 1978. *Republican Portugal: A Political History, 1910–1926.* Madison: University of Wisconsin Press.

Wiarda, H. J. 1989. *The Transition to Democracy in Spain and Portugal.* American Enterprise Institute for Public Policy Research.

Wilkinson, R., and K. Pickett. 2010. *The Spirit Level: Why Equality Is Better for Everyone.* London: Penguin.

Wills, G. 1992. *Lincoln at Gettysburg.* Simon and Schuster.

Wood, E. J. 2003. *Insurgent Collective Action and Civil War in El Salvador.* Cambridge, UK: Cambridge University Press.

Wood, G. S. 2002. *The American Revolution: A History.* New York: Modern Library.

Wood, E. J. 2000. *Forging Democracy from Below: Insurgent Transitions in South Africa and El Salvador.* Cambridge Studies in Comparative Politics. Cambridge, UK: Cambridge University Press.

Wuthnow, R., and M. Witten. 1988. "New Directions in the Study of Culture." *Annual Review of Sociology* 14: 49–67.

Tables and figures are indicated by an italic *t* and *f* following the paragraph number